VSTO
FOR
DUMMIES®

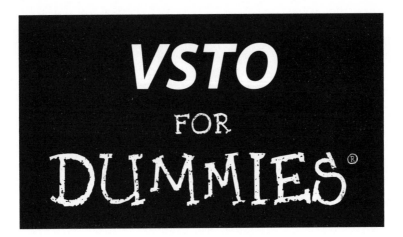

by Bill Sempf and Peter Jausovec

WILEY

Wiley Publishing, Inc.

VSTO For Dummies®

Published by
Wiley Publishing, Inc.
111 River Street
Hoboken, NJ 07030-5774

www.wiley.com

Copyright © 2011 by Wiley Publishing, Inc., Indianapolis, Indiana

Published by Wiley Publishing, Inc., Indianapolis, Indiana

Published simultaneously in Canada

WILEY

About the Authors

Bill Sempf: Bill started playing with computers in 1979 and hasn't looked back. In 1985, he was helping his father (also Bill) manage Apple IIe systems at the local library. Since then, Bill has built applications for the likes of Lucent Technologies, Bank One, Nationwide Insurance, and Sears, Roebuck and Co. He is the author of *C# 2010 All-in-One For Dummies and Visual Basic 2008 For Dummies;* a coauthor of Effective Visual Studio.NET, Professional ASP.NET Web Services and Professional VB.NET; a frequent contributor to MSDN, Builder.com, Hardcore Web Services, Cloud Computing Journal, Inside Web Development Journal and Intranet Journal; and an invited speaker for the ACM and IEEE, nPlus1, DevEssentials, the International XML Web Services Expo, and the Association of Information Technology Professionals. Bill is a graduate of The Ohio State University with a Bachelor's of Science in Business Administration, Microsoft Certified Professional, Certified Internet Business Strategist and Certified Internet Webmaster. His company is Products Of Innovative New Technology (usually called POINT), and you can reach Bill at bill@pointweb.net.

Peter Jausovec: Peter has worked with Visual Studio Tools for Office (VSTO) since the first version. He is currently employed at Microsoft where he helped test and design the Microsoft Visual Studio 2010 SharePoint developer tools, focusing especially on SharePoint Workflows.

Dedication

From Bill: To my wife Gabrielle and my son Adam. They put up with many a movie date with Daddy illuminated by his laptop screen.

From Peter: To my wife Nives.

Authors' Acknowledgments

This book has a long story behind it, which Bill will be glad to tell for the price of a beer at any of the community events he frequents. That story demands an acknowledgement of two particular groups — the developer community and Wiley.

When Bill came up with this title concept way back in 2006, he leaned heavily on the developer community for ideas and structure. This leaning turned into a true partnership, when Peter joined the fray as a co-author in 2008.

Then just a student, Peter would end up becoming a force in the development of this book, crafting the message presented and writing half the text. He then worked to update the older chapters to appropriately encompass VSTO 4.0 after he joined Microsoft's VSTO development team. His work, and the community that supports the creation of vital technologists like him, deserve everyone's recognition, support, and participation.

In that same vein, Eric Carter's early support from the technical perspective was very important to the book. Maarten van Stam's expertise in tech review has been fantastic, too. Both of those gentlemen have a deep and broad understanding of the technical issues of VSTO, and their help firming up the ideas presented was truly a cornerstone of the book.

Wiley, the company that publishes the *For Dummies* series, deserves a hat tip for sticking with this book. Many people, especially Katie Feltman and Kelly Ewing, allowed this to title draw out long beyond the timeline for most books while we waited for the technology to settle. We believe it was worth the wait and hope you do, too!

Publisher's Acknowledgments

We're proud of this book; please send us your comments at http://dummies.custhelp.com. For other comments, please contact our Customer Care Department within the U.S. at 877-762-2974, outside the U.S. at 317-572-3993, or fax 317-572-4002.

Some of the people who helped bring this book to market include the following:

Acquisitions and Editorial

Project Editor: Kelly Ewing

Acquisitions Editor: Katie Feltman

Technical Editor: Maarten van Stam

Editorial Manager: Jodi Jensen

Editorial Assistant: Amanda Graham

Sr. Editorial Assistant: Cherie Case

Cartoons: Rich Tennant
(www.the5thwave.com)

Composition Services

Project Coordinator: Patrick Redmond

Layout and Graphics: Carl Byers

Proofreaders: The Well-Chosen Word, Lauren Mandelbaum

Indexer: Christine Karpeles

Publishing and Editorial for Technology Dummies

> **Richard Swadley,** Vice President and Executive Group Publisher

> **Andy Cummings,** Vice President and Publisher

> **Mary Bednarek,** Executive Acquisitions Director

> **Mary C. Corder,** Editorial Director

Publishing for Consumer Dummies

> **Diane Graves Steele,** Vice President and Publisher

Composition Services

> **Debbie Stailey,** Director of Composition Services

Contents at a Glance

Table of Contents

Introduction

A couple of years back, before Visual Studio Tools for Office (VSTO) was released, one of the most popular tools for developing for Microsoft Office were macros and Visual Basic for Applications (VBA). With macros, you can automate a repetitive task inside Office applications. For simple Office applications, VBA is enough, but very soon, you'd want to use something more powerful, secure, and flexible.

This is where VSTO comes into play. With VSTO, you can do so much more than with plain VBA. There are many reasons you'd want to switch to VSTO, but the best one would definitely be the .NET framework. Yes, VSTO is built upon the .NET framework, which means you can use all the .NET goodness in your VSTO Office solutions.

With VSTO, you have all your client side needs covered. Now you want to move to the server side, and SharePoint is a very wise choice. But what is SharePoint? You can think of SharePoint as a place where all your (client side) documents and workbooks come together. SharePoint is a place to store, categorize, and share your Office documents. SharePoint is a huge topic that deserves a separate book. However, we do touch on SharePoint development in this book as well.

About This Book

The main purpose of this book is to attract existing Visual Basic for Applications (VBA) or Office developers and help them make the transition from unmanaged VBA world to managed .NET world. The logical choice to transition from VBA is to use Visual Studio Tools for Office. So, whether you're brand new to Office development or you're looking to get acquainted with both VSTO and SharePoint developer tools in Visual Studio 2010, this book is for you.

VSTO is well integrated into the .NET Framework. It's designed to work with Visual Studio. This isn't a book about Visual Basic for Applications, or VBA. This book is for people who already have Visual Studio and need to add Office development to their resume or for VBA developers who want to discover the power of Office development with .NET.

Conventions Used in This Book

When you're supposed to choose a series of commands, you see something like this: File⇨Open. This simply means choose the File command and then the Open command

What You're Not to Read

 If you see any text in this book that has this icon next to it, feel free to skip right over to the next paragraph. This icon alerts you to interesting information that you don't need to know.

Foolish Assumptions

In order to get the most out of this book, you should be familiar with basic concepts of programming. Don't worry; you don't have to be a master programmer to use VSTO to develop for Office application. All examples in the book are created with Visual Basic .NET programming language. If you ever used VBA or recorded any macros, you should be able to recognize similar programming constructs and concepts in Visual Basic .NET.

Throughout the book, we use Visual Studio 2010. If you've used any previous versions of Visual Studio, you shouldn't have any problems navigating through the user interface in the Visual Studio 2010. Even if you haven't used Visual Studio, we walk you through all the examples, step by step.

VSTO works only in Visual Studio Professional edition or better. You won't have a lot of luck trying to use any of the Express editions, LightSwitch, or WebMatrix with VSTO.

For the part of the book where we talk about SharePoint, we assume that you have basic knowledge on how SharePoint works. To be honest, we need a whole separate book if we want to explain SharePoint in every little detail.

How This Book Is Organized

To quickly find what you need, this book is organized into parts. Each part covers a different Office application that you can program against with VSTO and SharePoint developer tools for Visual Studio 2010.

Part 1: Introducing VSTO

In this part, you discover the basics of VSTO. You also find out what an Office add-in is and how to use Windows Forms control to make Office documents smarter. Finally, we focus on designing VSTO solutions.

Part II: VSTO Construction

In this part, we talk about building Word add-ins and customizing Word documents. You build an Excel add-in and discover the basics of the Excel object model. You also find out about the PowerPoint object model and develop an add-in that helps you with selecting images. You build an Outlook Job Jar add-in and find out about the Project add-ins. Finally, you discover the myriad development options in Visio.

Part III: Developing for SharePoint

This part is all about SharePoint development. Visual Studio 2010 shipped with a brand new set of templates that allow you to create different Visual Studio projects that target SharePoint 2010. You discover how to install SharePoint Foundation 2010 on a machine with client operating system. You also find out about different SharePoint project types and how deployment to the SharePoint server works.

Part IV: Finishing Up

In this part, you find out how the security in Office customizations works. You also discover everything you need to know to deploy your VSTO solutions.

Part V: The Part of Tens

No *For Dummies* book is complete without the lighthearted Part of Tens. In this part, we offer ten reasons you may want to ditch Web programming. We also give you a few cool ideas for VSTO projects, along with ten ways to integrate SharePoint.

Icons Used in This Book

So that you can pick out parts that you really need to pay attention to (or, depending on your taste, to avoid), we use some symbols, or *icons*, in this book.

If you see this icon, it means that we're mentioning some really nifty point or idea that you may want to keep in mind as you use the program.

This icon lets you know something you'll want to keep in mind.

Make sure that you read this text, which highlights common pitfalls and mistakes.

This information isn't necessary but is interesting, if you have techie leanings.

Where to Go from Here

If you're a complete beginner, we suggest you read the book's parts in the order we present them. However, if you've used VSTO before, feel free to look up the task that interests you in the book's Index or Table of Contents and start reading there. You don't have to read this book in order.

Part I
Introducing VSTO

In this part . . .

This part starts with installation and a look at the various editions of VSTO. Visual Studio Tools for Office is a big topic, but you can narrow the beginnings down to add-ins and documents. In this part, we show you how to build one of each, in the classic Hello World style. Finally, we look at designing VSTO applications.

Chapter 1

Getting Started with VSTO

In This Chapter

▶ Figuring out what you need to get started

▶ Picking a version

▶ Installing VSTO

▶ Building your first Office applications

*V*isual Studio Tools for Office is exactly what it sounds like it is — a set of tools that is part of Visual Studio and designed to enhance Office. In less politically correct terms, VSTO is Microsoft's answer to those who want to use the more robust .NET to get VBA-like functionality in their Office development.

VSTO has a lot of parts, does a lot of loosely related things, and means different things to different people. For that reason, we talk about what VSTO can do for you before we get into a little code in Chapters 2 and 3. In this chapter, we look at logistics with a tour through versions, options, and languages.

Harnessing the Power of VSTO

Visual Studio Tools for Office isn't a replacement technology for anything currently in the Microsoft pantheon of applications. VSTO doesn't replace Visual Basic for Applications, it doesn't replace scripting Office applications, and it doesn't replace Windows or Web forms.

VSTO is a set of tools that you can use with Visual Studio to supercharge Office. Put simply, VSTO provides tools to build add-ins and Customized Documents for Office applications like Word and Excel. That simplicity hides a wealth of power and functionality.

Talking about add-ins and Customized Documents

Add-ins, like the one in Figure 1-1, are little bits of programs that are managed by Office. You probably use add-ins all the time without even knowing it. If you have Adobe Acrobat installed and have the Save To PDF button in your toolbar, you've seen an add-in. OneNote puts an add-in in Office to allow you to move documents between Word and a Notebook, for example.

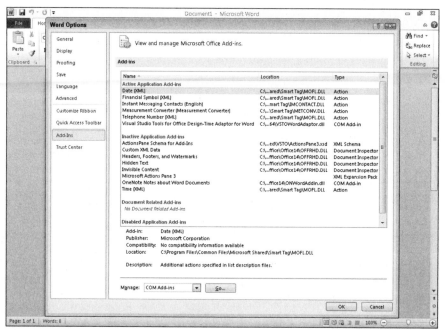

Figure 1-1:
Add-ins in
Word.

From the programmer's point of view, add-ins are just Windows applications that have a special home — an Office application. You can use VSTO to build add-ins, just as you could use Visual Basic 6 and other programming applications before VSTO. Add-ins have been around a long time. VSTO allows you to use managed code (for example, the .NET Framework) for the first time.

Customized Documents are new and take more explanation (see Figure 1-2). Customized Documents are regular Office documents (like an Excel spreadsheet) that have a .NET DLL associated with them that give them special powers. You can use code in the back-end of the document to fill in fields from a database, validate data, or respond to certain user requests.

VSTO is very different from what you're used to. It's not script code in a macro or in a Visual Basic for Applications project. After you make a document a Customized Document, it's a compiled project, just like a Windows application. VBA is also part of the document, while the code from a VSTO project is in a DLL linked to the document.

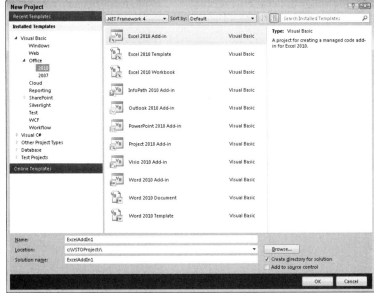

Figure 1-2:
Making
a new
Customized
Document
in Visual
Studio.

Customized Documents are cool but hard to use in the wild. Peter shows you an example in Chapter 3, and we also build more complex Customized Documents in Chapters 6 and 8.

At their core, Customized Documents are document-level only, while add-ins are application-level and can apply to all documents used by that installation of Office. They both use more or less the same path to get where they're going: Visual Studio Tools for Office.

Solving your problems with four VSTO features

Four important features are available in VSTO. By *features,* we're talking about the things that you need to remember when you're considering using this toolkit to solve your problems. VSTO allows you to do these four things to solve your problems:

- ✔ Add your custom functionality to existing Office applications, via add-ins.
- ✔ Leverage all the existing Office functionality in your applications, like Word document layout and Excel formulas, through communicating with those add-ins.
- ✔ Make documents that integrate fully with existing applications and databases.
- ✔ Use Microsoft SharePoint to increase communications between knowledge workers with add-ins and documents that communicate.

The following sections dig into each feature in more detail.

Add functionality to Office

PowerPoint does a lot when it comes to presentations. If you want to automatically generate sample images from the live photo repository in your company, though, you're in a tough spot. The good news is that VSTO add-ins can fix that issue.

Using an add-in, you can get the latest images from the project repository and make them available to a presentation author in real time. This add-in can provide them with the latest images for status reports and sales presentations. Without an add-in, you're back to searching through the Q drive, or whatever, and different people solving the problem different ways.

When you're building a solution for a company, automating common tasks is among the most common requests. Add-ins allow you to use Windows form elements, the Action or Task pane, and Smart Tags to do things specific to your company. What's more, these tools are available to every document that is created by the computer with the add-in installed.

Leverage Office functionality

Another consideration is the ability to leverage Office as an extension to your development platform. For example, while you can build pivot tables into your ASP.NET based reporting system, doing so takes a long time or requires the use of expensive third-party products. Or, you can use VSTO.

How, you ask? Just have your Reports button launch Excel with your custom add-in. Then users can get the data they want and then work with it using the tools they already know. Your Excel add-in provides a connection to the database, and the built-in security model ensures that your confidential data is safe.

Making good software quickly is the expectation of independent developers and IT departments alike these days. Leveraging functionality already purchased, and knowledge already gained, makes that goal easier to reach.

This ability sort of crosses over the two project types (documents and add-ins) in that both of those types can leverage different functionality. Documents leverage document level functions, and add-ins leverage the application level tools.

Make documents that think

Applications aren't the only piece of the puzzle. A Word letter template that knows how to check the Exchange server for names and addresses will make communication that much easier. And VSTO has just the ticket.

Customized Documents allow you to do just about anything in an Office document that you can do in a Windows application or in an old VBA project. Accessing databases, making calculations, and checking Web Services are all possible. Fields in a Word document can easily be bound to a data source using ADO.NET data binding.

Thinking out of the box is a core skill in information technology, and Customized Documents are right in there. While getting the ideas under your belt takes a while, you'll be surprised what you can do after you get a model for their use. Then, after you get the tool the way you want, it's mobile — transferable from installation to installation (at least in theory). Customized Documents are just that — documents. The logic follows the document itself from computer to computer under controlled circumstances.

Make connections between existing applications and Office

"Sure, we can get their sales data. Some of it is in this Excel spreadsheet, some in Outlook Business Contact Manager, and the rest in the Oracle ERP database that we access with this InfoPath form." VSTO to the rescue. Tying together Office applications has never been easier.

It doesn't matter how you look at it or what models you use, VSTO can make it so that your Office applications sing in unison through SharePoint. A Customized InfoPath form that knows where to go to get to the Excel data and the Outlook add-in will do the trick here. No matter what the combination, it's better than writing reams of VB Script.

Convergence is where it is at, too. Getting the disparate applications of the contemporary IT department to not only play nice but to be accessible by the knowledge workers is something special, and VSTO can make it oh-so-much smoother.

Exploring the Different Versions of VSTO

VSTO runs in a cycle that is between Office releases and Visual Studio releases, so sometimes it's tough to tell what version does what. We clear up any confusion in this section.

In this book, we cover only the version of VSTO that is part of Visual Studio 2010 and works with Office 2010: VSTO 4.0 Much of what we do in this book applies to many other platforms, except deployment, which is quite different. Due to the deployment story, I encourage you to use Visual Studio and Office 2010 whenever possible.

Visual Studio 2003 and 2005

Visual Studio Tools for Office weren't part of the default Visual Studio releases — instead, a separate product called Visual Studio Tools for Office was available. This product contained tools used in developing for Microsoft Office platform and was a complete edition (called SKU) of Visual Studio.

VSTO 2003 supported only Office 2003 and document-level customizations for Word and Excel. The next version, called VSTO 2005, included support for Outlook add-ins.

VSTO 2005 SE

Moving forward to 2005 when a new version — the so-called second edition of VSTO — was released. VSTO became part of Visual Studio 2005 Professional and higher SKUs, and the separate SKU for VSTO was removed from the lineup.

At this time, Microsoft released Office 2007, which included support for developing add-ins and document-level customizations. VSTO 2005 SE for Office 2003 also added support for application-level add-ins for Office products other than Outlook: Word, Excel, PowerPoint, and Visio.

Support for Office 2007 started with this version of VSTO as well, and you could create document-level customizations for InfoPath and add-ins for Word, Excel, Outlook, PowerPoint, Visio, and InfoPath. Note that in VSTO 2005 SE, you couldn't create Word or Excel document-level customizations targeting Office 2007 — that came in the next version.

VSTO 3.0

With VSTO 3.0, nothing changed if you were developing for Office 2003. VSTO 3.0 is built into Visual Studio 2008 Professional or higher SKUs. If you developed for Office 2007, you now had support for Word and Excel document-level customizations. In application-level or add-in world, VSTO 3.0 included support for Office Project. Apart from focusing only on Office client applications, Microsoft decided to add a project template to target Office Server System. Project templates for SharePoint 2007 workflow projects were added in this version in order to support Microsoft Office SharePoint Server 3.0.

Visual Studio 2010 and VSTO 4.0

The biggest feature for VSTO 4.0 in Visual Studio 2010 is support for 64-bit machines. Compared to previous versions, VSTO doesn't include any new project templates. If you think about it, there's not much the programmers could add to VSTO. With Visual Studio 2010, the focus of VSTO switched from supporting Office Client applications to SharePoint support.

Visual Studio 2010 contains a large set of project templates for developing against SharePoint 2010 (see Part III). Apart from SharePoint workflows, Visual Studio gained support for the following projects:

- ✔ Workflows
- ✔ List Definition
- ✔ List Instance
- ✔ Site Definition
- ✔ Content Type
- ✔ Module
- ✔ Empty SharePoint Project

Office 2003

Using the Shared Add-In project type, you can create Office 2003 add-ins with just a default install of Visual Studio of any version. This project type isn't VSTO; none of the libraries that I talk about here are available. The Shared Add-In project type uses the default COM Standard Add-In hooks and everything else is up to you.

COM is the Component Object Model that Office still uses. It is the predecessor of .NET, and still in use in a lot of systems, actually. C++ is the usual programming language of choice. We don't have to use C++, though, to use the add-in hooks provided by VSTO because all the classes are provided to us! Yay!

If you want to produce application-specific add-ins and Customized Documents for Office 2003, then you have to have a version of VSTO. How much power you get depends on what version you run:

- ✔ VSTO Version 2003 includes customized document projects for Word and Excel.
- ✔ VSTO Version 2005 adds add-in projects for Outlook, Word, and Excel.

✔ VSTO Version 2005 SE (found in Visual Studio 2008) further supports add-in projects for PowerPoint and Visio.

✔ VSTO Version 4 (found in Visual Studio 2010) adds features for Office development.

If you have a contemporary MSDN Professional subscription, the sum total accessible to you when working in Office 2003 includes

✔ Customized Documents:

- Word 2003
- Excel 2003

✔ Add-ins

- Word
- Excel
- Outlook
- PowerPoint
- Visio

Office 2007

Office 2007 has a new user interface and a new file format for all office documents. VSTO 2003 and VSTO 2005 don't support Office 2007 at all. VSTO 2005 SE adds add-in support for InfoPath, as well as the following:

✔ Word

✔ Excel

✔ Outlook

✔ PowerPoint

✔ Visio

✔ InfoPath

The document support for Office 2007 is found in Visual Studio 2008 and Visual Studio 2010 and includes Word and Excel.

What there is in Office 2007 — if you're running VSTO 2005 SE or Visual Studio 2008 — is support for some of the cool new Office user interface features:

✔ Custom task panes

✔ The Ribbon, in the form of Ribbon Extensions

✔ Outlook Form Regions

Earlier versions

Running Office XP or earlier? Upgrade. Office XP isn't supported, though interop assemblies are available for non-VSTO solutions using Visual Studio. You can also use a shared add-in because they speak COM. Nonetheless, VSTO add-ins don't run in Office XP.

Additionally, Office 2003 officially ended support when Office 2007 came out. That said, there is still VSTO support for 2003, but you can't expect it to last long. Microsoft provides support for current and previous versions only, and you can't assume that it will just keep supporting 2003 to be nice.

Installing VSTO

This book is about the Visual Studio 2010 implementation of VSTO targeting Office 2010. Throughout the book, we mention if functionality is different from Office 2007. Installing Visual Studio itself it actually pretty simple. You can, though, just get and install VSTO if all you're building is Office applications. Because you may be working in an earlier version and reading this book, I cover some other possibilities.

Requirements

According to Microsoft, hardware and software requirements are as follows:

- ✔ Hardware
  - Computer with a 1.6 GHz or faster processor
  - 1GB (32 bit) or 2GB (64 bit) RAM (Add 512MB if running in a virtual machine)
  - 3GB of available hard disk space
  - 5400 RPM hard disk drive
  - DirectX 9 capable video card running at 1024 x 768 or higher-resolution display
  - DVD-ROM drive
- ✔ Operating system (any one)
  - Windows Vista (x86 or x64), all editions except Starter Edition
  - Windows XP (x86 or x64), Service Pack 2 or later, all editions except Starter Edition
  - Windows Server 2003 (x86 or x64), Service Pack 1 or later, all editions

- Windows Server 2003 R2 or later (x86 or x64), all editions
- Windows Server 2008 (x86 and x64) or later (all editions)
- Windows Server 2008 R2 (x64) Enterprise Edition
- Windows 7 (x86 and x64) Ultimate Edition

✔ Office system software (any one)

- Microsoft Office 2010, Professional Edition
- Microsoft Office 2010, Professional Edition with InfoPath
- Microsoft Word 2010
- Microsoft Excel 2010
- Microsoft InfoPath 2010
- Microsoft Outlook 2010
- Microsoft Office SharePoint Server 2010(for SharePoint Workflows)
- Microsoft SharePoint 2010 (for SharePoint specific projects)

In order to use SharePoint specific project templates, you need to run a server operating system. The system requirements are different for those OSs. Developing for SharePoint 2007 requires Microsoft Office SharePoint Services installation on a 32-bit machine. If you want to use SharePoint 2010 projects, you need to install either a server OS or Vista or Windows 7 OS. Note that SharePoint 2010 is only supported on 64-bit machines.

Supporting software

In order to develop for Office, you must have Office installed (see Figure 1-3). If you have Office 2007 installed, you can build Office 2007 add-ins and Office 2007 documents. If you have Office 2010 installed, you can build Office 2010 add-ins. If you have any combination of Office installations, you get everything. If you have nothing, VSTO will install, but will complain a lot when you try to use it. In short: you won't be able to do much with VSTO if Office isn't installed.

Please run Windows Update a few times if you install VSTO. All this supporting software has security patches available. Unprotected machines on the Internet have a 12-hour lifespan. Don't be a victim.

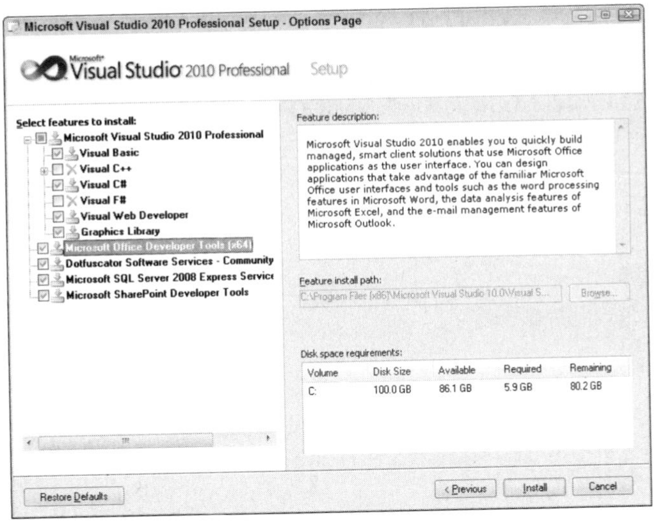

Figure 1-3:
Installing
VSTO.

Using VSTO in Visual Studio

VSTO uses Visual Studio as its Integrated Development Environment. A
bunch of features come baked in to the collaboration, including

- Drag and drop user controls (some specific to Office)
- IntelliSense (a sort of dynamic, built-in documentation) for functions and
  properties
- Debugging
- Deployment

Because of the collaboration between VSTO and Visual Studio, some of this
book is about using Visual Studio. If you are an experienced user of Visual
Studio, you may find the coverage repetitive, but, in true *For Dummies* style,
you're welcome to read only the information you need. Bear with us, though,
because a surprising amount of the information is new.

Using VSTO projects

From the starting user's perspective, a VSTO add-in or Customized Document
is implemented as a Project Type in the New Project dialog box. To see what
we mean, follow these steps:

1. **Launch Visual Studio 2010 by choosing Start⇨All Programs.**

2. **Choose File⇨New Project.**

3. **In the Project Types panel, open the Visual Basic tree (if it isn't already open) and click Office.**

   The New Project dialog box, shown in Figure 1-4, appears.

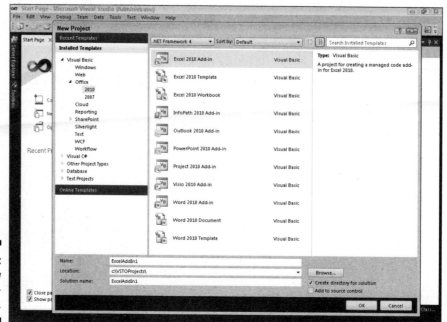

Figure 1-4:
The New
Project dia-
log box.

The contents of Figure 1-4's Installed Templates change based on your installed base. For more on templates, review the section "Exploring the Different Versions of VSTO." No matter what is in the templates list, you find subtle categories — add-ins and Customized Documents.

Working toward a finished product

Add-ins are application extensions that run within a host office program. Office applications are designed to run add-ins, as are many other Microsoft applications such as Internet Explorer and Visual Studio.

Add-ins add custom functionality to a host application. If you want to format an Excel cell a certain way, you'd just use a style or a custom number format. If you want to provide an Excel user with a way to use the latest ratios to convert all the dollars in a workbook to euros, you'd use an add-in. Basically, the functionality in an add-in is available to all documents.

Documents, which I usually call Customized Documents (to differentiate them from default documents, I guess), are actually files made to be opened by Office applications that have code you produce attached to them. Documents have a subcategory of their own — *templates* — which produces the template sort of document (like a .DOTX file, or a .XLTX file) that makes other documents.

Normal Customized Documents are just Office files with an attitude. They have a custom code library associated with them that gives special super powers.

For example, if you want to write a product catalog in Word, you'd just open Word and start typing. If you want that product catalog to get the list of products from a database, then you use a Customized Document. The functionality that you write will be available in just this one document, not every document the user opens.

Customized templates are interesting. You've probably used templates to make a custom work order for a company. You can include the logo and address of the company, and every time you need a new work order, the contents of the template are copied into a new spreadsheet. To teach that new work order how to save its contents to your accounting system, you use a customized template.

Starting with the end in mind

If you start with a project, you have to end with a result, right? You bet. You're not building scripts. You're building compiled applications, with executables and dynamic link libraries and configuration files. They just may not take the form you're expecting.

An installer

If you build an add-in project for Office 2003, you end up with an installer. The installer will be an .MSI file (for Microsoft Installer) that you can run on another Windows computer with the right version of Office already installed. The installer makes the add-in you wrote available to Office users on that computer. The VSTO installer is really the same as most other Visual Studio installers, except that it includes special Office registry keys.

After you've built this MSI, it's distributable, with certain security restrictions, to anyone. You can sell it, or give it away, or make it a download on your Web site or your corporate intranet. That installer will install a fully functioning application — it just requires the right version of Office to sit in, provided the security is set up.

A document file

Ever compiled something to a .DOC or .DOCX file? Neither had I until I used VSTO. It's a pretty cool feeling. When you make a document or document template project in Visual Studio, that's what you get — a file that you can open right up in an Office application.

The distribution of Customized Documents has a lot more restrictions, though. Theoretically, anyone can use them, but realistically, the end user (or their technical support engineer) has to do major security maneuvering to get the file to run. After those restrictions are met, though, you have a .DOCX or .XLSX file that is ready to do some of the user's work for them.

Chapter 2

Building an Add-in

*T*here is nothing quite like a finished piece of software. Ducks are all in a row and all documented. The t's are dotted, and the i's are crossed — or something like that. Everything is as it should be, except . . . or is it?

Fortunately, thanks to add-ins, you can change the behavior of a lot of software, including Microsoft Office products. The add-in is a piece of additional software that uses the basic functionality of an Office product to make something totally new. You can then use that new piece of functionality in the Office product.

In this chapter, you get a chance to change the way Word works. You're not changing the essential code, perhaps, but you are changing the way the user interacts with the software.

What's an Add-In, Anyway?

In a broad sense, an *add-in* is a component that you can include into an existing host to provide certain additional functions or features. A *host* or *host application* can be virtually any application that supports the add-in model. In the Microsoft Office and VSTO world, an add-in is simply a .NET assembly that gets installed as an extension of the Office suite (Word or Excel, for example).

Most commonly, you'd encounter something similar to an add-in (a plug-in) if you use your Web browser of choice to browse to a Web site that uses content that your browser doesn't recognize. In order to display the content, you create an add-in that contains the necessary functionality to render that content in a Web browser.

Developing add-ins pre-VSTO

In the pre-VSTO era, developing add-ins for Office wasn't an easy task. We don't want to get into too much detail about the pre-VSTO era but think about this: You had to implement an interface in order to get access to the Office object model. Before the host application could recognize an add-in, you had to register it in the registry — and we're not talking about one registry key. Multiple registry keys were necessary for host application to recognize the add-in. To keep it short, VSTO has made software developers' lives much easier.

Because nothing and nobody is perfect — not even people planning and developing software — add-ins are a great way to add functionality or even fix or workaround some bugs when the host application is already out there.

Add-ins are a great help for third-party software developers as well. Instead of developing new software from scratch, third-party developers can use existing software and just develop an add-in that is specific to the problem they're trying to solve.

With the help of Microsoft Visual Studio Tools for Office, you can develop your own add-ins and extend or add functionality to Office applications, including Excel, InfoPath, Outlook, PowerPoint, Visio, and Word. You can leverage all that code that was written and add to it to solve your specific business problems. Why would you build your own charting or statistical application if it's already implemented in Excel? Use those features and concentrate on the code that is specific to your problem.

Microsoft Visual Studio Tools for Office is a superb idea. It enables all developers, without exhaustive COM development knowledge, to develop their own add-ins for the Microsoft Office System with Microsoft.NET Framework. The VSTO team did a really great job handling all the plumbing that is necessary to communicate between add-in and host application, so you can focus on your own code. And yes, you can use everything from .NET Framework in your add-in; you can use your own class libraries, and you also have access to the huge Office object model with every imaginable class, property, and method.

Making a New Project

We bet you want to get started coding, and as in almost every programming book, you start with a legendary Hello World application or, in our case, Hello World add-in. In this example, we use Word as the host application, but you can use Visual Studio 2010 to create add-ins for other Office applications as well.

To make an add-in with Visual Studio 2010:

1. **Double-click the Visual Studio 2010 icon.**

   Visual Studio 2010 opens.

2. **Choose File⇨New⇨Project.**

   The New Project dialog box appears.

3. **Under Installed Templates, expand the Visual Basic node and then the Office node.**

   Subfolders for Office 2010 and Office 2010 projects appear.

4. **Click the Office 2010 subfolder.**

5. **Click Word 2010 Add-in.**

6. **Type** MyFirstWordAddIn **in the name text box.**

   Your work should look quite a bit like the one in Figure 2-1.

   If you chose a different starting configuration, then you might have the Visual Basic code in an Other Languages subfolder.

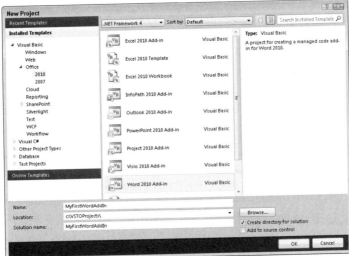

Figure 2-1: The New Project dialog box for your new add-in.

Depending on your language preference, the tree view on the left may show Visual C#, Other Languages, Visual Basic, and so on.

7. **Click OK.**

   Something very similar to Figure 2-2 appears.

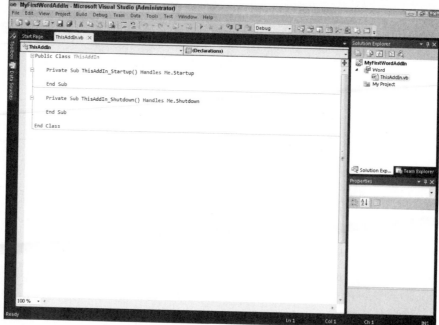

Figure 2-2:
A first view
of the Word
add-in
project
template.

The add-in solution created contains only one project with a single
file named `ThisAddIn.vb`. This file contains a partial class named
`ThisAddIn`, which represents your add-in.

Add-ins don't have any user interface. The good news is if you want a user
interface, you can create it in the same way that you'd create a new form or
user control in a Windows Forms project. Apart from standard controls, you
can also add a Ribbon control to your add-in.

Microsoft developers used partial classes to split the class definition over
two files. If you click the Show All Files button (second button from the left in
Solution Explorer) and expand `ThisAddIn.vb`, you see the second part of the
class named `ThisAddIn.Designer.vb`. This file contains all the necessary
plumbing to hook up with Word. Don't edit this file. It's generated by the VSTO
tooling in Visual Studio.

The add-in class autogenerated by the VSTO project already contains two
events: `ThisAddIn_Startup` and `ThisAddIn_Shutdown`. The first event
fires when Word is started, while the second one fires when you close Word.

A lightning bolt icon appears in front of the Method Name combo box. This is
true throughout Visual Basic, actually. The expanded Method combo box is in
Figure 2-3.

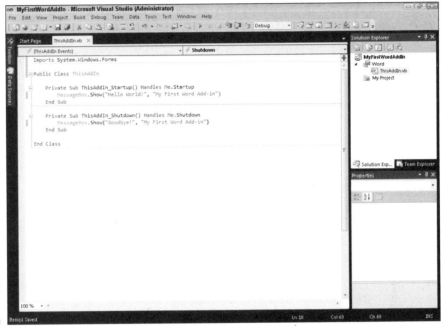

Figure 2-3:
The Method
combo box
in Visual
Basic.

In addition to two events on the add-in level, many more events are available on the application level. If you change the Class Name combo box to Application and open the Method Name combo box, all events on the host application are available.

Making the Add-In Do Amazing Things

To make the add-in functional, you need to add a little code. You can find a `Hello World` example in almost every book about programming, and this book is no different. The Hello World message should appear when you start Word.

Because all VSTO classes have a `Startup` event method, you put the code for displaying a message box inside that method. This method runs every time the add-in starts — in other words, whenever you start Word.

Just as `Startup` runs when you start Word, the `Shutdown` method runs every time you shut down an add-in. Shutdown happens when Word is closed.

Based on that, here are some steps to get you started with your first add-in:

1. **Double-click `ThisAddIn.vb` to open the source code of the project, if it's not already opened.**

2. **Type the following code at the start of the document, where the Import section is (above the class declaration):**

```
Imports System.Windows.Forms
```

With `Imports`, you're telling your project to use the functionality in a separate part of the .NET Framework, called an Assembly. In this case, the `System.Windows.Forms` assembly contains the `MessageBox` class definition and a bunch of other functionality. Apart from the `System.Windows.Forms Imports` statement, the reference project contains references to other assemblies as well. If you want to check all the references, expand the References folder in the Solution Explorer.

3. **Put the cursor inside the method `ThisAddIn_Startup` and type this code:**

```
MessageBox.Show ("Hello World!", "My First Word Add-in")
```

4. **Move the cursor to `ThisAddIn_Shutdown` event handler and type the next block of code:**

```
MessageBox.Show ("Goodbye!", "My First Word Add-in")
```

5. **Click Save.**

After you save the code file, your view should look like the one in Figure 2-4.

When you start the add-in, Word starts, the add-in is loaded, and the `Startup` event is fired, causing a message box to appear. A similar process happens when Word is closed — Word calls the `Shutdown` method, displaying a second message box. Press F5 to run the code and see what I mean.

The `Hello World` example is simple, but it's just a start. You can do much more with add-ins, including giving the user something more to work with than a dialog box. Designing forms and controls can be an interesting but time-consuming process.

If the designs throughout the book don't meet your needs, feel free to move the controls around, change the font and colors, and design the form your way. Because add-ins don't have a user interface by default, start yours by adding a new Windows Form item to the project, like the next example.

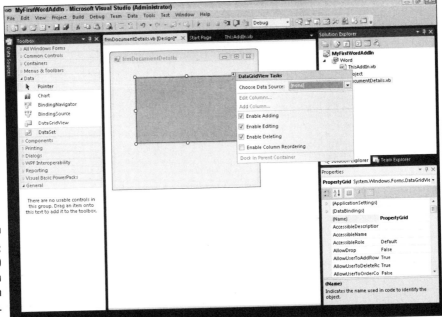

Figure 2-4:
Word 2010
add-in
project with
code.

Adding a user interface to your add-in

1. **Right-click the MyFirstWordAddIn project in the Solution Explorer and choose Add⇨Windows Form.**

   The new item dialog will be displayed.

2. **Type** frmDocumentDetails.vb **in the Name text box and click Add.**

   The New Item dialog box closes, and Windows Form is added to the project and opened.

3. **Click the Toolbox tab and, from the Data section, drag a DataGridView onto the Windows Form.**

4. **With DataGridView selected, click the Properties window and change the value of the name property to** PropertyGrid.

   For quick access to the Properties window, click the DataGridView control on the designer and press F4.

5. Click the DataGridView control on the Designer and click the small Play button on the top right side of the control.

The DataGridView Tasks window appears, as shown in Figure 2-5.

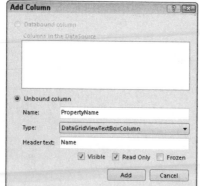

6. Uncheck the Enable Adding, Enable Editing, and Enable Deleting checkboxes and click Dock in Parent Container. The grid stays connected to the top, bottom, and sides on the window.

7. Click Add Column to add a column.

The Add Column dialog box, shown in Figure 2-6, appears.

8. In the Name text box, type PropertyName.

9. In the Header text box, type Name **for the Header text property.**

10. Check the Visible and Read Only checkboxes and then click Add to add the column.

11. Repeat Step 7 through 10 and add another column with name.

This time, name the column **PropertyValue** and the header text **Value**. Also, make sure that the Visible and Read Only checkboxes are still checked.

12. Click Add.

13. Click Close to close the dialog box.

You're returned to the editor.

14. Click Edit Columns on the DataGridView tasks panel.

The Edit Columns dialog box, shown in Figure 2-7, appears.

15. Change AutoSizeMode to Fill on both columns.

You have to click the columns to select them.

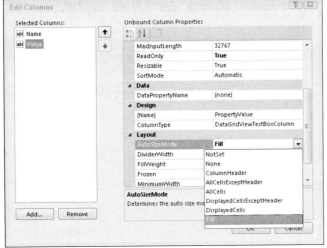

Figure 2-6:
Adding col-
umns to the
DataGrid
View
control.

16. **Click OK and return to the Editor.**

A user interface is now in the project.

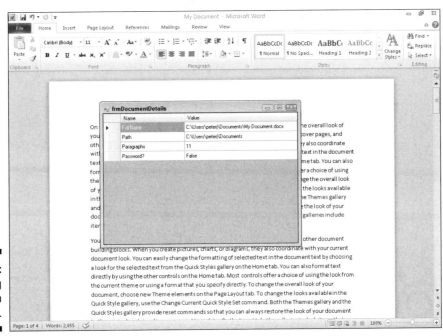

Figure 2-7:
Setting
column
properties.

Putting some data in that add-in

The add-in — which was once only a popup box — is now a full-fledged dialog with a data grid in it. We can show neat stuff in here. For this example, the Word object model provides the fodder. This kills two proverbial birds with one stone by showing you how to fill that box and showing off the Word object model at the same time.

In the next step list, you access the PropertyGrid control and add rows to it. The new row on the control contains a property name, such as Full Name or Path, and its value, such as Doc.Path or Doc.Paragraphs.

1. **Double-click ThisAddIn.vb to open it.**

   The code will open in the editor.

2. **Click the Class Name drop-down list and select Application.**

   The Class Name drop-down list is the control on the left side in the code view.

3. **Click the Method Name combo box and choose DocumentOpen.**

   The Method Name combo box is the control on the right side in the code view. After you click DocumentOpen, a method is added to the code.

   The parameter passed to the DocumentOpen method represents a Word document you're opening. You can use that parameter to modify the document or access and change its properties.

4. **Add the following code to the Application_DocumentOpen event handler:**

```
' Create an instance of our form
Dim propertyForm As New frmDocumentDetails
' Add the properties you want to the grid
propertyForm.PropertyGrid.Rows.Add("Full Name", Doc.FullName)
propertyForm.PropertyGrid.Rows.Add("Path", Doc.Path)
propertyForm.PropertyGrid.Rows.Add("Paragraphs", Doc.Paragraphs.Count.
        ToString)
propertyForm.PropertyGrid.Rows.Add("Password?", Doc.HasPassword.ToString)
' Show that form!
propertyForm.Show()
```

5. **Click Save.**

Unfortunately, we don't have the space to cover all the Windows Forms or Visual Basic terms in this book. If the Visual Basic code throws you for a loop, consider looking at *Visual Basic 2008 For Dummies* by Bill Sempf (coincidentally one of your coauthors).

The Doc parameter passed in to DocumentOpen event handler is of type Microsoft.Office.Interop.Word.Document, which basically means that it's a Word document. This object has about 170 properties and around 90 methods that directly allow the programmer to control the document in any way. Need to set a password? It's in there. Need to e-mail it for review? It's covered.

Making the Add-In Work

Due to all the manual steps need to make an add-in work in the pre-VSTO era, you can imagine that debugging was a real nightmare. You had to install pre-VSTO add-ins into the host application's space, which meant removing the add-ins from the scope of the development environment. The developer had to do a lot of logging and such to assist with debugging.

VSTO has fixed that problem. The only thing that developers need to do is to add break points and press the Start Debugging button or F5 key.

When you press Start Debugging (or F5 key on your keyboard), Visual Studio 2010 springs into action. The project is compiled and built. The add-in is then registered with the host application, the host application runs, and the add-in is loaded.

After you click Start Debugging, Word 2010 launches, and the message box you added to the Startup event handler appears. Try opening a document. Figure 2-8 shows the form as developed, with the document properties.

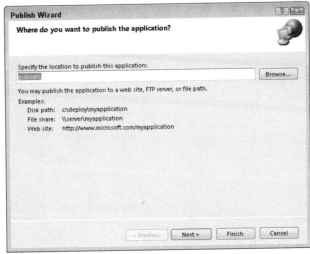

Figure 2-8: The add-in you just built — in action!

Careful: It's possible to have the dialog box appear behind Word on the desktop. We can fix that in code.

That, believe it or not, is all there is to it. The VSTO team put a lot of effort into the developer experience. We've been to hours of sessions by Microsoft on VSTO and built many samples and real-world applications with VSTO. Even though we know how much plumbing is necessary and the amount of work needed to develop add-ins pre-VSTO, we're still surprised every time how easy it is to debug in VSTO.

Seeing Your Add-In in Action

Sooner or later after you build your first add-in and you're running it on your development machine, you'll want to deploy it and make it available to other users.

We've used VSTO since the first version, so we know the pain that developers go through when deploying VSTO solutions. But no more! The first time we tried deploying an add-in with the latest VSTO version and Visual Studio, we were really impressed. We even had to deploy twice because we couldn't believe it.

1. **Right-click `MyFirstWordAddIn` in Solution Explorer and choose Publish.**

   The Publish Wizard dialog box, shown in Figure 2-9, appears.

2. **In the Location field, type the desired location for your add-in or leave the default one (`publish\`).**

3. **Click Next.**

   You see the next step in the Wizard.

4. **Leave the default radio button (From a CD-ROM or DVD-ROM) selected.**

5. **Click Finish.**

Figure 2-9:
You select
the location
for your
files in the
Publish
Wizard dia-
log box.

As you click the Finish button, Visual Studio 2010 rebuilds the project and publishes it to the location you specified in Step 2.

6. **Navigate to the location you specified in Step 2 and run** Setup.exe.

    By default, the Project Publish location is under the \publish folder in the Project Output folder. Of course, you can change this location and publish your project to another location on your hard drive or even publish it on the network or to the Web.

    The Publish command generates the executable setup file, VSTO deployment manifest, and Application Files folder, which contains all necessary project files. I talk more about the deployment and publishing in Chapter 17.

7. **Double-click** MyFirstWordAddIn **VSTO deployment manifest to install the add-in.**

    As you double-click the VSTO deployment manifest file, Microsoft Office Customization Installer dialog box appears).

8. **Click the Install button to install the customization.**

9. **When installation is finished, click Close to close the dialog box.**

All you need to do now is to start Word 2010 to see your add-in in action.

As you can see, deployment, once a major struggle, has become painless and simple. ClickOnce (the tool we used for the preceding steps) has dramatically improved the deployment process. This improvement means you can use ClickOnce features, such as automatic update checking, and your users will always automatically get the newest version of your add-in.

Chapter 3

Making Your Documents Smart

*I*n this chapter, you get started with Document Customizations. You create a simple Document Customization that displays a message box when the document is opened and closed. You also insert information into the predefined bookmarks. This chapter shows you how simple and easy it is to create Document Customization and make your documents smarter.

What Is a Smart Document, Anyway?

When we talking about a *smart document*, we're referring to an Office file, such as a Word or Excel template or document file, that is not just a plain document with text, pictures, and formatting but contains some component that makes it smart. The *smart* part of an Office document, in this case, means additional functionality that brings the document alive. This smart part is a .NET assembly created with VSTO technology.

If you've ever created any macros using VBA in Word, Excel, or other Office applications, then you've already created a type of a smart document. Macros you record are stored together with the document and live inside it.

The term *smart document* suggests two separate pieces to the puzzle: smart and document. The first piece, or smart part, is a .NET assembly created with VSTO. The second piece is an Office document, or *host,* which is hosting the smart component.

To use the proper terminology, instead of using smart documents, we use the term *document-level customizations* (as opposed to application-level customizations or add-ins, described in Chapter 2). Because VSTO supports customizing both documents and templates, we refer to the Document Customizations even if we mean template customization — in the end, documents and templates are very similar.

Customized Office documents act like any other Office document. Its the customization (the .NET assembly) that makes all the difference and provides extra functionality. Functionality is only available to a document that has the .NET assembly attached to it and not any document you'd open or create in Word. Having the functionality available to the document rather than Word or Excel itself is the main difference between add-ins or application-level customizations and smart documents or document-level customizations. Functionality of an add-in is available throughout the host application and in every document a user opens or creates.

An obvious and important difference between VSTO customizations and VBA customizations (or macros) is that brains of VSTO customizations live outside of the document (in .NET assembly) while VBA lives inside the document. You're probably familiar with all the macro viruses that are being e-mailed every day. Well, with VSTO, those viruses can't happen because code is separated from the document and additional security considerations are taken into account before the code is loaded or executed. (We talk about security in Chapter 16.)

You may wonder why you should use VSTO instead of VBA to create a smart document. Well, with VBA, you can't customize the Action pane, use Windows Forms controls, and have all the goodies of .NET in your VBA. Moreover, the VSTO team has created a managed version for some of the Office controls — like bookmarks in Word and list objects and ranges in Excel — and extended the existing, native Office controls and added new events to them. Do you want to add your own controls to the Action pane (see Figure 3-1)? In VSTO, it's not a problem!

While add-ins (see Chapter 2) are designed to modify and interact on an application level, smart documents or document-level customizations can do the same on a document level!

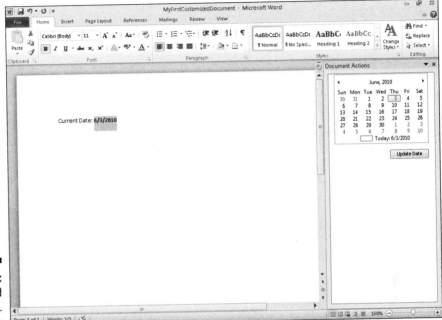

Figure 3-1:
Customized
Action pane.

Taking a Peek at a Quick Example

Document-level customizations have a lot of potential uses. Even though these customizations have a lot of differences from macros, you can think of VSTO as macros on steroids. With VSTO you have the entire suite of power of the .NET Framework. The possibilities are virtually endless.

We have to start somewhere with a quick example, so in this section, you create the `Hello World` example in a Word document.

Creating a new project

To create a new project, open Visual Studio 2010. Make sure you have the setup specified in Chapter 1!

1. **Choose File➪New➪Project.**

   The New Project dialog box appears.

Customizing a Word document? You bet!

Customizations of a document like `Hello World` seem a little more reasonable than the creation of an add-in because users are mostly familiar with macros and how they work. We've all written or used a little piece of code that saved off with the document and modified the contents of a cell in Excel or a margin in Word.

Document Customizations are a little different from macros. What happens here is the creation of a .NET assembly that is linked to the Office document. The code you write doesn't live in a document but in a separate file, and it's linked only to a document (via document properties). With a macro, your code travels inside the document. If you send your document with a macro to thousands of users and then discover a bug in your code, you have to fix the code and then resend the document to all those users.

With VSTO and ClickOnce deployment, you just change the code, publish your document, and the next time users open the customized document, they get the latest version with all the bug fixes and updates.

2. **In the Installed Templates, expand Visual Basic and then Office.**

3. **In the 2010 node, open the Word 2010 Document to select it.**

4. **Type** MyFirstCustomizedDocument **in the Save As field.**

   Your work should look something like Figure 3-2.

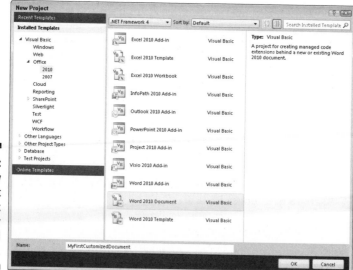

Figure 3-2:
The New
Project
dialog box
for your
customized
document.

5. **Click OK to create the project.**

   At this point, you also have the opportunity to select an existing document to customize, as shown in Figure 3-3.

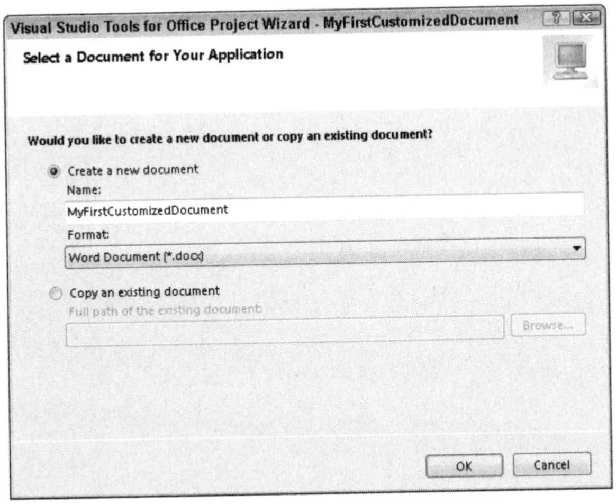

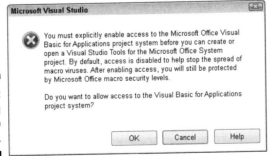

Figure 3-3:
Selecting a
document
for custom-
ization.

6. **Accept the defaults and click OK.**

   You should know, however, that the project template gives you the option to take an already laid-out document and add customizations to it. Using a template is a fairly significant feature, but we aren't going to use it right this second.

7. **Click OK if you see a security warning.**

   This warning, shown in Figure 3-4, appears if you're creating a VSTO Document Customization on this Visual Studio installation for the first time.

Figure 3-4:
Enabling
access to
VBA.

The Visual Studio environment does the totally unexpected: You're now running Word inside Visual Studio (see Figure 3-5).

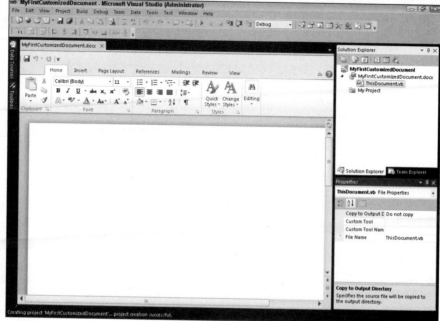

Figure 3-5:
A first view
of the Word
Document
project
template.

Adding basic customizations

If you worked through Chapter 2, adding code to the project will seem kind of familiar. Nonetheless, this time is different because it's a Document Customization and not an add-in, application customization.

When you create an add-in, a message box appears every time you start Word because an add-in is an application-level customization. In the following example, a message box appears only when the customized document is opened. If you still have the add-in from a previous chapter installed, you see that message box, but you also see another message box if you open a Customized Document.

Here are the steps for adding that Document Customization:

1. **Right-click `ThisDocument.vb` in the Solution Explorer and click View Code.**

    The code for the file `ThisDocument.vb` appears.

    Instead of clicking, you can press F7 to switch to Code View or Shift+F7 to switch back to Designer View. `ThisDocument.vb` file acts like a Windows Form and not a regular class file, which is why you have to explicitly request to view the code.

2. **Put the cursor inside `ThisDocument_Startup` method and add this code:**

```
MessageBox.Show("The Document has started!","My First Customized Document")
```

3. **Move the cursor to the `ThisDocument_Shutdown` event handler.**

4. **Add the next block of code:**

```
MessageBox.Show("The Document has left the building!",
"My First Customized Document")
```

5. **Click Save.**

6. **Press F5 to open Word and the customized document.**

   Word opens, and the customized document is loaded.

   A new message box, similar to the one in Figure 3-6, appears when the document is loaded. This message box appears because the document's `Startup` event is invoked — this is the first event that is fired when you double-click the document to open it. The next document event that is executed is the `Open` event. After you close Word, the document `Shutdown` event is called. If you dismiss the message box and close Word, a second message box appears.

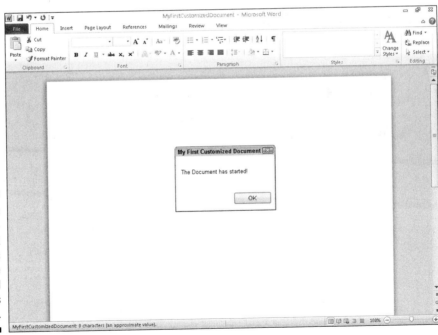

Figure 3-6:
This message box appears when the customized document is loaded.

The application events for Office programs like Word have been around for a while, but some of these document-level events are new. If you're new to Office programming, you may find these events unusual at first. If you've developed solutions for Office, you'll find these events refreshing and useful. Here's a sample list of these events:

- BeforeDoubleClick
- BeforePrint
- BeforeSave
- MailMergeAfterMerge
- MailMergeBeforeMerge
- SelectionChange
- SyncEvent
- WindowSize

The preceding events offer many benefits, such as the ability to have the document self-check, change the layout before a print job, or make a data connection during a sync or before a mail merge. These events can change the way you think about documents and allow you to satisfy most of your customers needs.

Getting a little more advanced

Those new events look interesting. so why not use them in an example? In Chapter 2, you can add a window that displays some of the document properties. In this example, we add application properties to the document right before it's saved.

1. **Start in Design View, like Figure 3-5.**

2. **Type the following text in the document:**

   ```
   Name of application:
   Resident path:
   User name:
   ```

3. **Open the Toolbox and expand the Word Controls section.**

4. **Drag the Bookmark control to the document surface.**

   The Bookmarks dialog box, shown in Figure 3-7, appears.

5. **Place the cursor after the colon in the first line of text and click OK.**

6. **Repeat Step 5 for the remaining two lines of text (path and user name) then save the project.**

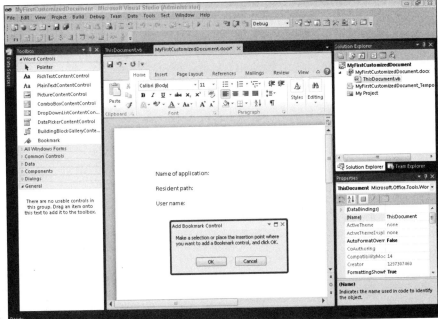

Figure 3-7:
The Bookmarks dialog box appears when you drag a Bookmark control to the document.

7. **Select the newly created bookmarks from the Properties window drop-down list and change the name properties to `bmNameOf Application`, `bmResidentPath`, and `bmUserName`.**

   To open Properties window, click F4 in Design View. Select the desired control from the dropdown.

8. **Press F7 to switch back to Code View.**

9. **Click the Class name drop-down list and select `ThisApplication`.**

10. **Click the Method name drop-down list and select the `DocumentBeforeSave` event.**

    The code for the `DocumentBeforeSave` event is added.

11. **Move the cursor to the `DocumentBeforeSave` method and type the following code:**

```
bmNameOfApplication.Text = Application.Name
bmResidentPath.Text = Application.Path
bmUserName.Text = Application.UserName
```

The finished code screen looks like Figure 3-8.

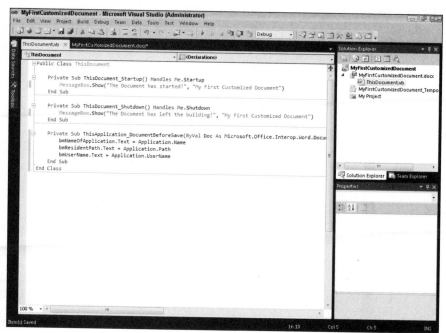

Figure 3-8:
The finished
code layout.

Seeing Your Work in Action

Part of the magic of VSTO is the debugger integration. If you don't have VSTO, you have to launch Word, hook into that process using the Visual Studio debugger, and then open your document.

When you're done, you have to detach the debugger, close the document, and then finally close Word. You'd do this debugging process for every run-through, unless you wanted to take your code out of the document object and test it manually using NUnit or Team System.

VSTO gives you F5 debugging for Office documents. Press F5 (or the Start Debugging button in Visual Studio 2010), and Word launches with your document in place. Breakpoints work, and the IDE traps exceptions. It's a beautiful thing.

To see your work in action, press F5. Here's what happens:

1. **Start Word and open your document**

   The first popup added in the first example in this chapter appears.

2. **Click OK.**

3. **Click Save to save the document and trigger the `DocumentBeforeSave` event.**

   The document information you added in `DocumentBeforeSave` event appears in the document, in normal text.

4. **Close the document.**

   The closing popup from the second example in the chapter appears.

5. **Click OK and close Word.**

   Finally, you return to your development environment.

Our version of the project looks like Figure 3-9, after we saved it.

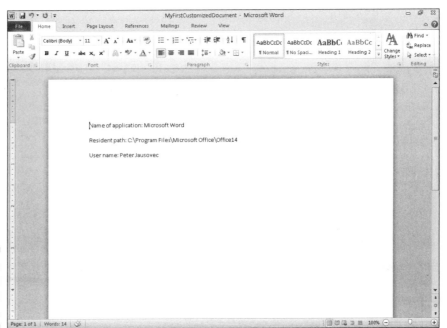

Name of application: Microsoft Word

Resident path: C:\Program Files\Microsoft Office\Office14

User name: Peter Jausovec

Figure 3-9:
The finished
Customized
Document.

The last thing to do is to deploy and distribute your customized document to the prospective users. Deploying is simple: Right-click a project name and click Publish.

Of course, you can access the Publish functionality:

1. **Choose Project⇨MyFirstCustomizedDocument Properties.**

   The Project Properties window appears.

2. Click the Publish tab.

Your screen should look something like Figure 3-10.

From this window, you can set more options on how the customization is deployed. In addition to the Publishing folder and the Document Customization version, you can also set the prerequisites needed on the client computer to successfully run the VSTO solution.

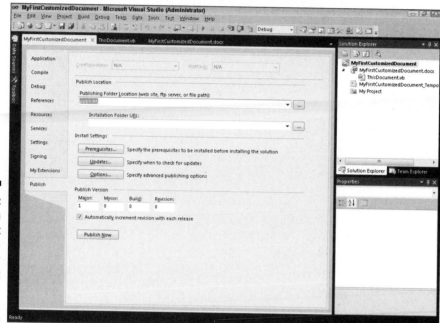

Figure 3-10: Publish project properties for our Document Customization.

In order for your VSTO customization to run, your users have to have .NET Framework 3.5 and Visual Studio Tools for Office Runtime installed.

Besides prerequisites, you can also specify how your customization should be updated. If you click the Updates button, you should see the dialog box shown in Figure 3-11.

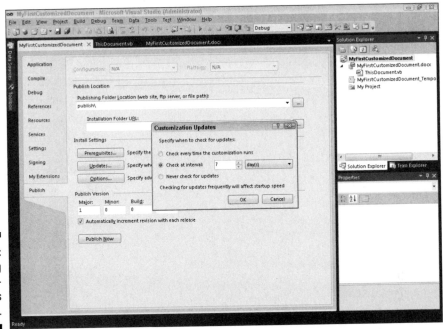

Figure 3-11:
Specifying
customiza-
tion updates
settings.

These dialog boxes may seem familiar to you if you've ever deployed any Windows Forms applications. The process for deploying VSTO solutions has become similar, almost identical to deploying Windows Forms applications. The brains behind this type of deployment are called ClickOnce.

Chapter 4

Designing for VSTO

- -

In This Chapter

▶ Keeping up with user expectations

▶ Using the project lifecycle

▶ Getting the most out of VSTO

▶ Keeping in mind design tips when building applications

▶ Benefiting from VSTO

- -

Chapters 2 and 3 showed the basics for the two major tools built into Visual Studio Tools for Office — add-ins and Customized Documents. While these are the tools, the design still needs to be handled. To handle the design, you, as the developer, need to know what VSTO can do for you.

This isn't a marketing slick for VSTO, but we do want to get across the features and benefits of the tool as a whole. The biggest part of using software like VSTO is thinking about how it can accomplish the goals when a sheaf of requirements is dropped on your desk.

We, like you, are working programmers. We understand that you need to solve problems every day. We believe that VSTO, and the Office Server System concept, will become a larger and larger part of both of our toolkits over the next three years.

In order to facilitate that transition, we offer up this honest look at what VSTO can and can't do.

Meeting the Growing Requirements of Users

We use Google every day. Google is becoming a ubiquitous application for computer programmers. In fact, the search engine is only part of Google. We use the mail software, the word processor, spreadsheet, and advertising tools, too. All told, millions of users take advantage of the more than 30 tools produced by Google.

We hope Google continues to revolutionize the Internet, even though it's making our lives very difficult. Why is Google making our lives — and your life — difficult? Once a week, we have a client say something like, "But how can this be so hard? I've been able to do it with Google for months!"

Most of our clients are used to the monologue that follows, pointing to Google's billions in venture capital and advertising revenue, and hundreds of programmers, engineers, and mathematicians. Nonetheless, the damage is done: Their expectations are set.

The reality is that the implementation of nearly perfect information — true or not — is making it more difficult to sell software. Small business owners especially want miracles for nearly nothing.

Dealing with high expectations used to be a matter of your code library, honestly. When Bill started in the Internet business in 1995, the fact that he had a directory full of prebuilt scripts assured that he could look a client in the eye and say,

"Sure! I can set up that mail form and fax a copy to your office."

Bill had done it before. A limited number of tasks was possible, honestly, so you could have even seen it all. Those days are over.

So much is now possible that it's not conceivable that anyone has a directory somewhere with a collection of Lisp programs that do everything that the client requests. For example, Bill recently had a client ask that Web site orders made after business hours be delivered to his home television. There just isn't an app for that!

In order to deal with these kinds of expectations, you need two sets of tools:

- ✔ A set of tools to help you get features built faster than ever
- ✔ A set of pre-existing features that you can build into new applications

Compacting the most work into the least time

When you're given a set of requirements, your choice of toolset and environment will dictate the length of time you spend fulfilling the requirements. If you build right against the hardware, using assembler, you will spend a lot of time building plumbing code. If you build Windows Forms in Visual Basic, a lot of that code will be taken care of for you as part of the .NET library, and you will code faster.

To press the most work into the least time, you need to use the most efficient toolset and the most functional environment. Using the VSTO library as your toolset and the Microsoft Office System as your environment comes very close to meeting that standard.

VSTO is specifically designed to utilize the way a user works with Office in getting things done. The technicians in us want to talk about events and handling them, but this chapter is about design. Suffice it to say that when a user attempts to tab out of a cell, you can attach code to that action.

Additionally, VSTO gives you the ability to see into the internals of an Office document. The data that the user enters or accesses is available programmatically to you, the programmer, at design time. This kind of access makes VSTO a quality enterprise development library.

The second piece of the puzzle is Office as an environment. In 1997, the big thing was coding for Netscape as an environment. The built-in neatness of HTML and hyperlinking and the like was considered too good to pass up. Compare that to coding for Office.

On one hand, you have a Forward and Back button. On the other hand, you have mail merge, a full personal management system, and time value of money calculations. As far as built-in functionality, Office has it all over web browsers.

Using pre-existing functionality

The more functionality you can effectively (thanks to the toolset) borrow from your environment, the more efficient you will be. Making use of the rich object model in .NET and also in Office is the goal of coding projects with VSTO.

Understanding why you're coding in VSTO is important. For example, say that you need to get time-sensitive data from an XML Web service and generate a graph of the trend shown. Your tools are ASP.NET or Excel.

Those experienced in intranet delivery can see that we're setting you up. Charting is notoriously difficult in any programming language and usually requires the purchase, installation, and learning curve of a third-party component. If you have an infrastructure to support, a component is a worthwhile investment. Otherwise, that same component is just a stumbling block.

Excel, meanwhile, has charts built in. With VSTO and the .NET Framework, you can get to Web Services and generate charts using the built-in Excel functions.

Planning for a Project

Preparation to create a new project consists of two distinct stages:

- *Planning* consists of defining the project and gathering the requirements.
- *Design* consists of recording the screens and logic that will fulfill the requirements and figuring out how to test to see whether they're right.

Rather than just write about how to follow this prescription, we walk you through the planning and design of a project that you can build in Part II. The sample project is a program that calculates dates. What the Office solution does and how it works are things that you figure out as part of the project development lifecycle.

The project lifecycle is a process best shown in Figure 4-1.

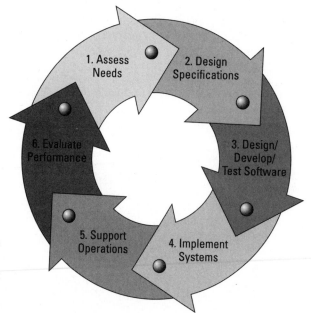

Figure 4-1:
The project
lifecycle.

You should complete projects using this process. If you've been coding in Visual Basic for a while, you may have noticed that a lot of programmers of other languages are sometimes disdainful of Visual Basic. Part of the reason is that you can easily write programs in Visual Basic without doing any planning. However, winging it isn't such a good thing.

This project lifecycle is just one of many design processes. You may hear a lot of industry terms thrown around, and these terms represent various angles on the same basic paradigm. Just remember that no matter what you call your development process, planning and design are good things.

In order to write a decent application, you must first have a plan. Even though steps may overlap, each step should be completed. Even in small projects, an hour spent in design is worth the time. Spending the time to find potential problems while planning is worth it because you'll spend ten times more time finding and squashing bugs in development and testing.

The first three steps of the project development lifecycle (refer to Figure 4-1) raise questions that you need to answer in order to figure out the requirements of your project. When planning an application for VSTO, the questions may look something like this:

- ✔ **Scope:** What does the software need to do? Which Office product supports that functionality best? What functionality needs to be added?

- ✔ **Requirements:** Exactly what is the program doing? How will the user enter input values? What results does the user expect?

- ✔ **Design:** How will the program calculate responses? What user interface elements will best show the data? How will data be stored and retrieved? How will the screen look?

Scoping out the system

Scope is the most important part of the design process because it defines exactly what the application will do. If someone asks you what your application does, you should be able to describe it while standing on one foot. Maybe more importantly, the scope defines what your application won't do — or what is _out of scope_.

Try writing the definition of the application in 101 words or less. Doing so enables you to keep the scope short because you're thinking about the meaning of every word.

Scope defines the application. When a user says that he expects that the Office solution should handle e-mail, you can reply that the feature was out of scope. If this requirement is expected, then you must alter the scope, which takes you back to the drawing board in the planning stages.

Gathering requirements

Requirements are the specific rules that govern the application. Think of requirements as the problems that you must solve in the design step of the project lifecycle.

If-possible requirements are surprisingly common. Basically, if-possible requirements consist of features that may not fit into the budget. Leave those items for last.

You place all the information you need to describe the application's functionality in a *requirements document,* which can be a Word file, a text file, a piece of notebook paper, or a cocktail napkin. Creating and using a requirements document helps ensure that the finished application does what it's supposed to do.

Designing the feature set

After the scope and requirements are figured out, some design needs to occur. Design is the step where you actually figure out how you're going to do what you set out to do in the first two steps. This phase is where knowing what VSTO will do for you is the most important. The rest of the chapter is about making that work.

In the next stage, the design document covers each point of the requirements document. You may want to number the points in your requirements document and in your design document to ensure that each requirement has a related design.

When the requirements are settled, you can describe the software from a technical perspective at the end of the design phase. In the following section, we cover these steps: drawing screens and defining logic.

Figuring Out What VSTO Can Do for You

The largest problem with describing VSTO is that it's tempting to just say, "It's .NET programming for Office." While this statement is true, it falls short of the mark. VSTO adds Office to .NET and .NET to Office. It's an interface that adds power to both sides of the equation. VSTO is individual applications working together.

Individual applications

Microsoft Office isn't a ubiquitous suite of applications throughout the world, but in the business universe, Office is common enough to consider a usable platform. VSTO capitalizes on this fact by allowing you, the developer, to utilize functionality in each individual Office application by creating add-ins that meet new business needs.

For example, calling Microsoft Word the gold standard of word processors will induce ire and nasty e-mails from everyone from LaTeX users to WordPerfect aficionados. None of those people are probably reading this book, so we can say it: Word is a rocking powerful word processor. There isn't much you can't do with Word in the text-processing world — from writing a book (like we're doing now) to generating sophisticated mailing campaigns to documenting software.

Some of Word's abilities, though, are overshadowed by their difficulty of use. For example, Mail Merge in an enterprise environment can overwhelm the most sophisticated of power users at times. Few users know that the Mail Merge wizard can merge from any data source that has an ODBC connector. That said, knowing that using a data source for a merge is possible and actually doing it are different things.

Using the Action Pane and a little VSTO programming, a developer can make an easy, drag-and-drop merge tool that

- ✔ Accesses a company data store of people, products, or anything else

- ✔ Provides an always-available list of fields from that data store

- ✔ Automatically creates a merge from a document template that includes those fields

Most readers have some experience building a Windows or Web application that accesses a company data store — making the Merge tool just takes the idea one step further. Rather than exporting the information from the data store or making and maintaining a complicated data connection, you can just provide an add-in that gives access to the fields.

Is the Merge tool something that hasn't already been done? Not really. All we've done is take an individual application — in this case, Word — and give it a little extra power, customized to our needs. In this case, you can use the existing tools for everything you've done so far. The add-in, however, makes using the data source a lot easier on the users.

Working together

With so many powerful applications, you want to be using them in concert as much as possible. Plan integration into your designs — these programs are interoperable, and you can create add-in logic that works in several office applications.

First, just as you can paste a PowerPoint graphic into a Word document, VSTO can speak to OLE objects in office applications. The `OLEObjects` collection in a document object gives unprecedented interoperability power.

Also, XML Web services provide some interesting features — especially with SharePoint Services and Excel Services. We cover this topic in Part III, but don't overlook loosely coupled transactions when you're creating interoperable office applications.

With the Solution model of Visual Studio, creating add-ins for several applications that all use the same referenced class file is simple. But did you know that you can make common Task pane content for many Office applications, too? It's yet another way to bring more features to your users with less fuss.

Designing Powerful Applications Quickly

What's a design chapter without tips? You should keep a few points in mind when designing for VSTO.

Defining your scope

Just like any other software project, you need to make sure that you know what you want to do before you start.

We have a client who is interested in the development process and is something of a power user. The more features he discovers in VSTO, Office, and Visual Studio, the more he wants to include in the software. The design is set, so we have to keep shooting him down to avoid bloat and delay.

Start your project knowing what you want to accomplish. Let the features of your software drive the design, and not the other way around.

The power of Smart Clients

Let the features of the Office applications work for you. Don't build formulas to calculate time value of money — use Excel. Don't make a table in HTML — use a Word Table. Don't buy a chart component — use PowerPoint. Use what's available and buy what isn't.

The problem here is often the not-built-here syndrome. A lot of developers and development shops won't use software unless they build it. They rebuild the wheel for fun. Try not to make that mistake. Smart clients have a lot of power. Use it!

Using powerful libraries

When designing for Office applications, you have three very powerful object libraries:

- ✔ VSTO itself
- ✔ The .NET Framework
- ✔ The Office Automation model

In the "that goes without saying" department: Learn the VSTO object model. The model has a lot to it that isn't really part of the Office libraries that you're used to. The blending of these libraries is the magic in VSTO applications.

Leveraging a good IDE

Visual Studio offers a lot of features that make the Office development experience much nicer. Use them. Even if you're primarily a Visual Basic Script programmer who is used to working in code without access to a debugger, take it easy on yourself and learn to use those tools in Visual Studio.

Visual Studio — like Visio, for example — has design tools that make the design process easier. The Windows Forms design panel itself is a great design tool. Use the tools to make the design process better for you and your users.

Understanding the limitations

Finally, despite all the cool things that VSTO can do, you need to make sure that you constantly keep in mind what it doesn't do well:

- ✔ VSTO isn't a public application solution. If you're trying to build something for public consumption, use ASP.NET.

- ✔ VSTO isn't the best boxed software solution. If you're selling problem-solving software in a box, then use Windows Presentation Foundation.

- ✔ VSTO isn't groupware. It's still designed for single users, although multiple users can use a VSTO customized document. (SharePoint is groupware though; don't forget about it.)

- ✔ A lot of Microsoft software already does things you could build with VSTO. Don't reinvent the wheel. If you want group presentation software, don't build a PowerPoint add-in; use LiveMeeting.

Getting Help from VSTO

The buy-versus-build decision is very prominent when looking at VSTO. In a Microsoft shop, existing Microsoft products, such as Small Business Accounting and Outlook Business Contact Manager, can solve a lot of problems.

At some point, however, a custom web application is your best choice. The fact is, VSTO may well be the better choice for many things in many situations.

A platform familiar to users

One of the biggest problems in getting employees to use the shiny new intranet is one of comfort. While that huge list of links on the left side of the screen may look impressive to the people paying the bills, it's just intimidating to the Accounting department.

Office is a fairly familiar interface. Even with the changes in Office 2010, studies have shown that Office 2003 users make the change and get back in their comfort zone in under an hour. People are just familiar with it.

Building an application in a familiar interface doesn't just make it faster and easier to build, but it makes people more likely to use it as well. So, if you have a choice between adding a page to the intranet that pumps out a Word document (and loads Word in the web browser, confusing the heck out of everybody) and building a Word document that just does what it needs to do out of the box, choose the comfortable path!

Library of work

When we moved from VB 6 to VB.NET, our biggest gripe was that the 10 or 12 DLLs that we carried around with custom libraries that handle data connections, encryption, Web site navigation, and the like would be obsolete. Then we found out that the same functions — almost to the letter — were available in .NET, and most of them were a lot better.

Working in VSTO is a lot like that situation. If you're accustomed to using VBScript to get things done and have a lot of pre-existing libraries with useful code, you'll find that .NET has all of it, and it's largely better — if only because it's precompiled and vetted by thousands of other developers through the global community.

Existing functionality

On the other side of things, the .NET Windows and Web developers will find that Office brings a lot of things to the table that are lacking in a Form or browser environment. Obviously, there is the document functionality itself, but the file handling is also useful, and the functions within the applications are usually available to do whatever you need. What better place to calculate ROI than in Excel, right?

Part II
VSTO Construction

In this part . . .

*M*icrosoft Office makes it easier for businesses to get things done. VSTO makes it easier to get things done with Office. Part II walks through each Office product supported by VSTO and breaks down the features that VSTO helps bring to the table.

Word and Excel start things off, with more sophisticated add-in and document projects than Part I covers. In this part, you take advantage of the Ribbon and other features of Office 2010 applications. Then the part moves into PowerPoint, Outlook, Visio, and Project.

Chapter 5

Building Word Add-Ins

*I*n this chapter, we dive into the world of Word add-ins and explain advanced topics, such as events, Ribbons, and custom Task panes. (For more on how add-ins extend the functionality of Office applications, see Chapter 2.)

Getting Used to the Ribbon

If you're new to Word 2010, the first thing you probably noticed was the Ribbon. The Ribbon replaced the menus and toolbars everyone was used to in previous versions of Microsoft Office. The Ribbon displays common commands related to your current working context. For example, say that you're writing a document using an older version of Word that doesn't have the Ribbon. Even though your document doesn't contain any tables, the table formatting menu is still visible, as well as other menus and toolbars.

Why would you have all those menus and toolbars cluttering the user interface and shrinking your workspace if you're not using even half of those commands? That's where the Ribbon comes into play.

With the help of the Ribbon, the Office user interface was decluttered — because menus and toolbars are replaced with Ribbon tabs and groups. The table formatting commands aren't cluttering your workspace anymore, and the Ribbon tab that contains table formatting commands is only visible when you're working on a table. Don't get scared by this radically different user interface; you'll get used to it fast.

Customizing the Ribbon with Add-Ins

With VSTO templates available in Visual Studio 2010, you can choose to customize the Ribbon either from application-level customizations or document-level customizations. To put it simply, you can customize the Ribbon from add-ins or from Word documents, Excel workbooks, or even Outlook add-in projects — yes, the Ribbon is now in Microsoft Outlook 2010 as well.

The difference between Ribbons in add-in or document solutions is that the Ribbon you customize from an add-in is available each time you start the host application (provided that add-in is installed), and the Ribbon you customize or create in a document-level customization is available only when you open that customized document. The process of creating and modifying Ribbons in application-level or document-level customizations is exactly the same.

Creating an Office add-in project with a Ribbon

To start an add-in project with a Ribbon project, follow these steps:

1. **In Visual Studio 2010, choose File⇨New Project.**

   The New Project dialog box appears.

2. **Under Installed Templates, expand the Visual Basic node and then Office 2010 node.**

   Subfolders for Office 2007 and Office 2010 projects appear.

3. **Click the 2010 subfolder and then click the Word 2010 Add-in template.**

   If you want a different type of add-in — say, Excel for example — you select the Excel Add-In template.

4. **Type** RibbonAddIn **in the Name text box.**

   The New Project dialog box looks like the one in Figure 5-1.

5. **Click OK.**

   Visual Studio opens your brand new add-in project in the Designer.

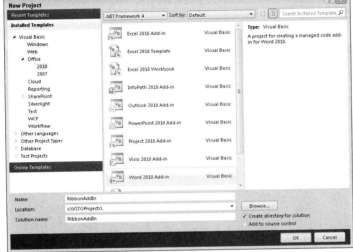

Figure 5-1:
The Word
2010 add-in
project in
the New
Project dia-
log box.

Adding a Ribbon to your project

After you create a project, you can follow these steps to add a Ribbon to the project:

1. **In Solution Explorer, right-click the project name and choose Add⇨ New Item.**

   The New Item dialog box appears.

2. **In the Office category, click the Ribbon (Visual Designer) template.**

   The New item dialog box with the Ribbon (Visual Designer) template selected now resembles Figure 5-2.

3. **Accept the default Ribbon name (Ribbon1.vb) and click Add.**

   The Ribbon is added to the project, and the Ribbon Designer opens in Visual Studio 2010.

You can now use the controls from the Toolbox to customize the Ribbon. Open the Toolbox and drag and drop a button control to the `Group1` control on the Ribbon Designer. Your workspace should look similar to Figure 5-3.

Figure 5-2:
The Ribbon
(Visual
Designer)
template
in the New
Item dialog
box.

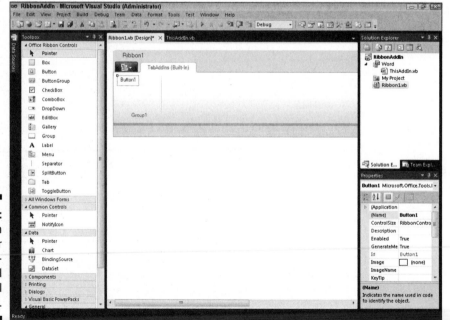

Figure 5-3:
The Ribbon
Designer
with the but-
ton control
inside Visual
Studio 2010.

To see your add-in with the Ribbon in action, press F5 to start Word 2010.

If you click the Add-Ins tab, the Ribbon appears (see Figure 5-4).

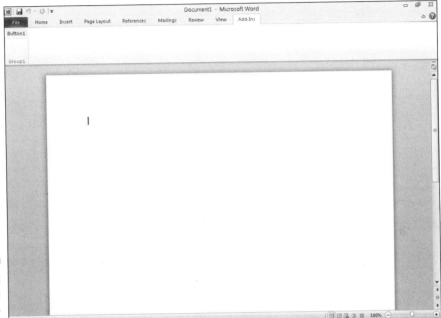

To find out more information about the Ribbon and how to use it, check out Chapter 6.

Building Custom Task Panes

The role of Task panes in Office applications is to display additional information or offer additional functionality to the users. An example of a Task pane in Word is the Research or Thesaurus Task pane. If you click the Review tab on the Ribbon in Word and then click the Thesaurus icon, a Task pane opens on the side, as shown in Figure 5-5.

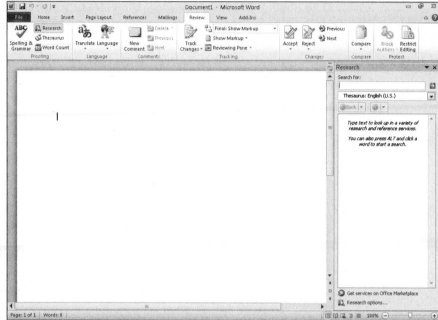

Figure 5-5:
The built-in
Task panes
in Word.

Beside the Task panes that are built in to Word and other Office applications, you can also create your own Task panes. To create a Task pane, you need to create an Office add-in project first and name it. (If you're not sure how to create an add-in project, see the earlier section "Creating an Office add-in project with a Ribbon.")

TIP

Creating a Task pane is the same as creating a regular Windows Forms user control.

To add a user control to the project:

1. **In Solution Explorer, right-click the project name and choose Add⇨ User Control.**

    The New Item dialog box appears.

2. **Type** MyTaskPane.vb **in the Name text box.**

3. **Click Add.**

    The dialog box closes, and the MyTaskPane.vb file appears in Solution Explorer.

After you close the dialog box, the designer for the user control appears automatically. If you open the Toolbox, you see all available Windows Form controls that you can add to the User Control designer. Yes, those controls are essentially the same as in Windows Form designer.

Adding controls to the Task pane

You can also add two text boxes and a button to the User Control designer. When the Task pane appears in Word, you can prompt the users to enter their first and last name. After they click the button, the entered values are inserted in the opened Word document. To add the controls:

1. **Starting with the project from the last example, expand the Common Controls tab on the Toolbox.**

   If the Toolbox isn't visible, choose View⇨Toolbox.

2. **Drag and drop the first TextBox control to the User Control designer.**

3. **Select the TextBox control on the User Control designer and choose View⇨Properties Window).**

   The Properties window appears.

4. **Rename the TextBox control by finding the (Name) property in the Properties window and change the value of the property to txtFirstName.**

   The first control appears on the User Control designer.

5. **To add a second TextBox control to the designer, repeat Steps 2–4 and name the control "txtLastName".**

6. **Add a Button control to the designer.**

   To do so, change the (Name) property value to "btnInsert" and the Text property value to "Insert". You can also add the Label controls right above the TextBox controls to make the whole user control look just a little bit better and user-friendly. After you're done, you should have something similar to Figure 5-6.

If you press F5 to start Word and run the add-in, nothing special happens. The Task pane you created doesn't appear in the Word user interface because you're missing the code to tell the add-in and Word application when to display the Task pane.

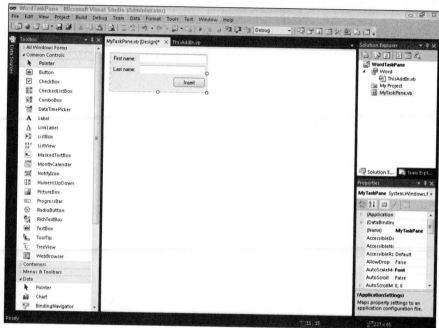

Figure 5-6:
Designing
the Task
pane.

Adding code to the Task pane

For the sake of simplicity, we show the Task pane as soon as the Word
application starts, and the Word add-in loads. In order to show the Task
pane, you need to add a couple of lines of code to the ThisAddIn.vb
file in Solution Explorer. To be more specific, your code should go in the
ThisAddIn_Startup method inside the ThisAddIn class that is in the
ThisAddIn.vb file.

To add code to your Task pane:

1. **In Solution Explorer, open the ThisAddIn.vb file.**

   The ThisAddIn_Startup method is the first method in this file.

2. **Add the following code to the ThisAddIn_Startup method:**

```
Private Sub ThisAddIn_Startup(ByVal sender As Object, ByVal e As System.
        EventArgs) Handles Me.Startup
Dim myCustomTaskPane As Microsoft.Office.Tools.CustomTaskPane
myCustomTaskPane = Me.CustomTaskPanes.Add(New MyTaskPane(), "My Task Pane")
myCustomTaskPane.Visible = True
End Sub
```

VS2010 generates the method like this (without the parameter listing):

```
Private Sub ThisAddIn_Startup() Handles Me.Startup
```

To make your life easier, the VSTO team implemented a `CustomTaskPane` class, which you can use to control the behavior of user-created Task panes. That's why you created `myCustomTaskPane` variable.

You can probably tell from the preceding code that adding custom Task panes isn't that hard at all — it's only a couple lines of code. All you need to do is to call the `.Add` method on the collection of custom Task panes and pass in the user control and title for the custom Task pane. The `.Add` method returns an instance of the `CustomTaskPane`. Just adding the user control to the collection of custom Task panes doesn't make the custom Task pane visible when the add-in starts, so you set the `Visible` attribute to `True`.

Adding functionality to the Task pane

Press F5 to start Word and load the add-in. The user control you designed appears in the Task pane. Figure 5-7 shows how Word looks with the custom Task pane you created.

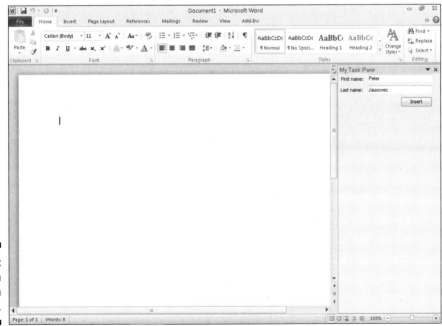

Figure 5-7:
Your custom Task pane in Word.

Although the Task pane appears in Word, it needs more functionality to be more useful. Right now, you can type your control's name control on the custom Task pane, but how do you insert that name in the document?

To add code that allows users to insert the name they typed into the text on the custom Task pane control to the Word document, follow these steps:

1. **Close Word and in Visual Studio, open the User Control designer.**

2. **Double-click the Insert button to add the event handler.**

   Don't worry; you don't have to create the event handler manually. Visual Studio 2010 automatically creates a Click handler for the button and opens the code.

3. **Add the code to the button event handler that reads the text from the first name and last name text box and inserts it to the Word document when someone clicks the Insert button.**

   Here's the code you should type inside the `btnInsert_Click` method:

   ```
   Private Sub btnInsert_Click(ByVal sender As System.Object, ByVal e As
           System.EventArgs) Handles btnInsert.Click
   Dim range As Word.Range = Globals.ThisAddIn.Application.ActiveDocument.
           Range(Start:=0, End:=0)
   range.Text = txtFirstName.Text + " " + txtLastName.Text
   End Sub
   ```

   The first line of the code method may look confusing, but it's actually fairly simple. Because you want to insert the text from text box controls to the Word document, you need a way to get to the document that opens when the add-in is started. You're basically traveling through the hierarchy all the way from the `Globals` class and then to the add-in (`ThisAddIn`), then to the Word application (`Application`), to the active document (`ActivateDocument`) that's loaded in Word, and finally to the `range` in the Word document.

   The second line of the code is pretty much self-explanatory — you use the `Text` property to set the text in the `range` object and to set it to the text users type in the `txtFirstName` and `txtLastName` control.

4. **Verify that the code works by pressing F5.**

   The custom Task pane appears.

5. **Type your first and last name into the text boxes on the Task pane and click the Insert button.**

   Your first and last names are inserted to the document. If you click the Insert button multiple times, the text is always inserted to the beginning of the document because the `Start` and `End` parameters defined in `Range` are set to 0.

The `Range` object represents one way of inserting text to Word documents. Chapter 6 talks about the `Range` object, other objects, and different ways of inserting and manipulating documents.

You can think of the range from the preceding code as a pointer pointing to a location in the document. Because you set `Start` and `End` parameters to 0, that pointer is pointing exactly to the beginning of the document.

Handling Events in Add-Ins

Events are a mechanism you can use to respond to something that happens in your add-in or in the host application (Word, Excel, Outlook, and other Office applications where add-ins are supported). Think about events in this way: If it's raining outside, you take an umbrella before you leave your house. As you take your umbrella, you're responding to the rain event. In this example, the rain is the event, and your response to the rain (the event) is to take the umbrella. You could also say that you're handling the event (rain) by executing an action (taking an umbrella) that is specific to this type of the event.

Events in both application and document-level customizations work in a similar way. An event happens, and you respond to it. You can choose which events you respond to or *handle*. If you're not planning to go outside, you probably won't handle the rain event by taking the umbrella.

In the simple add-in from the Chapter 2, the class in the `ThisAddIn.vb` file already contains two events: `ThisAddIn_Startup` and `ThisAddIn_Shutdown`. Most of the time, these events are used for initialization work when your add-in starts or for cleanup work after the add-in is shut down.

Most commonly, you handle events that are occurring either on the application or document level. Some of the interesting events on the application level are

- ✔ `DocumentBeforeClose`
- ✔ `DocumentBeforePrint`
- ✔ `DocumentBeforeSave`
- ✔ `DocumentChange`
- ✔ `DocumentOpen`
- ✔ `NewDocument`

Creating an event handler

You can respond to many other events, and you can also create your own events. Here's how you can create an event handler to respond to the event of creating a new document in Word:

1. **In Visual Studio 2010, create a new Word add-in project named `EventsAddIn`.**

   If you're not sure how to create a new project, see the earlier section "Creating an Office add-in project with a Ribbon."

   After Visual Studio creates the project, the `ThisAddIn.vb` file opens automatically. Notice that two drop-down lists appear at the top of the code. The first drop-down list on the left side contains objects that are available in your add-in.

2. **From the first drop-down list, select Application.**

   You choose Application because you want to handle an event that happens on the application level.

   The second drop-down list on the right side of the code contains all events that are available on the object you selected from the left drop-down list. By default, the selected item in this drop-down list is Declarations.

3. **From the Events drop-down list, select the `NewDocument` event.**

   Visual Studio creates an empty event handler for the `Application_NewDocument` event, which in code looks like this:

   ```
   Private Sub Application_NewDocument(ByVal Doc As Microsoft.Office.Interop.
           Word.Document) Handles
           Application.NewDocument

       End Sub
   ```

   The code you put in this method is called each time you create a new document in Word.

Accessing global document information

Think about this scenario: You want to create an add-in that adds a user name of the person who created the document to the each new document that is created. You already have the event handler, so to add the text to the document, you need only a couple of lines of code:

```
Dim rng As Word.Range = Globals.ThisAddIn.Application.ActiveDocument.
            Range(Start:=0, End:=0)
rng.Text = "User: " & Globals.ThisAddIn.Application.UserName
```

In the first line of code, we define the range in the document where the text will be inserted. Because you want to insert the text at the beginning of each new document, you set the `Start` and `End` parameters to 0. Finally, you set the `Text` property of the `Range` object to the text you want to insert into the document.

If you press F5 to start Word and run the add-in and then create a new document, the user name is inserted into the document, as shown in Figure 5-8.

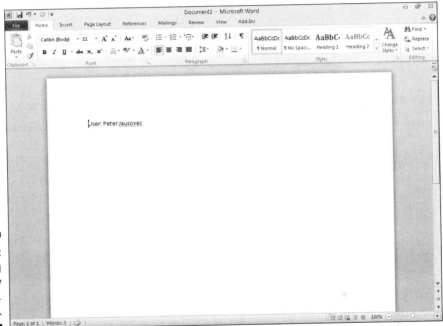

Figure 5-8:
Responding
to the New
Document
event.

Creating your own events

If the available events aren't enough, you can create your own events. To do so, you create a new class and add an event to it.

The simplest way to explain custom events is by using the bank account paradigm. In the following steps, you create an add-in and then add a class that represents a simple bank account. This bank account class supports only withdrawals. When the balance on the account is negative, an event happens. The bank account's starting balance is $1,000. To define a new class:

1. **Create a new Word 2010 add-in and name it `CustomEventsAddIn`.**

    If you're not sure how to create a new project, see the earlier section "Creating an Office add-in project."

2. **In Solution Explorer, right-click the `CustomEventsAddIn` project name and choose Add⇨ Class.**

   The New Item dialog box appears, and the Class template is selected.

3. **Type `BankAccount.vb` in the Name text box and click Add.**

   Visual Studio adds a new, empty class file to the project.

4. **Add the following code to the `BankAccount.vb` file:**

```
Public Class BankAccount
    Private accountBalance As Double = 1000
    Public Event NegativeBalance()

    ReadOnly Property Balance() As Double
        Get
            Return accountBalance
        End Get
    End Property

    Public Sub Withdraw(ByVal amount As Double)
        accountBalance = accountBalance - amount
        If (accountBalance < 0) Then
            RaiseEvent NegativeBalance()
        End If
    End Sub
End Class
```

This code defines a new class named `BankAccount`.

This class has one private variable called `accountBalance`. The value of this variable is set to $1,000 and represents the current balance on the bank account. You also created a read-only property called `Balance`, which returns the `accountBalance` variable. The `ReadOnly` keyword means that the value of this property can only be read and can't be set. The only way the account balance can change in this class is through the `Withdraw` method. When the `Withdraw` method is called, you subtract the amount the user provided to the method from the account balance. After the amount is subtracted from the account balance, you verify whether the new balance is negative (less than 0) and then raise the `NegativeBalance` event. This event is declared at the top of the class with the following line:

```
Public Event NegativeBalance()
```

Taking an interface to the bank

To see how the bank account behaves, you can create a custom Task pane and add some controls to it. In the Task pane, you display the current bank account balance to the user and give him the option to withdraw any amount from the account. When the user withdraws more money than he has on the bank account, the `NegativeBalance` event is raised. You respond to that event by showing the account balance with red color.

1. **Add a new user control to your project and name it `BankAccountTaskPane.vb`.**

   If you're not sure how to do so, see the section "Adding controls to the Task pane," earlier in this chapter.

   Now you can add two label controls, a text box, and a button control to the User Control designer.

2. **Drag and drop the first `Label` control from the Toolbox to the designer and change the Text property of the control to `Current Balance:`.**

3. **Drag and drop the second `Label` control and place it right next to the Label from previous step.**

4. **Change the `Name` property of the `Label` control to the `lblCurrent Balance`.**

5. **Drag and the `TextBox` control right below the two label controls and rename it `txtAmount`.**

6. **Finally, drag and drop a `Button` control and place it next to the `TextBox` control.**

7. **Change the `Text` property to `Withdraw` and the `Name` property to `btnWithdraw`.**

   Your user control in the designer should look similar to Figure 5-9.

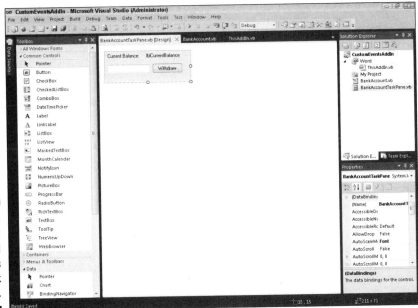

Figure 5-9:
This simple user control represents a bank account.

Giving the bank some class

In order to use the `BankAccount` class from the user control, you need to create an instance of the `BankAccount` class. Open the code view of the `BankAccountTaskPane.vb` file by right-clicking the `BankAccountTaskPane.vb` file in Solution Explorer and choosing View code. To create an instance of the `BankAccount` class, add the following line of code below the `BankAccountTaskPane` class declaration:

```
Public WithEvents myAccount As New BankAccount
```

The preceding line creates an instance of the `BankAccount` class, and the `WithEvents` keyword specifies that you want to use events that this class raises.

Next create a constructor for the `BankAccountTaskPane`. In the constructor, you set the account balance from the `BankAccount` class to appear in the `Label` control. Finally, you add an event handler for the `Withdraw` button control. In this event handler, you call the `Withdraw` method to withdraw the amount that the user enters in the `txtAmount` text box control from the bank account balance.

1. **In the Design Pane, select the `BankAccountTaskPane` object from the left drop-down list.**

2. **Select the New event from the right drop-down list.**

   A constructor is added in the `BankAccountTaskPane` class.

3. **Type the following code right after the `InitializeComponent()` call in the constructor called `New ()`:**

   ```
   lblCurrentBalance.Text = myAccount.Balance
   ```

4. **Switch back to the `BankAccountTaskPane.vb` designer and double-click the Withdraw button to add the click handler.**

   Code view opens, and the `btnWithdraw_Click` method is added to the code.

5. **Add the following code to the `btnWithdraw_Click` method:**

   ```
   myAccount.Withdraw (txtAmount.Text)
   lblCurrentBalance.Text = myAccount.Balance
   ```

The last thing you need to do to add the code to respond to the `NegativeBalance` event you declared in the `BankAccount` class. With the `BankAccountTaskPane.vb` file open, select `myAccount` object from the drop-down list on the left side. From the right drop-down list, select the `NegativeBalance` event. An event handler for the `NegativeBalance` event is added to the code. You want to respond to this event by changing the balance font color to red:

```
lblCurrentBalance.ForeColor = Drawing.Color.Red
```

Following is the complete listing of class `BankAccountTaskPane.vb`:

```
Public Class BankAccountTaskPane
    Public WithEvents myAccount As New BankAccount

    Public Sub New()

        ' This call is required by the designer.
        InitializeComponent()

        ' Add any initialization after the InitializeComponent() call.
        lblCurrentBalance.Text = myAccount.Balance
    End Sub

    Private Sub btnWithdraw_Click(ByVal sender As System.Object, ByVal e As
            System.EventArgs) Handles btnWithdraw.Click
        myAccount.Withdraw(txtAmount.Text)
lblCurrentBalance.Text = myAccount.Balance
    End Sub

    Private Sub myAccount_NegativeBalance() Handles myAccount.NegativeBalance
        lblCurrentBalance.ForeColor = Drawing.Color.Red
    End Sub
End Class
```

Calling up the pane from Word

The last thing you need to do is to make the user control appear on the Task pane when the user starts Word.

1. **Double click the `ThisAddIn.vb` file to open Code View.**

2. **Add the following code to the `ThisAddIn_Startup` method:**

    ```
    Dim accountTaskPane As Microsoft.Office.Tools.CustomTaskPane
    accountTaskPane = Me.CustomTaskPanes.Add(New BankAccountTaskPane, "Bank
            Account")
        accountTaskPane.Visible = True
    ```

    You may be familiar with this code — we use it in previous examples.

3. **Press F5 to start debugging.**

    The Custom Task pane opens (see Figure 5-10).

4. **To verify the bank account behavior, enter an amount into the text box and click the Withdraw button.**

    The text on the label that shows the current balance changes accordingly.

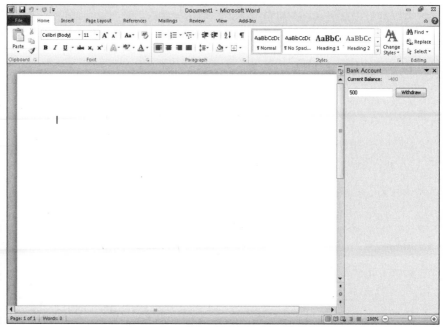

Figure 5-10:
The bank
account
Task pane in
action.

5. **Try withdrawing more money than the balance of the account is.**

   The negative balance event is raised, and the text on the label appears
   in red.

Putting the Account Panel All Together

In this chapter, you create a simple and, to be honest, a bit useless Ribbon.
But you do create a Custom Task pane that actually does something. To
make the Custom Task pane even better, you can combine the Ribbon with
the Custom Task pane.

Instead of displaying a Custom Task pane when an add-in is loaded, you can
hook it up to a button on the Ribbon. When the user clicks the button, the
Custom Task pane appears. The next time the user clicks the button, the
Custom Task pane disappears.

Adding a Ribbon control

Instead of creating a new add-in project from the scratch, you can use the
bank account add-in project from "Building Custom Task Panes." The bank

account example already has a Custom Task pane, and you only need to add the Ribbon control.

1. **Open the bank account add-in project in Visual Studio.**

   If you haven't created this project, refer to the section "Building Custom Task Panes," earlier in this chapter.

2. **Add a new Ribbon to the project.**

   To do so, open the Add New Item dialog box and select Ribbon (Visual Designer) template from the list of templates. You can use the default Ribbon name (Ribbon1) and click Add to add the Ribbon to the project.

3. **Drag and drop the `ToggleButton` control to `Group1` on the Ribbon designer so that you toggle the Custom Task pane's visibility.**

   You can make the button look nicer by changing the group and `ToggleButton Label` property.

4. **Click the `Group1` on the Ribbon Designer and change the `Label` property in the Properties window to Custom Task Pane.**

   The `Group1` control label on the Ribbon Designer changes accordingly.

5. **Click the `ToggleButton1` on the Ribbon Designer and change the `Label` property in the Properties window to Toggle Visibility.**

   The `ToggleButton` label changes.

Making the Task pane appear and disappear

You can add code to make the Task pane either appear or disappear. You can now delete any code from the `ThisAddIn_Startup` method we added in "Giving the bank some class." Instead of adding the Custom Task pane from the add-in `Startup` method, you can handle the Task pane from the Ribbon code. To do so:

1. **In the Ribbon Designer, double-click the toggle button control to add the `Click` handler and open the `Ribbon1.vb` code.**

2. **Add the following line of code right after `Public Class Ribbon1` line:**

```
Dim BankAccountTaskPane As Microsoft.Office.Tools.CustomTaskPane
```

   With this line of code, you're declaring the `myCustomTaskPane` variable on the class level, so you have only one instance of the Custom Task pane control.

3. **Add the following code to `ToggleButton1_Click` method:**

```
If BankAccountTaskPane Is Nothing Then
        BankAccountTaskPane = Globals.ThisAddIn.CustomTaskPanes.Add(New
        BankAccountTaskPane(), "Bank Account")
End If

BankAccountTaskPane.Visible = CType(sender, RibbonToggleButton).Checked
```

Instead of creating and adding new `MyTaskPane` to the `CustomTaskPanes`
collection each time the user clicks the button, you check whether
`myCustomTaskPane` has been created yet, and if not, you create it. In
the second statement, you set the `Visible` property to the toggle button's `Checked` property. If the toggle button is checked (pressed), the
value is `True`, the `Visible` property of `myCustomTaskPane` is set to
`True` as well, and the Custom Task pane is visible. Otherwise, when the
button isn't checked, the Custom Task pane isn't visible.

4. **Press F5 to run the application and verify the behavior.**

Because you removed the code from `Startup` method, the Custom task
pane isn't visible yet. To display it, click the Add-Ins tab. You should see
a group with the Toggle Visibility button on it (see Figure 5-11).

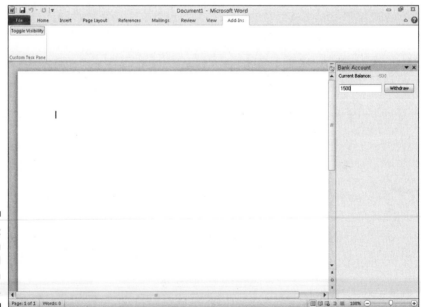

Figure 5-11:
The custom
Ribbon and
Task pane in
Word.

5. **Click the Toggle Visibility button.**

The Custom Task pane is there. Notice how the Toggle Visibility button
is checked? If you click the button again, the Custom Task pane should
disappear.

Chapter 6

Customizing Word Documents

Microsoft Word is one of the most popular applications from the Microsoft Office suite. The basic idea of Word is create a document, write text, format the document, and perhaps add pictures, tables, and charts. You can then save the document and print it, e-mail it, or even upload it to the SharePoint document library where others can download it, update it, and upload it again, repeating the whole cycle.

With the help of the Visual Studio Tools for Office, you can write customizations that can manipulate documents at almost every point in the document lifecycle. For example, if your work requires you to add certain data to the document before the document is printed, VSTO can help you with that task. If you need to automatically create a PDF version of the document or upload a document to the FTP server each time user saves it, VSTO can help you do all this and more.

Exploring the Word Object Model

You can use the Word object model to access specific methods or properties and change applications' or document behavior, style, and so on. The various objects in the Word object model are arranged in a hierarchical order. At the top of the Word object model is the `Application` object. Next is the `Document` object. If you drill down even more in both of these objects, you'd see that the Word object model is gigantic, with hundreds of objects and thousands of methods and properties.

The most commonly used objects from Word object model are the

- ✔ Application object
- ✔ Document object
- ✔ Selection object
- ✔ Range object
- ✔ Bookmark object

Changing properties and calling methods on other objects

You can change properties and call methods on other objects in the object model in the same manner. For example, you can access the Document object from `Application.ActiveDocument` — this property returns the active document, opened in Word. As an example, use the `Characters` property to count the number of characters in the active document. The following single line of code returns the number of characters in the active document:

```
Application.ActiveDocument.
    Characters.Count
```

On the document object level, you can also use the `CheckGrammar` method to check the grammar in the document (instead of using the `CheckGrammarAsYouType` property — see the section "The Application object"). In case you have multiple documents opened simultaneously, you have to specify which document instance you want to invoke the `CheckGrammar` method for.

You can also use `Application.Active Document` to reference a Word document, but it works only on the active document.

If you want to check a specific document that is opened, you can access the `Application.Documents` collection and get the collection of all opened documents. In order to get to the specific document, you can use the index to get the document `Application.Documents[1]`.

In the following code, we assume that multiple documents are open. The following code displays the number of all opened documents and then goes through the `Documents` collection and displays the name of each document.

```
MessageBox.Show("# documents:
    " & Me.Application.
    Documents.Count.
    ToString())

Dim document As Word.Document
For Each document In
    Me.Application.Documents
    MessageBox.Show("Document
    name: " & document.Name)
Next
```

The Application object

The top object in the hierarchy is the Application object. This object represents the Word application and is the parent to all the other objects in the object model. Properties and methods of this object usually work with the Word application. So, if you want to control the Word environment, the Application object is your friend.

For example, what object, property, or method from the Word object model can you use to change settings in Word? You can use the Options property in Application object. If you want to check the grammar in the document as you type, you set the CheckGrammarAsYouType property to True.

Likewise, you can change the color of comments using the CommentsColor property.

Every setting you make or change on the Application object applies to the Word application, not the document that is currently opened.

This code listing shows you how to set the CheckGrammarAsYouType property and change the comments color:

```
Me.Application.Options.CheckGrammarAsYouType = True
Me.Application.Options.CommentsColor = Word.WdColorIndex.wdDarkRed
```

The first line enables the grammar checking as you're typing, and the second line changes the comments color to dark red.

The Document object

From the object model, you can manipulate documents the same way you would through the Word user interface. You can probably do it even faster than going through the Word user interface. But before you can write any text to the document, you need to create or open it. The Word object model contains methods you can use to create, open, save, and close documents.

The following code creates a new document in Word:

```
Application.Documents.Add ()
```

Just that one line of code is enough to create a new document in Word. If you want to base your document on a template, you can pass the Word template name — for example, normal.dot — to the Add method:

```
Application.Documents.Add("normal.dot")
```

In order for this line to work, the document template has to be saved in the default Word template folder, which is usually located in `C:\Users\ [UserName]\AppData\Roaming\Microsoft\Templates`, where X is the name of your hard drive and `UserName` is your username (assuming that you're using Windows 7).

The example in this chapter uses Word templates. Why are we using templates and not documents? Templates can be very useful if you're planning to create multiple documents that have same formatting and contain the same text. For example, say that you're creating an invoice that has your company logo, company colors, and special formatting. Why would you create the same invoice with the same layout and formatting over and over again if you could just create a template and enter the necessary specific for that invoice? You design the template once, and you don't worry about that formatting anymore — it's all about reusing the work you've already done.

As you read the following sections, you may be wondering what is going on with our variable naming. The only reason we use short variable names in our examples is to make them fit nicely on a page. We don't like it when one line of code spans through multiple lines because it makes it hard to read and understand. We don't like the names we're using in these examples, but we'd rather use short names so that the code is easier to understand. We encourage you to use meaningful names in your code — use `saveFileDialog` or `open-FileDialog` instead of `dlg` or `openedDocument` instead of `doc` — it's easier to understand.

Opening a document

Opening a document is similar to creating one. Instead of using the `Add` method, you use the `Open` method and pass in the path to the document as a parameter. In order to get the document path, you can use the `OpenFileDialog` class, which is a standard dialog box that appears whenever you try to open a file. When the user selects a file and clicks Open, the document opens, and the title appears. Here is the code to open a document:

```
Dim dlg As New OpenFileDialog()
If dlg.ShowDialog() = DialogResult.OK Then
    Dim doc As Word.Document
    doc = Me.Application.Documents.Open(dlg.FileName)
    MessageBox.Show("You opened document: " & dlg.FileName)
End If
```

Saving and closing a document

Saving and closing a document works similarly to opening one (see preceding section). To save a document, you use the `Save` or `SaveAs` method. To close the document, you use the `Close` method. You can pass in additional parameters to these methods. For example, you can pass in a document path to the `SaveAs` method if you want to save the document to specific location. And when closing a document, you can pass the parameter to save or not to save changes when closing.

Here is the simplest way to save the active document:

```
Me.Application.ActiveDocument.Save()
```

The preceding code saves the document to a temporary location. If you want to set a document name and save it to specific location you can use `SaveFileDialog` and then call `SaveAs` method:

```
Dim dlg As New SaveFileDialog()
If dlg.ShowDialog() = DialogResult.OK Then
    Me.Application.ActiveDocument.SaveAs(dlg.FileName)
End If
```

The preceding code saves the document with the name you specify in the save dialog box. If you don't care about your document, you don't have to save it. Just close it:

```
Me.Application.ActiveDocument.Close()
```

The Range and Selection objects

You can use the `Range` and `Selection` objects to manipulate text inside Word documents. These objects represent a collection of words, characters, and paragraphs. To put it simply, `Range` and `Selection` objects represent text in the document.

Whereas a document has only one `Selection` object, you can define multiple `Range` objects. `Selection` in Word document is a piece of text you select with keyboard or a mouse. If you modify the `Selection` object, the actual selection in your document changes. With the `Range` object, you can modify any part of the document, and your selection doesn't change at all.

Selecting text

You can use the `Selection` object to select the text from character 1 to 30 and display it in a message box:

```
Me.Application.Selection.Start = 1
Me.Application.Selection.End = 30
MessageBox.Show(Me.Application.Selection.Text)
```

If you create a sample Word 2010 document project and insert the preceding code into the `Startup` method and run the project, the text from characters 1 to 30 is highlighted and displayed in the message box, as shown in Figure 6-1.

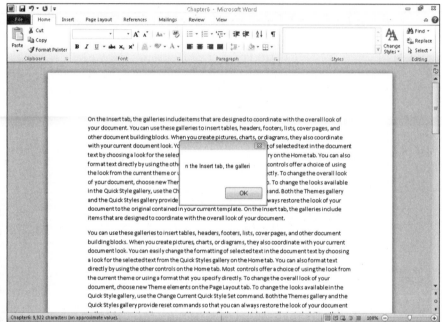

Figure 6-1:
A high-lighted selection in a Word 2010 document.

Instead of using a `Selection` object, try using a `Range` object instead:

```
Dim rng As Word.Range
rng = Me.Application.ActiveDocument.Range(1, 30)
MessageBox.Show(rng.Text)
```

You notice that visually nothing changes in the document. Text isn't highlighted as it was when you used `Selection` object.

You can do plenty more things with the `Range` object. Take a look at the following examples:

```
Dim rng As Word.Range
rng = Me.Application.ActiveDocument.Range(1, 30)

MessageBox.Show("# sentences: " & rng.Sentences.Count)
MessageBox.Show("# words: " & rng.Words.Count)
MessageBox.Show("# characters: " & rng.Characters.Count)
```

The preceding code is self-explanatory — you're displaying the number of sentences, words, and characters in a range.

You can also use `Font` property on `Range` object to change the font style:

```
Dim rng As Word.Range
rng = Me.Application.ActiveDocument.Range(1, 30)
rng.Font.Italic = 1
rng.Font.Bold = 1
rng.Font.Color = Word.WdColor.wdColorBlue
```

Using the `Range` object, you can set the text to bold and italics. Text color also changes to blue. You can change many more properties, such as `Shading`, `Size`, and even `Animation`.

Moving around a document

To move around the document, you can use `Characters`, but it can get very frustrating. You should start with the largest unit of text — `Paragraph`. In the following example, you read the second paragraph from the document and align it to the right side:

```
Dim paragraph As Word.Paragraph
paragraph = Me.Application.ActiveDocument.Paragraphs(2)
paragraph.Alignment = Word.WdParagraphAlignment.wdAlignParagraphRight
```

The `Paragraph` object has fewer properties than `Range`. If you want to use a specific property that is only available on the `Range` object, you can use `Paragraph.Range` to get that `Range` object.

Inserting text

Probably one of the most important things you need to know is how to insert and delete text from documents. Nothing surprising on how to do this task — just use `Range` object.

You can use two methods to insert text: `InsertBefore` and `InsertAfter`. Methods aren't available on the `Paragraph` object, so you have to get the `Range` object first and then call the desired method:

```
Dim paragraph As Word.Paragraph
paragraph = Me.Application.ActiveDocument.Paragraphs(2)

paragraph.Range.InsertBefore("This is before paragraph!")
paragraph.Range.InsertAfter("This is after paragraph!")
```

You select the second paragraph and then insert text at the beginning and at the end of that paragraph.

You can also use some other insert methods on the `Range` object, such as `InsertParagraph`, `InsertParagraphAfter`, `InsertParagraphBefore`, `InsertBreak`, and so on.

You can delete text with the `Selection` object. The `Delete` method will just remove the text selected by the user. (For more on the `Selection` object, see the section "Selecting text," earlier in this chapter.)

The Bookmark object

You can basically think of a *bookmark* as a named location — instead of using numbers for starting and ending position, you can refer to the bookmark by name.

The `Bookmark` object is similar to the `Range` and `Selection` objects. The `Bookmark` object has a starting position and an ending position, just like the `Range` object. You can use bookmarks to mark a certain location in the document.

Microsoft extended the original Word bookmark control and it now has some additional functionality if you use it from Visual Studio Tools for Office. We describe this additional functionality in the section "Showing you the data" later in this chapter.

Working with Tables

Tables in Word consists of rows and columns. To access a specific row or column, you can use the `Rows` and `Columns` properties:

```
Dim tableRange As Word.Range = Range()
Dim myTable As Word.Table = tableRange.Tables.
          Add(tableRange, 2, 3)
myTable.Rows(1).Range.Text = "Row 1."
myTable.Columns(2).Cells(1).Range.Text = "Column 2."
```

The preceding example creates a table with two rows and three columns. The `tableRange` variable represents the location for the table. The interesting thing to note is that every time you have a Range object, you can easily insert a table into it.

 Notice that we did not use the index 0 to access the first row or column in the table. Be aware that indexes for arrays in Office begin with the number 1 and not 0 as in other programming languages.

Both Rows and Columns object have the Cells object. With the help of Cells and an index, you can access every cell inside the table. With all these rows, columns, and cells, tables in Word sound a lot like Excel — indeed, it's quite similar. Because you can get the Range object from Rows and Cells, you can also easily set text formatting.

To set table formatting, check out this example:

```
myTable.Borders.OutsideLineStyle = Word.WdLineStyle.wdLineStyleDouble
myTable.Borders.OutsideLineWidth = Word.WdLineWidth.wdLineWidth025pt
```

The preceding code sets the double line around the table. You can also use a bunch of other line styles. Take a look at the WdLineStyle enumeration. With IntelliSense, you can type Word.WdLineStyle; when you type the dot, you get a list of all values you can use.

Designing a Smart Word Template

In this section, you design a smart Word template that a fictitious company can use for creating a marketing letter. You first need to ask yourself which information a marketing letter needs to contain. The following basic information should appear on a marketing letter:

- **Company details** (company name)
- **Salesperson details** (name, address, e-mail)
- **Marketing text** (price, product, description)
- **Contact details** (Web site, phone number, and so on)

You can also, of course, include additional information on your letter template, if you like. But for this example, you'll keep it simple — you can still go back and add some more text and information to the template. You also won't worry about the template design at this point.

Figure 6-2 shows a marketing letter template with placeholders for information. After you create the template in Word 2010, save it because you'll use it as a base for this book's VSTO project.

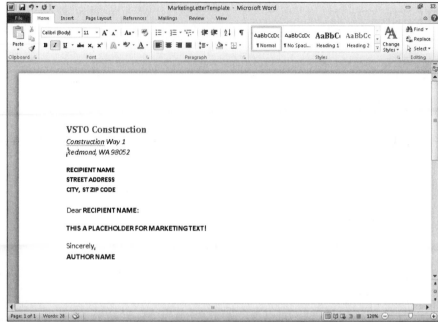

Figure 6-2:
A simple
marketing
letter tem-
plate in
Word 2010.

In Figure 6-2, parts of text (such as author name, recipient name, company name and so on) appear in bold. The boldfaced text marks the portions of text that are different for each customer who receives the marketing letter.

The template! It's alive, alive!

You usually design templates or documents inside the respective application (for example, Word 2010). You can easily design it inside Visual Studio 2010 as well, but we prefer to use Visual Studio for development.

You can use Visual Studio 2010 to breathe life into your template. Follow these steps to create a new Word 2010 Template project based on an existing template:

1. **In Visual Studio 2010, choose File⇨NewProject.**

   The New Project dialog box appears.

2. **Under Installed Templates, expand the Visual Basic node and then Office 2010.**

3. **Select the Word 2010 Template.**

4. **In the Name text box, type the name for your solution.**

   For this example, name it MarketingLetterGenerator because you'll be generating marketing letters.

5. **Click OK.**

   The wizard page, shown in Figure 6-3, appears.

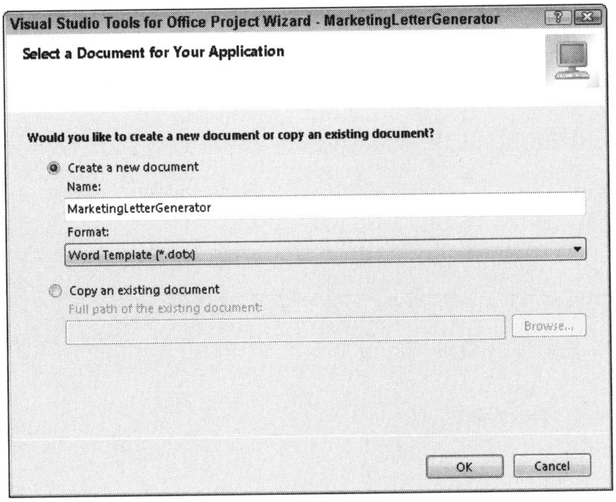

Visual Studio Tools for Office Project Wizard - MarketingLetterGenerator

Select a Document for Your Application

Would you like to create a new document or copy an existing document?

◉ Create a new document
Name:

MarketingLetterGenerator

Format:

Word Template (*.dotx)

○ Copy an existing document
Full path of the existing document:

Browse...

OK   Cancel

Figure 6-3:
Wizard page with selected template.

6. **Choose the Copy An Existing Document option.**

   If you haven't created the template yet, you can select the Create A New Document option and design the Word template inside Visual Studio.

7. **Click the Browse button and browse to the Word template you create in the earlier "Designing a Smart Word Template" section.**

8. **Click OK.**

   The Word 2010 template project is created.

When you click the OK button, Visual Studio 2010 generates the solution and the project. By default, the Word template you created opens in Visual Studio 2010.

If you try to run the solution, you'll notice that nothing special happens. Word 2010 starts, and the marketing letter template you created opens. That's pretty much everything this project does for now.

Coding up a salesperson

In order for the template to do something useful, you need data and customers so that you can start sending those marketing letters. Because creating a database and data is outside the scope of this book, we use a pre-created database, AdventureWorks, which you can download from `http://msftdb-prodsamples.codeplex.com`.

On that site, under the Files section, click the `AdventureWorksDB.msi` link and run the setup. After the setup is completed, follow these steps to add tables from the AdventureWorks database to your project:

1. In Visual Studio 2010, choose Data⊏>Add New Data Source.

The Data Source Configuration Wizard dialog box, shown in Figure 6-4, appears.

Figure 6-4:
From the Data Source Configuration Wizard, you can select your data location.

2. Select the Database option (if not already selected) and click Next.

The Choose a Database Model dialog box appears.

3. Select Dataset and click Next.

The Choose Your Data Connection dialog box appears.

4. Click the New Connection button.

The Choose Data Source dialog box, shown in Figure 6-5, appears. From this dialog box, you can create a new connection to the AdventureWorks database.

Figure 6-5:
You can
select a
data source
from this
dialog box.

5. **Select Microsoft SQL Server Database file from the Data Source drop-down list and click Continue.**

    The Add Connection dialog box, shown in Figure 6-6, appears.

Figure 6-6:
Pointing to
the data-
base file
from Add
Connection
dialog box.

6. **Click Browse to browse to the database file and click Open.**

    The database file name is `AdventureWorks_Data.mdf`, and it should be under `C:\Program Files\Microsoft SQL Server\MSSQL.1\MSSQL\Data`. When you click Open, you return to the Add Connection dialog box.

7. **Click OK to return to Data Source Configuration Wizard.**

    A new connection to the Adventure Works database is added to drop-down list in the Data Source Configuration Wizard.

8. **Click Next on the Data Source Configuration Wizard.**

    A dialog box asks whether you want to copy the database to the project.

9. **Click Yes.**

Visual Studio adds the Data Sources to the project.

10. **Click Next.**

The wizard page with the list of database objects, shown in Figure 6-7, appears.

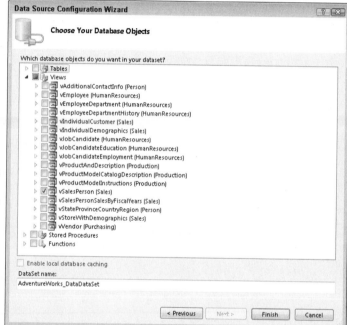

Figure 6-7:
A list of
tables,
views,
stored pro-
cedures,
and func-
tions in your
database.

11. **Expand the Views node and put a checkmark in front of vSalesPerson (Sales).**

12. **Click Finish.**

The database is added to the project.

After the database and template are in place, you can continue developing the user interface.

If you looked closely at Figure 6-4, you probably noticed that you could use more data sources, not just the database. You could, for example use SharePoint or a Web Service as your data source. The nice thing about working with data in Visual Studio 2010 is that it doesn't really matter where the data is coming from.

Showing you the data

In order to display the data from the database, you need a form with controls that hold the data from the database table.

Instead of creating a new form, adding controls to it, and then inserting that data from the control into the document, you can enter data directly to the document.

Taking a look at the Data Source window

Before doing anything else, you need to bring up the Data Source window by choosing Data⇨ Show Data Sources. You see the Data Sources window, shown in Figure 6-8.

Figure 6-8:
The Data
Sources
window
with the
vSalesPer-
son table.

The name of the root node in the Data Sources window is AdventureWorks_ DataDataSet, which represents the database you added to your project in the previous section. Underneath this node is the vSalesPerson node, which is the data table (or data view) where the information you need is located. Entries below the vSalesPerson node represent the columns in the data table.

Also notice the small icon that appears in front of every node. This icon represents a type of the control that displays the column data once the control is dragged and dropped to the designer. If you click one of the columns (for example, Title), you see an arrow that, when clicked, reveals different controls that you can use for that column.

Selecting controls

Selection of controls depends on the designer that is currently opened. If you have a Windows Form or User Control designer open, you can choose from the TextBox, ComboBox, Label, LinkLabel, or ListBox controls. You also have an option to set the column control to None, which means that no data is displayed for that column after you drag and drop it to the designer.

Because we aren't using a Windows Form, open the Document designer by double-clicking ThisDocument.vb. When you click the column names, you now have more choices! In addition to the typical controls, you can also choose from the following controls:

- ✔ PlainTextContentControl
- ✔ RichTextContentControl
- ✔ ComboBoxContentControl
- ✔ DatePickerContentControl
- ✔ BuildingBlockGalleryContentControl
- ✔ Bookmark

Content controls were first introduced in Microsoft Office 2007. They appear on the document and are used for entering and displaying data.

By default, every column is set to use PlainTextContentControl to display data, but you can change it to any other control you like.

You need to display only these data columns:

- ✔ FirstName
- ✔ LastName
- ✔ AddressLine1
- ✔ AddressLine2
- ✔ City
- ✔ StateProvinceName
- ✔ PostalCode

Adding databound content controls to the template

You can add new controls to the template you created in the section "Designing A Smart Word Template," earlier in this chapter:

1. Open the Document designer and the Data Sources window.

You have to drag and drop data columns to the document.

2. Click the `FirstName` data column in the Data Sources window and make sure that the selected control is `PlainTextContentControl`.

3. Drag and drop `PlainTextContentControl` into the document, next to the RECIPIENT NAME line.

4. Drag and drop the `LastName` column into the document, next to the Recipient Name line.

5. Delete the RECIPIENT NAME text.

   That text was just a placeholder so that you knew where to put the databound controls.

6. Repeat the same for the other data columns you need.

   You need to add the following data columns:

   - `FirstName`
   - `LastName`
   - `AddressLine1`
   - `AddressLine2`
   - `City`
   - `StateProvinceName`
   - `PostalCode`

   After you're done, your document should look like Figure 6-9.

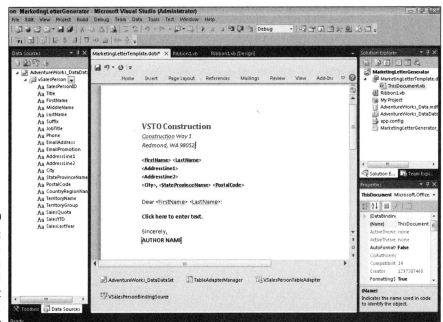

Figure 6-9:
Your template with databound content controls.

The template looks almost the same as it did before you added the databound content controls. A databound control is almost the same as a regular, nondatabound control. The only difference is that a display value is already assigned to the databound control. And that value is retrieved directly from the database! As a result, you don't have to write any lines of code to get the data from the database.

You have two more placeholders you need to wrap with controls. For AUTHOR NAME, use the `Bookmark` control. In comparison to the native bookmark control, VSTO team has extended controls functionality and wrapped the native `Bookmark` control into a new managed `Bookmark` control. With the new, managed `Bookmark` control, you can use events like `Selected`, `BeforeClick`, and `BeforeDoubleClick`. Best of all, the new `Bookmark` control supports data binding. You can bind the data from a data source and display it in a Bookmark:

1. **Switch to Toolbox and choose the `Bookmark` control under Word Controls tab.**

2. **Drag and drop the `Bookmark` control to the designer.**

   A dialog box appears and instructs you to make a selection in the document where you want your `Bookmark` control.

3. **Select the AUTHOR NAME text at the end of the document and click OK.**

   Gray brackets now surround the text, signifying a **`Bookmark`** control.

4. **Click the drop-down list in the Properties window, click `Bookmark1` control, and rename it to `bmkAuthorName`.**

   To rename any control from the property grid, find the `Name` or `(Name)` property and change its value.

5. **Repeat Steps 1 to 4 for the marketing text placeholder.**

   Instead of using `Bookmark` control, use `RichTextContentControl` and rename it to `MarketingText`.

If you run the solution (press F5), you'll notice that the same set of data is always displayed. The reason is that you didn't tell your control which record to pull out of the database, so the first record from the database is always displayed. What you need is a way to move through records in the database.

Programming the Ribbon

The biggest and most obvious change to the user interface of Office is the Ribbon. The Ribbon replaces the menus and toolbars used in previous versions of Office. Commands in Office are reorganized in tabs and chunks. You can imagine the tabs as menus (or toolbars) and chunks as menu items (or toolbar icons).

The main reason for the user interface change was the discovery of functionality. Instead of opening three or more dialog boxes to check that one radio button you care about, you can now more easily find that functionality in the Ribbon.

Some functionality is also displayed only when you can actually use it. Think about this example: What's the point in having buttons and toolbars for working with tables displayed all the time if you don't even have any tables in your document? In Office 2010, when you click inside the table, you see only the functionality specific to tables on the Ribbon.

But what is so great about the Ribbon? Well, the best thing for developers is that you can modify it and access it programmatically and make it work for you. And with VSTO and the new version of Visual Studio, which introduced the so-called Ribbon Designer, this modification is a fairly simple task. When compared to working with the old `CommandBar` object model and no designer in previous versions of Office, you can do more stuff in less time. Behind the scenes Ribbon is a simple XML file. If you don't like designers, you can open up the XML file and modify the Ribbon in a hardcore way.

Browsing the Ribbon controls

The Ribbon supports an extensive set of controls you can use. It has a couple of new controls like Galleries, but most of the Ribbon's controls have the same behavior and look and feel as standard Windows Forms controls, such as buttons, check boxes, combo boxes, edit boxes, and so on.

You can take two paths in Visual Studio 2010 to work with the Ribbon. The first path is more hardcore and involves creating and modifying an XML file by hand. The second one is more user-friendly and involves the Ribbon Designer.

Yes, that's right—the Ribbon has a designer inside Visual Studio 2010; you can just drag and drop the desired controls to the Ribbon from the toolbox shown in Figure 6-10, and you're all set. With the Ribbon Designer inside Visual Studio 2010, you have a good control on Ribbon.

We encourage you to use the Ribbon Designer for now, but if you know what you're doing and you need to fine-tune the Ribbon more, you can do it by modifying the XML file directly. (For more information on modifying the XML file, see the nearby sidebar.)

Figure 6-10:
Ribbon-
specific
controls on
the toolbox
inside Visual
Studio 2010.

Directly editing the Ribbon XML

If you decide at some point that you've had enough of the Ribbon Designer and you want to use an XML file, you can export the Ribbon to XML file. Visual Studio 2010 creates a Ribbon XML file and Ribbon code file. The latter contains comments on how to enable Ribbon XML file in your code.

Unfortunately you don't have an option to import the Ribbon from XML file and display it in the designer. It's good to be aware of this limitation if you're exporting and changing XML file.

You're probably wondering what the Ribbon looks like in XML. Well, take a look at the following snippet from `Ribbon.xml` file:

```
<ribbon>
 <tabs>
  <tab idMso="TabAddIns">
   <group id="group1"
   label="group1">
    <button id="button1"
   label="button1"
   showImage="false" />
   </group>
  </tab>
 </tabs>
</ribbon>
```

It is not so hard to decipher the preceding snippet of code. Based on the preceding XML file, you can easily figure out that the Ribbon has one tab and one group, with one button inside that group.

Adding a Ribbon to marketing letters

Adding a Ribbon to existing or new project is pretty straightforward. If you created the `MarketingLetterGenerator` Word project in the section "Designing a Smart Word Template," earlier in this chapter, you can just add the Ribbon to the project.

Adding a Ribbon to the VSTO project is the same as adding any other project item, such as custom controls and forms. To add a Ribbon:

1. **In Visual Studio 2010, open the `MarketingLetter` project:**

   You can create this project in "Designing a Smart Word Template," earlier in this chapter.

2. **Right-click the project name in Solution Explorer and choose Add⇨ New Item.**

   The Add New Item dialog box appears.

3. **Select the Office node from the Categories tree view on the left side of the dialog box.**

4. **Select the Ribbon (Visual Designer) from the Templates drop-down list on the right side of the dialog box.**

5. **Type the name for the ribbon in the Name text box.**

   We use the default name, `Ribbon1.vb`.

6. **Click Add.**

   The Ribbon is added to the project. You see a nice-looking Ribbon Designer, shown in Figure 6-11.

A new tab named Office Ribbon Controls appears in the toolbox. Click the little plus sign beside the name to expand it. This tab contains the list of controls you can use on the Ribbon Designer. The Ribbon you created already contains one `Group` control, so you can already start adding controls to the group. You can add only a couple of controls — `Group` and `Tab` — directly to the Ribbon. These two controls act like a container for other controls and are used to logically group the commands on the Ribbon.

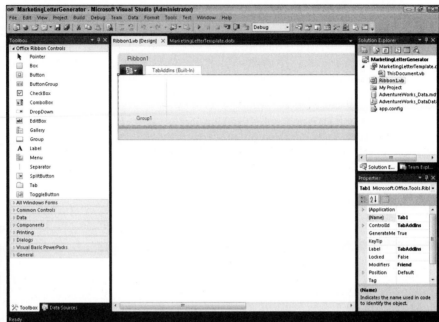

Figure 6-11:
Ribbon
Designer
inside Visual
Studio 2010.

Adding controls to the Ribbon

Because a `Group` control is already on the Ribbon, you can go ahead and drag and drop two `Button` controls to the `Group1` control. You work with controls on the Ribbon, change properties, and add event handlers in the same way you do any other Windows Forms control.

If you want to change the text that appears on the tab, you have to click it and open the Properties window. From the Properties list, click the `Label` property and type the name for your tab.

You can add custom controls to another place on the Ribbon. Click the big Office button on the left side in the Ribbon Designer. Another user control-like designer pops up. This is the so-called Office Menu. Controls added to the Office Menu Designer are visible in the Office application (Word, in this case) when you click the Office button.

After you run the project, the tabs and controls you added to the Ribbon appear next to the built-in Office tabs. You can change the behavior by using the `StartFromScratch` property on the Ribbon. By default this property is set to `False`, but if you set it to `True` and run the project, only your customized Ribbon appears. `StartFromScratch` is only one property, but it can let you completely change your Word user interface.

Putting the finishing touches on the Ribbon

The Marketing Letter project already has the new tab. You now should add two buttons to the default group that is already on the Ribbon. Change the Group label to Marketing Letter Generator, and the button captions to Next and Previous. When the user clicks one of the buttons, you see different data from the database.

When you add the two buttons, they're arranged vertically, which isn't too user-friendly. To get the correct arrangement, drag and drop the ButtonGroup control to the group and then move those two buttons into the ButtonGroup control, as shown in Figure 6-12.

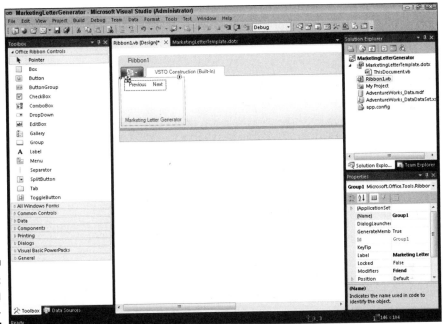

Figure 6-12:
Designing
the Ribbon.

Instead of displaying plain text only on controls, you can take advantage of the Image property and set the image to your controls.

Instead of just providing an empty text box on the Ribbon, you can read the author name through document properties and place it in the text box. Here's how:

1. **Put an EditBox control just below the button group.**

2. **Change the Label property to Author name and change the Name property to txtAuthorName.**

3. **Switch to Ribbon Code View (right-click `Ribbon1.vb` and choose View Code) and locate the method `Ribbon1_Load`.**

   It should be the only method in that class. The code in this method is executed when the Ribbon is loaded. This method is a good place to put in the code for author name.

4. **Type the following code in `Ribbon1_Load` method:**

   ```
   txtAuthorName.Text = Globals.ThisDocument.Application.UserName
   ```

From the preceding code, you can access the `UserName` property, which you can also set from the Word 2010 user interface. If you click the Office button and Word Options, you see the User name text box, which is where your code gets the value. After you have the user name, you set it to the text box on the Ribbon.

You can play around with other properties on the `Application` object. For example, you can access the user initials if you use this property:

```
Globals.ThisDocument.Application.UserInitials.
```

Moving to a new record

You still have some work to do in order to enable your users to move through the records in the database:

1. **In the Ribbon Designer, double-click the Previous and then the Next button.**

   Two empty button click event handlers appear in the code.

2. **Enter this code in the method that handles the Previous button click event:**

   ```
   Globals.ThisDocument.VSalesPersonBindingSource.MovePrevious()
   ```

   You're calling the `MovePrevious` method on the binding source, and you're telling the binding source to show you the previous record in the database. You don't need to worry about refreshing the data or rebinding it to the controls; it's all done automatically.

3. **Add the code for the Next button:**

   ```
   Globals.ThisDocument.VSalesPersonBindingSource.MoveNext()
   ```

   In this case, only the method name is different. Of course, you see the next record in the database instead of the previous one.

Seeing your work in action

After you have the author name already in the text box on the Ribbon, you need to transfer the name to the document — to be more exact, to the bookmark you named `bmkAuthorName`. Here's what you need to do:

1. **Open the Ribbon Designer in Visual Studio.**

2. **Drag and drop another button to the Ribbon and name it** Sign the document.

3. **Double-click the new button to get its event handler.**

4. **Add this code to the event handler:**

```
Globals.ThisDocument.bmkAuthorName.Text = txtAuthorName.Text
```

That's almost everything you need to do. The document has one more control on that isn't used — the marketing text. You have several options on how to use the marketing text control:

✔ You can type the marketing text directly into the document each time a new document is created.

✔ You can read the marketing text from a database and then insert it to the document.

✔ You can create a Task pane where you can let the users browse through different types of marketing texts and that allows them to insert the text into the document.

For this example, you will type the text directly when you open the document.

Your Ribbon with all the controls you added should look like Figure 6-13.

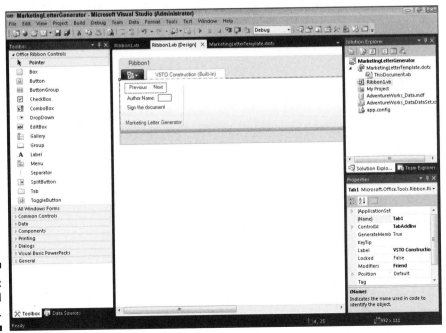

Figure 6-13:
The finished
Ribbon.

When you press F5 to run the project, Word opens (see Figure 6-14). Click the Next and Previous buttons, and the data instantly changes in the document. Click the Sign the Document button and see your name inserted.

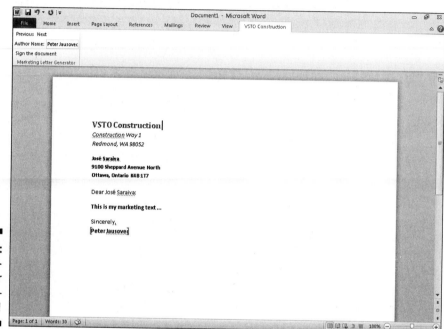

Figure 6-14:
The market-
ing letter
generator —
it works!

Chapter 7

Building an Excel Add-In

. . . .

In This Chapter

▶ Using VSTO to create new functionality in Excel

▶ Creating a dialog box

▶ Using and accessing worksheet and workbook properties

. . . .

*A*n add-in that lives inside the Excel application is just a little bit different from an add-in that lives inside Word, Outlook, or any other Office application VSTO supports. The concept of an add-in in Excel is the same as described in Chapter 2. The only difference is the application that hosts the add-in.

Because the concept of Excel worksheets differs from Word documents, in this chapter, we create a sample that is specific to Excel. (If you want to find out more information about add-ins, refer to Chapter 2.)

Creating a New Project

When you create a new Word document, you have only one design surface in front of you — and that design surface is your Word document. The Excel equivalent of a Word document is an Excel workbook. Excel workbooks can have multiple worksheets.

To create an Excel 2010 add-in:

1. **In Visual Studio 2010, choose File⇨New⇨Project.**

   The New Project dialog box appears.

2. **Expand the Visual Basic node and the Office node.**

   Subfolders for Office 2007 and Office 2010 projects appear.

3. **Click the 2010 subfolder and then click Excel 2010 Add-in.**

4. **Type** `MyFirstExcelAddin` **in the Name text box and click OK.**

   The Excel 2010 add-in project is created.

As you probably noticed, the Excel add-in code file looks almost exactly like the Word add-in code file. The code has the `ThisAddIn_Startup` method and the `ThisAddIn_Shutdown` method.

Designing a Dialog Box

You can create a dialog box that prompts the user for a name when he tries to add new worksheets to the workbook. First, you have to add a Windows Form to the project:

1. **Right-click the project name and choose Add➪Windows Form.**

   The New Project Item dialog box appears.

2. **In the name field, type** frmWorksheetSettings.vb.

3. **Click Add.**

   A file called `frmWorksheetSettings.vb` is added to the project structure in the Solution Explorer, and the Form Design View opens.

   If Design View doesn't appear, double-click the `frmWorksheet Settings.vb` file in the Solution Explorer to open it.

4. **Rename the form caption.**

   To do so, open the Properties window (click the Form and press F4) and change the `Text` property to New Worksheet Settings. As soon as you press Enter, the text in the Form title bar updates.

5. **Change the `MaximizeBox` and `MinimizeBox` property to `False` in the Properties panel.**

   By default, these two properties are set to `True`, which means they appear on the form.

   Because you want the form to behave as a dialog box, you should either remove or hide the Minimize and Maximize buttons. The Minimize and Maximize buttons are usually in the right upper corner of the form.

   As soon as you change the properties to `False`, the Minimize and Maximize buttons disappear from the form, and the only button left is the Close button.

6. **Change the `FormBorderStyle` property value to `FixedDialog` to prevent users from changing the size of the form.**

   By default, this property has the value set to `Sizable`. As the name suggest, the form with the sizable border style is resizable, which you don't want.

   Your form should look similar to Figure 7-1.

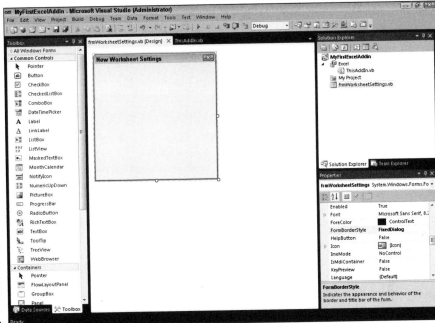

Figure 7-1:
Form with
changed
properties.

7. **Because you want to allow users to name the new worksheet, add a text box and a label to the form.**

   To do so, open the Toolbox (if it's not opened already) and drag and drop a `Label` control and a `TextBox` control onto the Form design surface. (You can open the Toolbox by choosing View➪Toolbox.)

8. **Change the label's `Text` property to `Worksheet name`.**

   To do so, open the Properties window and change the `Text` property value from `Label1` to `Worksheet name`.

9. **Change the control's name the same way you changed the `Text` property in Step 8.**

   Click the desired control (`TextBox`, for example) on the designer. In the Properties window, change the property value of the `(Name)` property to `txtWorksheetName`.

   With the Form properties changed and your label and text box control on the form, your form should look like Figure 7-2.

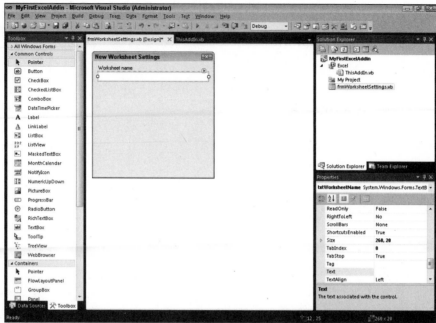

Figure 7-2:
Label and
text box
controls on
the form.

The control's Name property behaves differently from other properties, such as the Text property. Because you can access the control from the code, the control name should correspond to some standards. For example, you can't use spaces or special characters in a control name, so the control names My Control or Hey!!!Control Name aren't valid.

In order to use the worksheet name that the user provided, you have to make the text box control accessible outside of the frmWorksheet Settings class.

10. **Change the Modifiers property, which is by default set to Friend, to Public.**

A couple of controls are missing from the form — you need to provide a way for users to set the name and close the form and to cancel or close the form without accepting the changes.

11. **Drag two button controls from the Toolbox to the form and name them btnAdd and btnCancel.**

12. **Change the Text property to New Sheet so that users will know what clicking the button will do.**

13. **Resize the form and, position the controls any way you prefer.**

We used the layout shown in Figure 7-3.

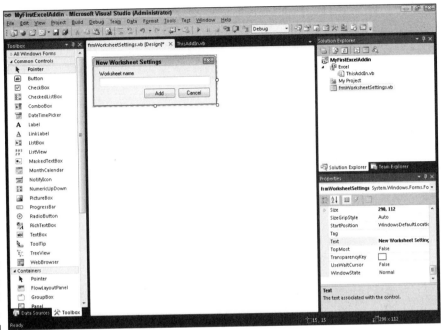

Figure 7-3:
The finished
dialog box.

You probably noticed as you were moving controls around the form that Visual Studio displays guidelines to help you position and align a control with other controls on the form.

You're creating a reference to the form in the `ThisAddIn.vb` class, and you need a way to know when the user clicked a specific button so that you can respond correctly. The `DialogResult` property on the button represents a result produced by clicking the button.

For the Add button, you can set this property to OK, which means that user wants to add a worksheet. (You can easily use the value Yes or any other value.) For the Cancel button set the DialogResult property to Cancel.

14. **Click the Add button on the form and open the Properties window.**

15. **Find the `DialogResult` property and change it to OK for the Add button and to Cancel for the Cancel button.**

Using the dialog box in your add-in

After you design the dialog box (see preceding section), you can start coding. Leave the Form file opened and open or switch to `ThisAddIn.vb` file. Your work starts in `ThisAddIn_Startup` method. Because you want to display the dialog box you created before the user names a new worksheet, you should search for an event that occurs before anyone adds a worksheet.

Adding event handlers in Visual Basic is simple. On the top of the Code View are two drop-down boxes. From the left drop-down box, you can select the object; from the right drop-down box, you can choose appropriate events associated with the selected object.

Adding a worksheet is an event that fires on the application level, so you should search for it under the `Application` object — click the drop-down list on the left side and find the `Application` object. Then click the right drop-down box to display the available events. The `WorkbookNewSheet` event fires each time the user adds a new sheet to the workbook, which is exactly what you're looking for. Select the `WorkbookNewSheet` and add the following event handler method to the code:

```
Application_WorkbookNewSheet(ByVal Wb As Microsoft.Office.Interop.Excel.
                Workbook, ByVal Sh As Object) Handles Application.WorkbookNewSheet
```

Even though no event fires before the new worksheet is added, you can use the parameters that are passed to the previous method to finish your work.

So-called before or after events are fired before or after something happens. In the context of the `Application` object in Excel, a before event called `WorkbookBeforeSave` fires before the actual workbook is saved. The `WorkbookBeforeSave` event is useful if you want to execute a piece of code before the workbook is actually saved. These types of event usually have a way to cancel them, which means that you can cancel the `Save` event and the workbook won't be saved.

In the handler for `WorkbookBeforeSave`, you can display the dialog box (to get the name of the worksheet) and set the new worksheet name. The `Wb` parameter from the preceding method represents your workbook, and `object Sh` represents the new worksheet. Before you can set the name of the new worksheet, you have to cast it from the object type to the Worksheet type, which is in the `Microsoft.Office.Interop.Excel` namespace. But even before you can cast the object, you need to write the code to show the dialog box you created in the previous section. Type the following code in the `Application_WorkbookNewSheet` method:

```
Dim form As New frmWorksheetSettings()
If (form.ShowDialog() = Windows.Forms.DialogResult.OK)Then
                CType(Sh, Excel.Worksheet).Name = form.txtWorksheetName.Text
Else
                CType(Sh, Excel.Worksheet).Delete()
End If
```

In the first line, you created a new form. The second line calls the `ShowDialog` method, which shows the dialog box and returns the `DialogResult`. `DialogResult` tells you which button the user clicked. In the preceding `If` statement, you are checking whether the user clicked the OK button. If he clicked the OK button, you get the name the user typed, and you can assign it the worksheet name.

The second part of the `If` statement deserves a bit of explanation. Because you use the event that triggers after the worksheet is added, you have to delete the worksheet if the user clicks the Cancel button. You can also decide to go with the default name instead of deleting the worksheet. So, in the second part of the `If` statement, which executes only if the user clicks Cancel or closes the dialog box, you call the `Delete` method, which is provided to you by the `Worksheet` class.

Seeing your work in action

You need to test the code and the dialog box you created. Press F5 to start Excel and load your add-in. When Excel starts, click the New Worksheet button, located next to the worksheet tabs at the bottom left. Every new workbook created in Excel contains three worksheets. The button to the right of the last worksheet tab is the new worksheet button — click it!

You should see the new add-in, which is similar to Figure 7-4.

Type some text into the dialog box's text box and click Add. The worksheet name changes to the name you specified in the dialog box.

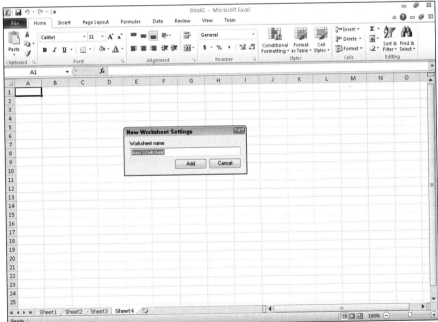

Figure 7-4:
The add-in and dialog box in action!

To verify what happens when you click the Cancel button, click the Add New Worksheet button once again and then click the Cancel button on the dialog box. When the dialog box opens, the new sheet is already created, but as soon as you click Cancel or close the dialog box, the new sheet is deleted.

To return to Visual Studio, you can close Excel or stop debugging from Visual Studio. Now start Excel as you normally would start it by choosing Start⇨Programs. With this new instance of Excel, add a new worksheet and notice that your dialog box appears. That's right — the add-in you created is installed in Excel, and it appears even if you don't start the add-in from Visual Studio. To be honest, the functionality of this add-in can get irritating if you're working with Excel on daily basis. If you want to remove or uninstall the add-in, follow these steps:

1. **In Excel, click the Office button and choose Options.**

   The Excel Options dialog box appears, as shown in Figure 7-5.

2. **From the Excel Options dialog box, click the Add-Ins button.**

   On the right side of the dialog box, the list of active and inactive application add-ins appears.

3. **Select COM Add-Ins from the Manage drop-down list, shown in Figure 7-6, and click Go.**

   The COM Add-Ins dialog box, shown in Figure 7-7, appears.

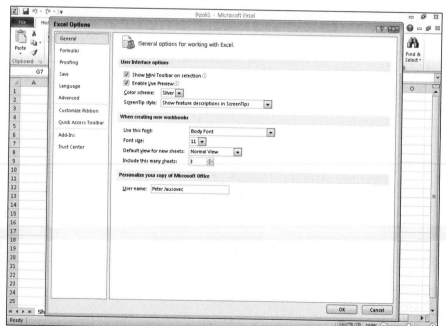

Figure 7-5:
The Excel
Options
dialog box.

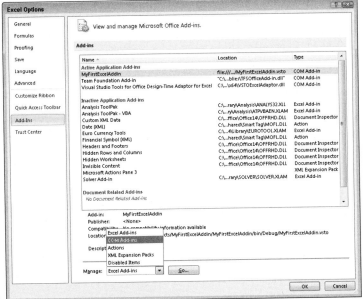

Figure 7-6:
Managing
COM
add-ins in
Excel.

4. **Click the add-in named `MyFirstExcelAddin`.**

5. **Click Remove to remove the add-in from Excel.**

6. **Click OK to close the dialog box.**

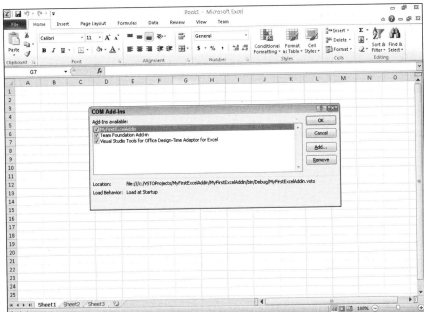

Figure 7-7:
The COM
Add-Ins
dialog box.

Now try adding a new worksheet again. The dialog box isn't showing because you removed it. The next time you run the add-in from Visual Studio, the add-in gets installed, and you have to follow the preceding steps to remove it, if you want to do so.

Chapter 8

Putting Customers into Excel

· ·

In This Chapter

▶ Accessing remote data

▶ Working with the Action pane

▶ Lining up Word and Excel controls

· ·

*V*STO is designed with business in mind. Office is the reigning tool for line-of-business applications worldwide, and VSTO is the programming toolset for that tool. In this chapter, you put some business into Excel by customizing an Excel document.

You start by constructing some basic functions around a business problem with Excel. Then, we show you some neat tricks with the Action pane that represent some of the most common uses of VSTO technology in the real line of business applications.

Customizing Excel Workbooks

Workbooks, worksheets, charts, and tables in Excel are parts of a document, just as paragraphs, words, images, and pages are in Word. The principles we explain in Chapter 6 also apply to Excel workbooks. Even though Excel is a different application than Word, some concepts apply to both applications. In fact, when you add controls, data sources, ribbons, and Task panes to Word or Excel, the only difference is the host application itself.

Excel, like Word, has a `Range` object, which represents a group of cells or a single cell. The VSTO Excel project is structured similar to the Word project in Chapter 6 but has four different code files:

```
Sheet1.vb
Sheet2.vb
Sheet3.vb
ThisWorkbook.vb
```

The first three classes represent each worksheet inside an Excel workbook. The class ThisWorkbook represents the whole workbook — similar to the class ThisDocument in Word. Of course, if you add more worksheets to the workbook, Visual Studio adds a class file for each one.

From those four code files, you can access each sheet by typing code like Globals.Sheet1, which takes you to the first sheet, Globals.Sheet2 to the second one, and so on for any other sheet in the workbook.

Getting to core Excel functions

The Range and Cells classes are all you need for basic functions, such as getting a value from a cell or setting a value to cells on the worksheet. For example, to read a value from cell A1 and write a value to cell B3, you can write

```
Dim number As Integer
number = Globals.Sheet1.Range ("A1").Value
Globals.Sheet1.Range("B3").Value = number + 10
```

If you take the preceding example and say that cell A1 contains number 10, then the value in cell B3 should be 20 after you run the code. The easiest way to do the math, though is to write a formula to add the two numbers:

```
Globals.Sheet1.Range("A3").Formula = "=SUM(A1:A2)"
```

If you think that writing formulas from code is just like writing them within Excel, you're right. The formula in the preceding code adds the values from the cell range A1:A2 and writes the result in cell A3. In the same way that you call the SUM function, you can also call other built-in Excel functions, such as AVERAGE, SQRT, DATE, and so on.

How about changing the text formatting? Well if you have a Range object, you can just call some methods and set some properties on the object. For example, to make the text bold and change the font color to red, type the following code:

```
Globals.Sheet1.Range("A3").Font.Bold = True
Globals.Sheet1.Range("A3").Font.Color = RGB(255,0,0)
```

To set the color, you call the RGB method, which accepts three integers — each one represents a color value. Because you want to use the color red, you set the first value to maximum and other two values to 0. If you want to use the color green, you set the middle value to 255 and first and the last one to 0.

Creating invoices in Excel

Although many companies use Word documents as invoices, you can also use an Excel template. In fact, Excel is more appropriate for invoices than Word because it is a line-of-business application for accounting types. For our backend, we use the same database we used for the Word solution in Chapter 6 — AdventureWorks. Download this database from http://MSFTDBProdSamples .codeplex.com.

To create an invoice in Excel:

1. **In Visual Studio 2010, create a new Excel 2010 Template project based on an empty template named Invoices.**

   To do so, click Add⇨New Project and select the Excel 2010 Template project in the New Project dialog box.

   Next you need to add a database to the project.

2. **Choose Data⇨Add New Data Source.**

   You see the New Data Connection Wizard.

3. **Select Database (if not already selected) and click Next.**

4. **Select Dataset and then click Next.**

   From this window, you create a new connection to the AdventureWorks database.

5. **In the Choose Your Data Connection dialog box, click the New Connection button.**

   The Add Connection dialog box appears.

6. **Click the Browse button to browse to the database file.**

   The database file name is AdventureWorks_Data.mdf, which should be under C:\Program Files\Microsoft SQL Server\MSSQL.1\MSSQL\Data depending on your Windows installation.

7. **Click OK to return to the Data Source Configuration Wizard dialog box and then click Next.**

   A dialog box asks you whether you want to copy the database to the project.

8. **Click Yes and then click Next one more time.**

   A wizard page that contains a list of database objects appears, as shown in Figure 8-1.

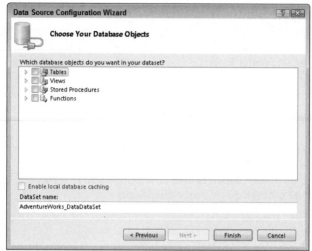

Figure 8-1:
All database
objects.

9. **Expand the Tables node and put a checkmark in front of the table Product (Productions).**

10. **Click Finish.**

   Your database is added to the project.

   If you've done everything correctly, your workspace should look like Figure 8-2.

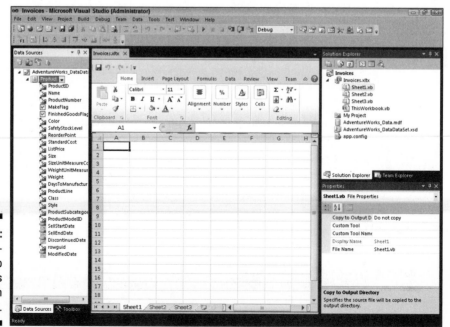

Figure 8-2:
A prop-
erly setup
Invoices
project with
data source.

Next you need to create a user control for choosing the products and then inserting them into the invoice.

11. **Right-click the project name in the Solution Explorer and choose Add⇨User Control.**

    The Add New Item dialog box appears.

12. **Type ucProducts in the Name text box.**

13. **Click Add.**

    The User control is added to the project.

14. **Open the Data Sources dialog box by choosing Data⇨Show Data Sources.**

    The Data Sources window contains the data table Product you added in Step 9, as shown in Figure 8-3.

    If you expand the Product node, you see all the columns in this data table. The icons before each are column are exactly the same as the icons for some of the Toolbox controls. These icons are called *display controls* because they display data once on the form or user control designer. If you drag a Name column (which has a TextBox control icon) onto the form, you would get a TextBox control, which is bound to the Name column in the database. Figure 8-4 shows the list of controls you can use to display data from the database.

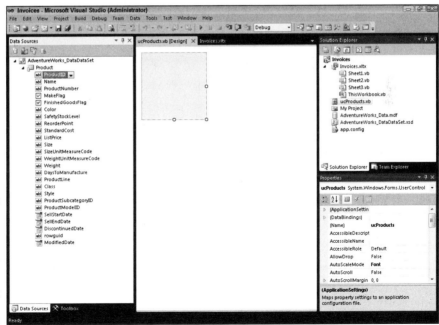

Figure 8-3:
The Data Sources window with the Product data table.

Figure 8-4:
The list of
controls you
can use to
display data.

15. **Change the display control for the `Name`, `ProductNumber`, and `ListPrice` columns to `Label` and drag and drop those columns to your User Control designer.**

    To change the display control for columns, simply click the column name and then click the drop-down arrow to open a context menu with the available displayed controls.

16. **When you're done changing the display controls, drag and drop the columns to the User Control designer and arrange them on the User Control designer to look something like Figure 8-5.**

    As you drag those controls to the User Control designer, Visual Studio created and configured a couple of components and a navigation bar control automatically. The components located at the bottom of the User Control designer are used for connecting to the database and binding the data to the controls as well as navigating and moving through different records in the database.

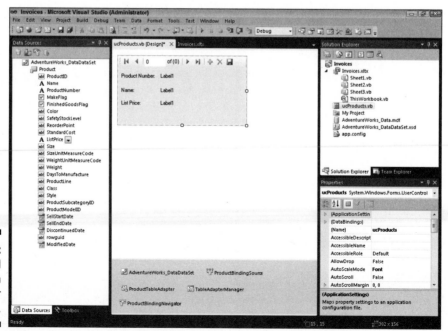

Figure 8-5:
Databound
controls on
the user
control.

Working with the Action pane

Instead of putting a user control on a form, you can place it on the Custom Action pane inside Excel to display product information and enable your users to search for products. You can think of the Action pane as a kind of a placeholder for the controls — similar to a Windows Form or user control. The Research pane is one example of an built-in Action pane control inside Excel or Word.

In order to display the Action pane, you need to add it to the collection of controls on the Action pane. We can do that with one line of code.

1. **Open Solution Explorer by choosing View⇨Solution Explorer.**

2. **Right-click the `ThisWorkbook.vb` file and choose View code.**

   You can also select the `ThisWorkbook.vb` file and press F7. The Code View for `ThisWorkbook.vb` file opens.

3. **Type the following code inside the `ThisWorkbook_Startup` method:**

   ```
   Me.ActionsPane.Controls.Add (New ucProducts ())
   Me.ActionsPane.Visible = True
   ```

   The first line of code adds an instance of your user control to the `ActionsPane` control collection. The second line makes sure that the Action pane is displayed each time the workbook opens.

4. **Press F5 to debug the solution.**

   Excel opens, you see something similar to Figure 8-6.

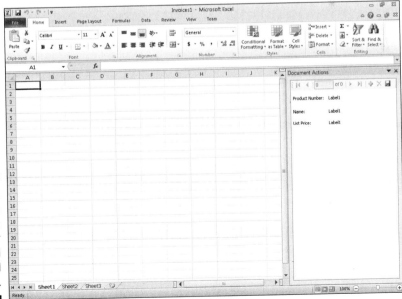

Figure 8-6:
The Action pane with your user control inside Excel 2010.

Working with the Custom Task Pane

VSTO developers can leverage another customizable pane — the Custom Task pane —when developing Office add-ins.

The difference between the Action pane (see preceding section) and the Custom Task pane is that the latter is available to every document or workbook inside the Office application, while the Action pane is available only to a customized document or workbook. If you try to open or create a new workbook in Excel, the Action pane doesn't appear. With a VSTO Office add-in, you can could create a Custom Task pane that is available to your users no matter which document or workbook they open.

If you run the Excel Template solution, you may notice that it doesn't look right. The template doesn't display any data from the database. At this time, the controls aren't bound to the database yet — instead of the Products data, you see the text `Label1`.

Adding real data

To display real data in your controls, follow these steps:

1. **In Visual Studio, right-click the `ucProducts.vb` file and choose View Code to open the code file.**

2. **From the left drop-down list, select the item named `ucProducts Events`.**

3. **From the right drop-down list, select the `Load` event.**

   The `ucProducts_Load` method is added to the code. Your workspace should look similar to Figure 8-7.

You add the `Load` event handler because you want to load the data from the `Products` data table and show it in the user control. Showing data when the control is loaded seems like a good option.

Adding event handlers from the Visual Basic language is extremely simple. When you switch to the code, two drop-down boxes appear at the top. You can select the controls from the left drop-down box and the events handlers from the right one. As soon as you select an event, the code for the event handler is automatically added to the code file.

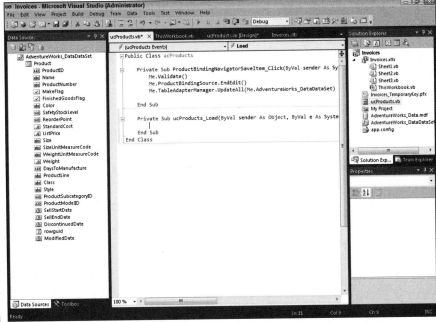

Figure 8-7:
Load event
in the
ucProd
ucts.vb.

Binding VSTO controls

Every time you add a data source to the project, a couple of components are added automatically. You can see those components if you switch to the designer of a form where the databound controls are located. You can use those components to fill the `Product` data table when the control is loaded. Go to the `ucProducts_Load` event handler (), created in the preceding section, and add this code:

```
Me.ProductTableAdapter.Fill (AdventureWorks_DataDataSet.Product)
```

The preceding line calls the `Fill` method on the `Product` table adapter component and passes in the `Product` data table from the AdventureWorks data set. This way, you get your data displayed in the controls. If you run the solution again, data from the database appears on the Action pane, as shown in Figure 8-8.

A lot of products are in the database selected in Figure 8-8. Using the buttons on the navigation control to find the desired product seems a waste of time. Implementing at least a very simple searching mechanism would allow users to search through the table of products in the database. To do so:

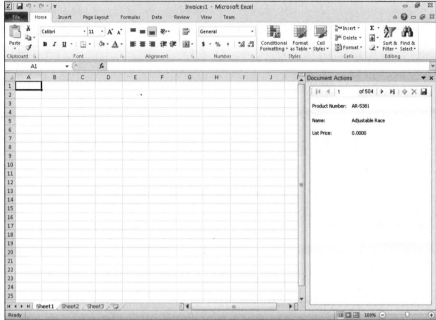

Figure 8-8:
Data
from the
database
displayed on
the Action
pane.

1. **Open the `ucProducts.vb` in Designer View.**

   To do so, double-click the `ucProducts.vb` file in the Solution Explorer.

2. **Drag and drop a `TextBox` and a `Button` control to the design surface.**

   When users enter something in that text box and click the button, you can search for the product in the `Products` data table.

3. **From the Properties window, set the `Name` property of the text box to `txtSearch`, the button's `Name` property to `btnSearch`, and the `Text` property on the button to `Search`.**

   When you're done, your work should look like Figure 8-9.

4. **Double-click the Search button on the user control to create an event handler and add this code:**

```
Dim recordNo As Integer
recordNo = ProductBindingSource.Find("Name", txtSearch.Text)

If (recordNo = -1) Then
MessageBox.Show("Product '" & txtSearch.Text & "' was not found!")
Else
ProductBindingSource.Position = recordNo
End If
```

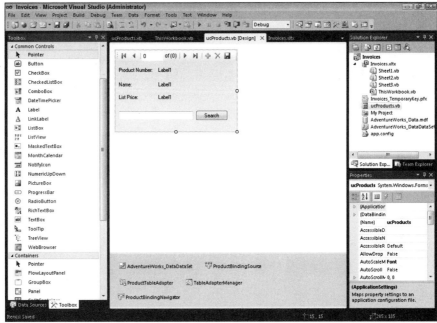

Figure 8-9:
The Search
text box and
button in
place.

In the preceding code, you're passing in the column name (Name) from the database and the text (txtSearch.Text) you want to search to the Find method. This method returns an integer that represents the index of the record in the database.

If the Find method returns the value -1, it means that the item with the name specified wasn't found, so a message box appears. If the record number is any other number, it means that the product was found, and you set the Position property on the binding source to the record number. Because this is a primitive search, you can extend this method so that it supports searching with wildcards — for example, searching for Ite* yields the results Item, Item 1, Item 2, and so on.

5. **Press F5 to run the project.**

   Data appears in the Action pane. If you use the navigation controls at the top of the Action pane, you can actually move through different records in the table.

6. **Try entering something into the search text box and click the Search button.**

   If the item doesn't exist, a message box (see Figure 8-10) appears.

7. **Enter the word** Chain **into the text box and press the Search button.**

   This time the message box isn't displayed because a product was found in the table.

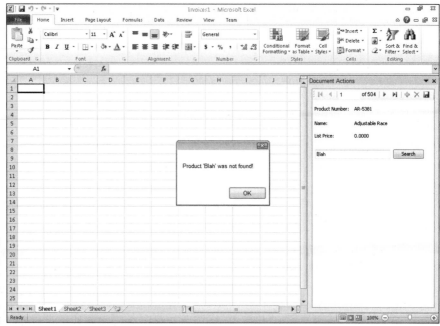

Figure 8-10:
The prod-
uct wasn't
found.

Using Excel Controls

Same as Word, Excel supports a number of managed controls. Beside all .NET controls, you can add two Excel-specific controls to worksheets:

- ✔ NamedRange: You can think of the NamedRange control the same way as a regular Excel range. The difference is that NamedRange has a name, and you can use that name to reference it. For example, if you add a NamedRange control MyNamedRange to cell A1, you no longer need to use Range("A1").Value to get the value; instead, you use MyNamedRange.Value. Named ranges can be pretty useful, and it's more readable than referencing ranges and cells with characters and numbers.

- ✔ ListObject: The ListObject control is used to display data in a series of rows and columns. If you want to add a table from the Data Sources dialog box to the worksheet, the data appears in a ListObject.

If you've done any VBA development, then these two controls probably sound familiar. When compared to native Excel controls, NamedRange and ListObject controls have some additional functionality, such as event handlers.

Using the ListObject control to add data

You can use `ListObject` to add data to an invoice. To do so, you need a list object that has three columns: product number, product name, and list price.

1. **Double-click `Sheet1.vb` to open Sheet1 in Excel.**

   Excel opens in Visual Studio 2010.

2. **Expand the Excel Controls tab in the Toolbox.**

3. **Drag and drop the `ListObject` control to the Excel sheet.**

   The Add ListObject Control dialog box, shown in Figure 8-11, appears.

4. **While the Add ListObject Control dialog box is open, select the cells in row 5 and expand the selection to column C.**

5. **Click OK to add the `ListObject` control to the worksheet.**

   The `ListObject` control, shown in Figure 8-12, is added to the worksheet, and it has three columns.

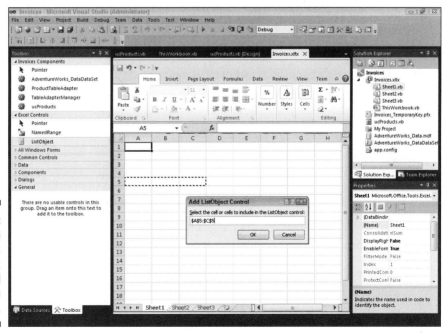

Figure 8-11: Adding the `List Object` control to the worksheet.

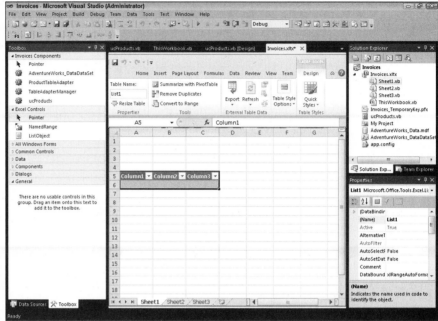

Figure 8-12:
The List
Object
control
on the
worksheet.

6. **From the Properties window, select List1.**

7. **Change the ListObjects' Name property value to lstProducts.**

   Because columns have default names, you should change them to reflect the name of the values they hold.

8. **Rename the ListObject cell in row A to Product number, cell in row B to Name, and cell in row C to List Price.**

   To rename the columns, click the respective cells on the worksheet and start typing — just as you do in Excel. The worksheet with the renamed ListObject cells is shown in Figure 8-13.

   You need to write a few lines of code to insert the data that was selected in the Action pane into the ListObject in the Excel spreadsheet.

9. **Switch back to the ucProducts.vb designer by double-clicking the ucProducts.vb file.**

10. **Add a new button to the designer and change the Name property to btnInsert and Text property to Insert.**

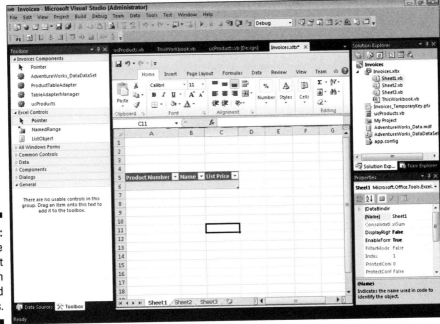

11. **Double-click the Insert button and add the following code to insert the data into the `ListObject` control on the worksheet:**

```
Dim row As Excel.ListRow
row = Globals.Sheet1.lstProducts.ListRows.AddEx()
Globals.Sheet1.Range("A" + row.Range.Row.ToString()).Value =
        ProductNumberLabel1.Text
Globals.Sheet1.Range("B" + row.Range.Row.ToString()).Value = NameLabel1.
        Text

Globals.Sheet1.Range("C" + row.Range.Row.ToString()).Value =
        ListPriceLabel1.Text
```

At the beginning of the code, you get a new `ListRow` object by calling the `AddEx` method on the `lstProducts.ListRows` property. Then you get the specific cells (for example, A6, B6, and C6) and set the values from database. Each time you click the Insert button code adds a new row to the `ListObject`.

Adding a few more columns

The set of steps in the preceding section actually missed a couple of things. You still need to add a Quantity column and Line Total column to the invoice. But instead of changing the user interface on the Action pane, you can make these changes in the Workbook Designer itself.

To add columns in Workbook Designer:

1. **Double click `Sheet1.vb` to open the Excel designer.**

2. **Click next to the last column in the `ListObject` and start typing** Quantity.

   The column is automatically added to the existing `ListObject` — this is really cool!

3. **Repeat the procedure for the Line Total.**

   The Excel sheet should look like the one in Figure 8-14.

   In order to get the correct value in Line total column, you need to create a formula to calculate the total.

4. **Switch back to the `ucProducts.vb` Code View, scroll to the event handler for inserting the data (`btnInsert_Click`), and add this line at the end of the method:**

```
Globals.Sheet1.Range("E" + row.Range.Row.ToString()).Formula = "=D" + row.
        Range.Row.ToString () + "*" + "C"+ row.Range.Row.ToString ()
```

The code you just added sets the formula for column Line total to multiply the price and quantity. The complete code listing for the `btn Insert_Click` method should be exactly like this:

```
Private Sub btnInsert_Click(ByVal sender As System.Object, ByVal e As
        System.EventArgs) Handles btnInsert.Click
Dim row As Excel.ListRow
row = Globals.Sheet1.lstProducts.ListRows.AddEx()
        Globals.Sheet1.Range("A" + row.Range.Row.ToString()).Value =
        ProductNumberLabel1.Text
        Globals.Sheet1.Range("B" + row.Range.Row.ToString()).Value =
        NameLabel1.Text
        Globals.Sheet1.Range("C" + row.Range.Row.ToString()).Value =
        ListPriceLabel1.Text
        Globals.Sheet1.Range("E" + row.Range.Row.ToString()).Formula
        = "=D" + row.Range.Row.ToString() + "*" + "C" + row.Range.Row.
        ToString()
        End Sub
```

Because you have the Line Total, you should also have the total for all line totals — basically the sum of all Line Totals.

5. **Go back to the Workbook Designer by double-clicking the `Sheet1. vb` file and drag and drop a `NamedRange` control right above the `ListObject` and name it `rngTotal`.**

6. **Click the cell where the named range is and insert the following formula:**

```
=SUM(lstProducts[[#All],[Line total]])
```

This formula sums all Line total rows in `lstProducts ListObject`. If you run the solution and add products to the invoice, you should see the line totals updated and the whole total value you just added.

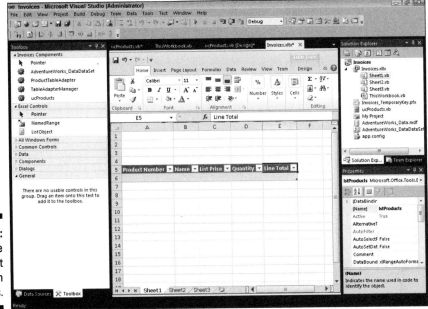

Figure 8-14: The ListObject with columns.

You can see the final product in Figure 8-15. It almost looks like an invoice. If you want, you can make the template look nicer, add some additional text with customers name, and so on.

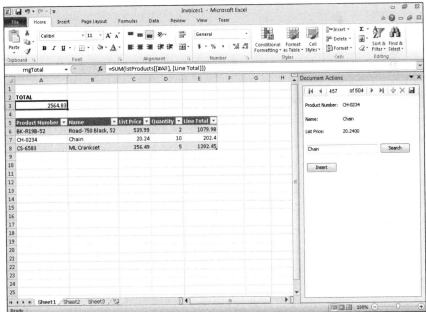

Figure 8-15: The finished Invoicing template.

Displaying data on the worksheets

An easy way to display the data on the worksheets in Excel is to drag and drop the whole `Products` table (or just specific fields) to the designer:

1. **In Visual Studio 2010, double-click `Sheet2.vb` to open `Sheet2`.**

2. **Open the Data Sources window.**

   You see the data table and its columns.

   In the "Adding a few more columns" section, you can use Windows Form controls to show the data, but you can also use Excel controls like `NamedRange` or `ListObject`.

3. **Select the `Product` data table and click the drop-down menu.**

   You see that the default display control is set to `ListObject`.

4. **Drag and drop the whole `Product` table to the designer.**

   All fields from the data table are inserted to the `ListObject` control in Excel, as shown in Figure 8-16.

5. **Run the project and switch to `Sheet2`.**

   The whole `Products` data table is displayed, as shown in Figure 8-17.

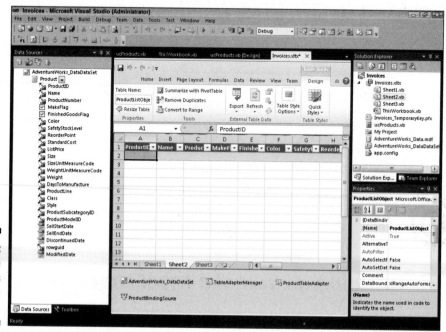

Figure 8-16: The entire Products table on the worksheet.

	ProductID	Name	Product	MakeFl	Finishe	Color	SafetyS	Reorde	Standa	ListPric	Size	SizeUn	Weight	Weight	DaysTo
201	527	Spokes	SK-9283	FALSE	FALSE		1000	750	0	0					0
202	528	Seat Lug	SL-0931	FALSE	FALSE		1000	750	0	0					0
203	529	Stem	SM-9087	TRUE	FALSE		500	375	0	0					1
204	530	Seat Post	SP-2981	FALSE	FALSE		500	375	0	0					0
205	531	Steerer	SR-2098	TRUE	FALSE		500	375	0	0					1
206	532	Seat Stays	SS-2985	TRUE	FALSE		800	600	0	0					0
207	533	Seat Tube	ST-9828	TRUE	FALSE		500	375	0	0					1
208	534	Top Tube	TO-2301	TRUE	FALSE		500	375	0	0					1
209	535	Tension P	TP-0923	FALSE	FALSE		800	600	0	0					0
210	679	Rear Dera	RC-0291	FALSE	FALSE	Silver	500	375	0	0					0
211	680	HL Road Fr	FR-R92B-5	TRUE	TRUE	Black	500	375	1059.31	1431.5	58	CM	LB	2.24	1
212	706	HL Road Fr	FR-R92R-5	TRUE	TRUE	Red	500	375	1059.31	1431.5	58	CM	LB	2.24	1
213	707	Sport-100	HL-U509-F	FALSE	TRUE	Red	4	3	13.0863	34.99					0
214	708	Sport-100	HL-U509	FALSE	TRUE	Black	4	3	13.0863	34.99					0
215	709	Mountain	SO-B909-N	FALSE	TRUE	White	4	3	3.3963	9.5	M				0
216	710	Mountain	SO-B909-L	FALSE	TRUE	White	4	3	3.3963	9.5	L				0
217	711	Sport-100	HL-U509-B	FALSE	TRUE	Blue	4	3	13.0863	34.99					0
218	712	AWC Logo	CA-1098	FALSE	TRUE	Multi	4	3	6.9223	8.99					0
219	713	Long-Slee	LJ-0192-S	FALSE	TRUE	Multi	4	3	38.4923	49.99	S				0
220	714	Long-Slee	LJ-0192-M	FALSE	TRUE	Multi	4	3	38.4923	49.99	M				0
221	715	Long-Slee	LJ-0192-L	FALSE	TRUE	Multi	4	3	38.4923	49.99	L				0
222	716	Long-Slee	LJ-0192-X	FALSE	TRUE	Multi	4	3	38.4923	49.99	XL				0
223	717	HL Road Fr	FR-R92R-6	TRUE	TRUE	Red	500	375	868.6342	1431.5	62	CM	LB	2.3	1
224	718	HL Road Fr	FR-R92R-4	TRUE	TRUE	Red	500	375	868.6342	1431.5	44	CM	LB	2.12	1
225	719	HL Road Fr	FR-R92R-4	TRUE	TRUE	Red	500	375	868.6342	1431.5	48	CM	LB	2.16	1

Figure 8-17: The Products table populated in Excel.

Working with Charts in Excel

You'll probably agree with us when we say that charts, lists, and pivot tables are among the most powerful and appealing features in Excel (as well as other numerous financial, statistical, and other features).

You can create charts from Visual Studio 2010 in two ways.

- ✔ You can add a chart by right-clicking the project name and choosing Chart.
- ✔ You can create a chart from code.

The first option is more friendly to the developer because you can change some chart properties from the Properties window instead of changing it from the code.

Adding a chart the Excel way

To add a new chart to the project and display the data from `lstProducts` list object:

1. **Right-click the `Invoices.xltx` file in the Solution Explorer.**

2. **Choose Add New Excel Chart.**

   The `Chart1.vb` file is added to the project.

3. **Double-click the `Sheet1.vb` file.**

   The worksheet opens in Excel inside Visual Studio

4. **Drag and drop a `Button` control from the Toolbox to the Excel surface.**

5. **Change the `Name` property of the button control to `btnAddChart`.**

6. **Change the `Text` property of the button control to `Add Chart`.**

   The Excel `Sheet1` in Visual Studio looks Figure 8-18.

7. **Double-click the button to add an event handler.**

   The Code View of the worksheet opens.

8. **Add the following code to the button event handler:**

```
Globals.Chart1.SetSourceData(lstProducts.Range)
```

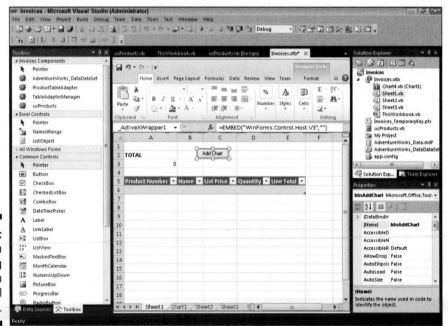

Figure 8-18:
The button
for adding
charts on
the Excel
worksheet.

Creating a chart from code

With `SetSourceData` method, you can tell the chart where to pull the data from. `SetSourceData` accepts the `Range` parameter. Because you want to plot the data from `lstProducts` list object, you're passing in the `Range` of that list object.

To create a chart from code:

1. **Press F5 to start the project.**
2. **Insert products from the Action pane into the Excel worksheet.**
3. **Click the Add Chart button you added to the Excel worksheet.**
4. **Switch to Chart1 tab.**

   The data that is in the `lstProducts List` object is presented on the chart.

Isn't it amazing? You wrote only one line of code to show that chart in Figure 8-19, and it looks great!

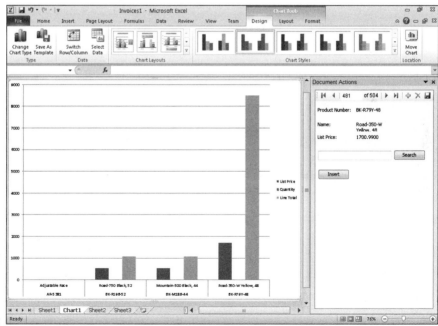

Figure 8-19:
A chart in Excel.

Chapter 9

Presenting PowerPoint

. . . .

. . . .

*I*n this chapter, you use VSTO to change the way PowerPoint works. PowerPoint is the most used presentation software in the world and is quite powerful. Nonetheless, part of the power is in its simplicity.

You can use VSTO to create add-ins that make PowerPoint work better in your company, although PowerPoint is a really flexible application on its own. All you can do is make PowerPoint better.

Introducing PowerPoint

PowerPoint is presentation construction software. It's designed to give nontechnical users complete control of a basic presentation model: text, images, and movement within a presentation, as well as management of the presentation itself. PowerPoint is the de facto standard presentation software the world over. If you run a conference center, the Windows machines are expected to have PowerPoint installed.

PowerPoint 2007 added the Ribbon along with the new XML file format. PowerPoint 2010 now includes many of the other features that presenters have been looking for:

✔ **Presenter view:** If you're using two monitors, you can see your notes on the second monitor, along with your presentation on the first. You see only the presentation on the first monitor.

✔ **Security:** Ever handed out a presentation with all your jokes still in the presenter notes? Those days are over: You can delete all your personal information. All other Office security features are available, too.

✔ **XPS export:** XML Paper Specification provides much nicer cross-platform support than PDF, HTML, or a bunch of JPEGs.

✔ **Custom slide layouts:** If you want to change the slide layouts (the dotted lines with the "Put a title here" text), you can save them for later use.

✔ **Text effects:** Finally, you can wrap text around line art — something we've been waiting for seemingly forever.

What's more, nearly all of these features are programmable.

Changing the Way PowerPoint Runs

The PowerPoint object model contains two big important classes: the `DocumentWindow` and the `Presentation`. The `DocumentWindow` runs PowerPoint, and the `Presentation` handles the presentation itself. (For more on the `Presentation`, see the next section.)

The `DocumentWindow` is the instance of PowerPoint that is hosting your slide deck. The members of the class represent the editing ability of PowerPoint and the environment itself. DocumentWindow is the key to the tool — the Presentation object is the key to the data in the presentation.

The difference between those objects is important, though somewhat confusing. If you look at the object map, it has an overwhelming quality. Please remember that only two things really matter in the PowerPoint model — the window and the deck — and your experience will be better.

A `DocumentWindow` is one of the collection of windows that PowerPoint keeps open to allow the user to work on a presentation. When you're in PowerPoint (or any other common Windows application) and click View to see the documents currently open in that application, you're seeing `DocumentWindows`.

All those `DocumentWindows` are part of a collection from the add-in's perspective. Just like an array, an add-in can reference the members of the collection with an index, such as `myDocumentWindows(2)`.

The `DocumentWindow` foremost on the desktop is the active `DocumentWindow`. An add-in can use the `Active` property to check to see whether a given `DocumentWindow` is the active one, or it can make a particular `DocumentWindow` active with the `Activate` method, such as `myDocumentWindows(2).Activate`.

The deck running in a specific `DocumentWindow` is specified with the window's `Presentation` property.

Working with individual panes

One thing that makes PowerPoint so nice to use is the multiple panes that maintain the information the presentation author needs. Visual Studio has a similar concept, with the Solution Explorer and the Toolbox, for example. PowerPoint has the Outline, Slide, and Notes panes (see Figure 9-1).

Because you're concerned primarily with changing the way PowerPoint runs in this section, changing the active pane is useful. If you happen to be creating an add-in that loops through all the text in a slide and deposits it in the Notes view, you need to activate the Slide pane, loop through the text shapes, and copy the test. Then you activate the Notes pane to paste, before changing slides.

The panes are indexed as follows:

Pane	*Index*
Outline	1
Slide	2
Notes	3

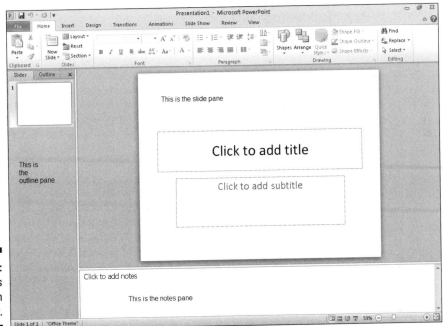

Figure 9-1:
The panes available in PowerPoint.

Activating the Notes pane for the window selected in `myDocumentWindows` is simply

```
myDocumentWindow(2).Panes(3).Activate
```

To change the size of the panes, however, you don't actually have to reference the panes. The `SplitHorizontal` property of the `DocumentWindow` object handles the size of the Outline pane, and the `SplitVertical` property handles the size of the Notes pane.

Altering a selected item

Another property of the `DocumentWindows` that gives some high-powered access into the inner workings of PowerPoint is the `Selection` property. When you refer to `myDocumentWindows(2).Selection`, you're referring to whatever happens to be selected by the user at that moment.

If you think handling selections this way may be a programming nightmare, you aren't alone. The VSTO developers handled selections nicely, though, and they aren't hard to use at all. Three collections are properties of every selection: `ShapeRange`, `SlideRange`, and `TextRange`. If one of these properties doesn't apply (for example, you have an image selected but not text), then the Selection is simply `Nothing`.

So the `ShapeRange` gives a collection of all the selected shapes. (For more on shapes, see the section "Changing a Presentation Itself," later in this chapter.) Everything on a PowerPoint slide is a shape. The `ShapeRange` that you get back from a Selection can contain the drawings, shapes, OLE objects, pictures, text objects, titles, headers, footers, slide number placeholder, and date and time objects on a slide.

You use the `SlideRange` when slides themselves are selected on the Outline pane. If no slides are selected, then `SlideRange` is just `Nothing`. If you want to change the template used by a selection of slides, for example, this collection is for you. Anything that you can do to a slide you can do to all the slides in a `SlideRange`.

The `TextRange` is the most common object that you expect to be selected. This object represents the highlighted text inside one shape on one slide. You can format or maneuver the text in a `TextRange` like any other text in any other Office application.

Note that all these collections are `ReadOnly`, but their contents are not. For example, you can't change what has been selected, but you can change the text in a `TextRange`.

Making your selection

In authoring a presentation, you have the ability to control items on the stage that the user has selected. The `Selection` property of the `DocumentWindow` (usually accessed using the `ActiveWindow` object) returns the object selected by the cursor, like the following code:

```
Dim active As DocumentWindow = Globals.ThisAddin.Application.ActiveWindow
active.Selection.TextRange.Font.Bold = MsoTriState.msoTrue
```

Usually, when you're working with the `Selection` object, you want to check the `Type` of the object returned because you don't know what it is. For example (like the following code), if you have a button that changes the font to bold, and the user selects an `Image` object and then clicks that button, you won't have a font to change!

```
Dim active As DocumentWindow = Globals.ThisAddin.Application.ActiveWindow
If active.Selection.Type = PpSelectionType.ppSelectionText Then
    active.Selection.TextRange.Font.Bold = MsoTriState.msoTrue
End If
```

Looking at items different ways

The `View` property of the `DocumentWindow` returns a handle to the current document views: normal view, slide view, outline view, slide sorter view, notes page view, slide master view, handout master view, or notes master view. Two parts are especially interesting: the `Zoom` and the `PrintOptions`.

That's where the interesting part ends, though, because `Zoom` and `PrintOptions` are exactly what you'd expect them to be. They're memorized on a view-by-view basis, though, so you'll find them to be an important feature if you're heavily manipulating the master views as part of your add-in.

Changing a Presentation Itself

Presentation is the data that you're working with. If you want to insert text or an image, change items on the stage, or otherwise actually edit the slide deck itself, then the `Presentation` object is where you want to look.

Like the `DocumentWindow`, the `Presentation` has its own members and contained objects. The contained objects are just what you'd expect in a presentation: design templates, slides, shapes, and the like. In order to build an add-in that affects the contents of a deck, you usually have to ask the `DocumentWindow` for the active presentation and then use the returned object to make changes.

Presentations are in a collection and are indexed by number and by filename. While you can use the number, we can't imagine how it would be too helpful:

```
Dim myPresentation as Presentation = Application.Presentations(1)
```

We prefer

```
Dim myPresentation as Presentation = Application.Presentations("My Really Cool
        Presentation.pptx")
```

The Application object is a cross-Office object that points to the `DocumentWindow` in PowerPoint. In Word, it points to the running Word application, and it's the same in Excel and so on. Also, remember that the `ActivePresentation` object points to the Presentation that is currently active in PowerPoint, no matter what it's called.

The `myPresentation` variable contains a handle to the presentation that you requested (even if it isn't active), and you can use all these features.

Changing the design

You may want to change your presentation's design by adding or removing shapes or features, changing fonts or colors, or even switching the master slide around.

`Shape` is the basic object on a PowerPoint slide, and it's where you have the first level of control. If you want to add an image on a slide then you add a shape of the Image type.

You have to finding a shape before you can change it. The easiest way to find a particular shape is if you named the shape when you added it program-matically. If you didn't name the shape, then you need to loop through the `Collection` and `Check` parameters.

After you find your shape, you edit it by using a host of simple properties that are part of the `Shape` object. Combine these properties with a few slick methods, and you have remarkable control:

- ✔ `AlternativeText` — Is great if you're exporting to HTML.
- ✔ `BlackAndWhiteMode` — Affects how the image is shown monochromatically.
- ✔ `Fill` — Gets a `Fill` object that does what you expect.
- ✔ `Glow` — Adds a glow effect.
- ✔ `Left, right, top, bottom` — Moves things around, figuratively.
- ✔ `Rotation` — Moves things around, literally!
- ✔ `Visible` — Makes an object visible.

Fonts, like the other design features, are stored in a collection as a property of the presentation. The `Font` collection resides at all levels of the presentation — from the deck level (`Application.ActivePresentation`, for example) down to a shape's `TextRange`. To bold all the fonts in a presentation, for example, you do the following:

```
For Each currentFont As Font In Application.ActivePresentation.Fonts
    currentFont.Bold = MsoTriState.msoTrue
Next
```

All these properties are about the same — a collection holds all the related objects, and you have control at multiple levels. Colors are about the same, but you have more lateral control. Shapes, backgrounds, fonts all have colors collections that you programmatically have access to:

```
Application.ActivePresentation.Slides(1).Background.Fill.ForeColor.RGB = 212
```

The `Designs` collection manages the slide masters and presentations masters for a deck. Designs are a little confusing because everything seems to have a `Design` property. Masters, presentations, and slides all track `Designs`, for maximum flexibility by the user interface. The quantity of Design properties all acts to make the programming model a little more complex.

The bunch of `Designs` isn't as bad as it seems, though. Think of this collection this way. The `Design` represents the settings that are carried from slide to slide — the master information, really. Fonts, color schemes, and default shapes are all handled by the `Design` (specifically the `SlideMaster` property). You can change the look of a specific slide totally and completely all at once by changing the `Design` — especially when you're organizing the slide deck.

Organizing the slides

In the `Color` example in "Making your selection," we use a `Slides` collection. You can use the `Slides` collection to move things around; it holds all the slides in order of the presentation. To add a slide programmatically, you give PowerPoint the index where you want the slide to live and then the slide's layout:

```
Dim active As Presentation = Globals.ThisAddin.Application.ActivePresentation
Dim custom As CustomLayout = active.SlideMaster.CustomLayouts.Item
            (PpSlideLayout.ppLayoutClipartAndText)
active.Slides.AddSlide(4, custom)
```

The preceding code is akin to right-clicking between two slides in the `OutlinePane`, clicking between two slides, and then selecting New Slide. You can see that you get some of the layout options in Figure 9-2.

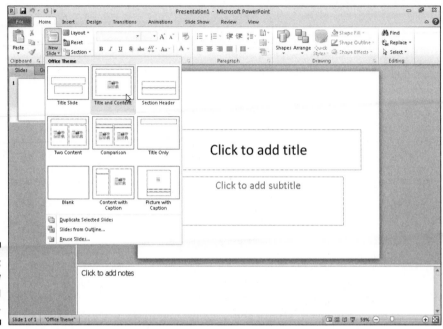

Figure 9-2:
The New
Slide dialog
box.

In the `ppSlideLayout` collection, you have access to all the layouts, and you can make your own, too. Here's a look at the custom layouts supported by the PowerPoint object model:

- `ppLayoutBlank`
- `ppLayoutChart`
- `ppLayoutChartAndText`
- `ppLayoutClipartAndText`
- `ppLayoutClipArtAndVerticalText`
- `ppLayoutFourObjects`
- `ppLayoutLargeObject`
- `ppLayoutMediaClipAndText`
- `ppLayoutMixed`
- `ppLayoutObject`
- `ppLayoutObjectAndText`
- `ppLayoutObjectOverText`

- ✔ ppLayoutOrgchart
- ✔ ppLayoutTable
- ✔ ppLayoutText
- ✔ ppLayoutTextAndChart
- ✔ ppLayoutTextAndClipart
- ✔ ppLayoutTextAndMediaClip
- ✔ ppLayoutTextAndObject
- ✔ ppLayoutTextAndTwoObjects
- ✔ ppLayoutTextOverObject
- ✔ ppLayoutTitle
- ✔ ppLayoutTitleOnly
- ✔ ppLayoutTwoColumnText
- ✔ ppLayoutTwoObjectsAndText
- ✔ ppLayoutTwoObjectsOverText
- ✔ ppLayoutVerticalText
- ✔ ppLayoutVerticalTitleAndText
- ✔ ppLayoutVerticalTitleAndTextOverChart

If you're familiar with PowerPoint, you probably recognize all these layouts.

Presenting the slide show

The `SlideShowWindow` supports the actual running of the slide show, and the VSTO tools let you change the way it runs in a number of ways. To run a slide show, use the `Run` method of the `SlideShowSettings` class, which will return a `SlideShowWindow` to you. You can use that returned object to control certain facets of the slide show:

```
Dim active As Presentation = Globals.ImagePicker.Application.ActivePresentation
Dim thisWindow As SlideShowWindow = active.SlideShowSettings.Run
```

The `SlideShowWindow` has a `ViewProperty` that gives you access to the actual running presentation. You can move the presentation forward and back with the First, Next, Previous, and Last buttons. The presentation itself has a handle so that you can change it on the fly with real-time data. You can change the cursor with the `PointerColor` and `PointerType` properties. The `ViewProperty` is a powerful set of tools.

Changing Options

You have the option to show the context-sensitive smart tag that appears when the user pastes — you know, the formatting option one, with the Keep Source/Match Destination/Text Only options? You can turn off the context-sensitive smart tag, if you liken:

```
With Application.Options
    If  .DisplayPasteOptions = False Then
        .DisplayPasteOptions = True
    End If
End With
```

You can also turn the `AutoCorrect` option on and off:

```
With Application.AutoCorrect
    .DisplayAutoCorrectOptions = msoFalse
    .DisplayAutoLayoutOptions = msoFalse
End With
```

Using the Document Inspector

PowerPoint 2007 offers a host of new features, and the Ribbon is just the start. The Document Inspector allows you to remove all (or just a little) personal information from a presentation with just a few clicks. What's more, you can customize the Document Inspector using VSTO.

The Document Inspector is accessible by implementing `IDocument Inspector` in your class. Under your class declaration, type `Implements IDocumentInspector`. Three new functions (`Fix`, `GetInfo` and `Inspect`) appear for you to add custom code to. The new functions represent the functionality of the Document Inspector in the user interface, and you can directly call them in your add-in:

```
Public Class myInspector
    Implements IDocumentInspector
    Public Sub Fix(ByVal Doc As Object, ByVal Hwnd As Integer,
ByRef Status As Microsoft.Office.Core.MsoDocInspectorStatus,
ByRef Result As String) Implements Microsoft.Office.Core.IDocumentInspector.Fix

    End Sub
    Public Sub GetInfo(ByRef Name As String,
ByRef Desc As String)
Implements Microsoft.Office.Core.IDocumentInspector.GetInfo
```

```
    End Sub
    Public Sub Inspect(ByVal Doc As Object,
ByRef Status As Microsoft.Office.Core.MsoDocInspectorStatus,
ByRef Result As String, ByRef Action As String)
Implements Microsoft.Office.Core.IDocumentInspector.Inspect

    End Sub
End Class
```

You can discover more about the Document Inspector in this great article by
Frank Rice:

```
http://msdn2.microsoft.com/en-us/library/aa338203.aspx.
```

Adding to PowerPoint

VSTO is the bridge between the developer and Office (see Chapter 1). It's the
language that a programmer can use to converse with the business users.
Bridges, conversations, whatever you want to call them — you're adding
them to the Office product here.

When adding to PowerPoint, there are things you can and can't do. Chapter 4
discusses designing to the requirements first and the capabilities second.

In short, you can write an add-in for PowerPoint using VSTO. In other words,
you can write a program that affects a user's machine and his specific install
of PowerPoint. You're writing a program, just like you're creating an .exe file
installed on a PC.

That add-in has a lot of power in PowerPoint. The two main bits VSTO you
can control are the environment and the data file . In the realm of the environment, you can manage the Tasks pane, Ribbon, context menus, and auxil-
iary tools.

When it comes to the decks themselves, you have comprehensive access
when working in 2010. Anything that you can do using the user interface in
PowerPoint you can do using the code in VSTO. From formatting to reorder-
ing, the control is yours.

However, you can't build a document project in PowerPoint — yet. Unlike
Word, where you can actually code up a .docx file, give it to a user, and have
it communicate with your database, you can't build a custom .pptx file as of
this writing.

An Example: Custom Art Selector

This sample requirement is that every time an item number appears in a title of a slide, the up-to-date image that relates to that item is inserted right there on the slide. We have to make it easy to get to — it is something that a presentation author can do after finishing a presentation if they wish.

The idea in this example is that the sales guy doesn't have to worry about having the most up-to-date art or where the art is stored. The presentation author can title a slide with the product code, write about it, and then whoosh! Here comes the image, ready to be placed in just the right spot.

To that end, you're going to write an add-in that knows the location of the central company image repository. The add-in will — on pressing a button in the Ribbon — go through the slides, look for item numbers, and, if it finds them, insert the appropriate image in the correct spot on the slide.

Creating a slide template

For this example, you use the slide's title to determine whether an image should be placed on the slide. As such, you can use the default template for this example, but most people will use a cool custom template. For this example, all you need to do is make sure that the template has a `Title` object on the page.

PowerPoint has a number of shapes that you can add, such as

- Callout
- Chart
- Comment
- Connector
- Curve
- Label
- Line
- Media
- OLE
- Picture
- Placeholder

- Polyline
- Shape
- Table
- Textbox
- Texteffect
- Title

Each one is a component object of the slide, which you can access from the Shapes connection of the `Slide` object. This method is how you get to the `Title` of each slide.

You can programmatically add a shape to a slide, or you can add it via the user interface. If you click the Insert tab of the Ribbon, you see that most of the shapes in the preceding list are in the buttons. `Title`, however, is not in the list. Your best bet is to keep the title that is a part of the default new slide.

Building an add-in

To create a new PowerPoint add-in, start Visual Studio 2010 and create a new project, specifically the PowerPoint 2010 Add-in project in Visual Basic, as shown in Figure 9-3. We called our project ImagePicker.

Watch out for debugging

We found it interesting that — at least in PowerPoint — debugging caused the security module to try and disable the add-in. When we'd run into a runtime error or stop the application at a breakpoint, we would often get notified by PowerPoint. We click No, and the debugging didn't seem to cause any additional trouble.

When working with PowerPoint add-ins, you need a deck to try things out with. We use the `OurProducts.pptx` deck to do the example in this chapter — you can feel free to reuse it as you need to.

Make sure that you have everything on one machine — PowerPoint 2010, Visual Studio 2010, and the latest VSTO install.

Figure 9-3:
Add a new
PowerPoint
add-in
project.

A class file is the project's primary focus. This file comes already set up with the `Startup` and `Shutdown` event handlers, which you use to set up the variables that you need and take them out of memory when the method is done.

So that you can easily access parts of the framework that you need for this project, you have to add a few `Imports` statements:

```
'Gives us access to the Presentation
Imports Microsoft.Office.Interop.PowerPoint
'This is where the Global objects are
Imports Microsoft.Office.Core
'We need this for the Dictionary of images
Imports System.Collections.Generic
```

These statements go up above the `Public Class` declaration.

You also need a variable, such as a generic dictionary, to store the collection of images:

```
Private Shared ImageLibrary As New Dictionary(Of String, String)
```

This code goes right under the `Class` declaration so that the members in the class can use it.

Building an Image Library

When the add-in starts up, it will need to change the location specified and gather a library of images that the add-in knows it can use to populate the slides. Changing the location isn't PowerPoint specific; it's just old-fashioned .NET code.

We built a new subroutine called `LoadImageLibrary` that flips through the files in a directory and adds them to a `Dictionary` object. We used the name of the file (without the extension) as a key, and the full path to the file as the value. This way, we can look up the image path in the dictionary using the name of the product, as long as the image name and the product name are the same:

```
Private Shared Sub LoadImageLibrary()
    'Go find the images directory and get a list of names
    Dim imageDir As New System.IO.DirectoryInfo("C:\ProductImages")
    'Load them into a class level generic list
    For Each imageFile As System.IO.FileInfo In imageDir.GetFiles
        ImageLibrary.Add(imageFile.Name.Substring(0,  imageFile.Name.
            IndexOf(".")), imageFile.FullName)
    Next
End Sub
```

Of course, you can always set the path differently, depending on the needs of the specific software that you're writing. The path to the images probably isn't hard-coded in the software — that's what the Application Settings are for. Using the Application Settings is just an illustration, though. Keep good software practice in mind.

You want your code to run as soon as the add-in loads up. You could run at other times, but running at load time gives you an excuse to use the `Startup` and `Shutdown` methods. To populate this `ImageLibrary`, add the `LoadImageLibrary` to the `ImagePicker_Startup` subroutine:

```
Private Sub ThisAddIn_Startup() Handles Me.Startup
    LoadImageLibrary()
End Sub
```

Picking the images

After you have a good list of images in the `ImageLibrary`, the add-in needs to flip through the pages of the current presentation and look for the keys in the titles. You use the PowerPoint `Presentation` object (see the earlier "Changing the Presentation Itself" section) to do so:

1. **Get a reference to the active presentation with the `Globals` object, provided as part of the add-in core.**

2. **Loop through the `Slides` collection.**

3. **Look at the title of the slide.**

4. **If the title of the slide is a key to an entry in the `ImageLibrary` dictionary object, add the referenced image file to the slide.**

The code for the subroutine looks like this:

```
Public Shared Sub PickImages()
    Dim active As Presentation = Globals.ThisAddIn.Application.ActivePresentation
    'For each slide in the presentation
    For Each slideToCheck As Slide In active.Slides
        'Check the title for the product name
        If ImageLibrary.ContainsKey(slideToCheck.Shapes.Title.TextFrame.
            TextRange.Text) Then
            'If we get it, drop a picture of the image on the page
            slideToCheck.Shapes.AddPicture(ImageLibrary.Item
                (slideToCheck.Shapes.Title.TextFrame.TextRange.Text),
                MsoTriState.msoFalse, MsoTriState.msoTrue, 20, 100)
        End If
    Next
End Sub
```

The only really sticky line of code is the `AddPictures` method, which takes a bunch of weird-looking parameters. You may wonder how you're going to remember those enumerators. Fortunately, you don't have to. In Figure 9-4, Visual Studio reminds you what the possible values are and what it is that you're populating.

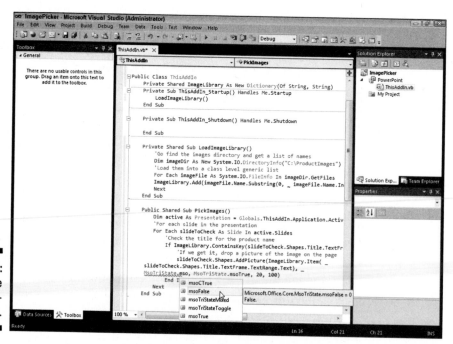

Figure 9-4:
IntelliSense
for enu-
merators.

Making a button on the Ribbon

The last feature we want to add to the add-in is giving the user a way to run the `PickImages` subroutine. In the old days, you'd add the function to the menu. Today, you add a button to the Ribbon.

1. **Add a new item to the project and make it a Ribbon for the Visual Designer, as shown in Figure 9-5.**

Figure 9-5:
Adding a
Ribbon to
the project.

The Ribbon has a lot of options, which we cover elsewhere in the book (see Chapter 6). For now, the basics will suffice.

2. **Drag a button from the Office Ribbon Controls group of the Toolbox onto the Ribbon Designer, as shown in Figure 9-6.**

3. **In the Properties panel, change the text of the button you just added to PickEm.**

4. **Click the Group in the designer and change the text to Image Picker.**

5. **Double-click the PickEm button to add a default event handler and change to code view.**

6. **In Code View, call the `PickImages` subroutine by adding the method call to the `Button1_Click` subroutine body:**

```
Private Sub Button1_Click(
  ByVal sender As System.Object,
  ByVal e As Microsoft.Office.Tools.Ribbon.RibbonControlEventArgs)
  Handles Button1.Click
    ThisAddIn.PickImages()
End Sub
```

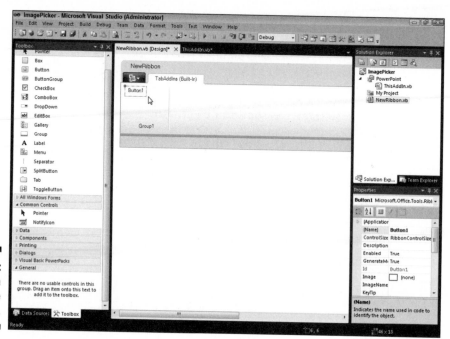

Figure 9-6:
Adding a
button to the
Ribbon.

This new group appears under the Add-Ins tab of the Ribbon in PowerPoint on any machine where it's installed. Clicking the button runs the function for the currently loaded presentation.

Running the example

To run, press the F5 button on your keyboard.

1. **Press F5 to enter Debug mode.**
2. **Open the sample presentation (`OurProducts.pptx`) in PowerPoint when it loads.**
3. **Click the Add-In tab.**
4. **Click the PickEm button.**

The images are loaded for the slides with product names in the title files.

Chapter 10

Building an Outlook
Job Jar Add-in

. . . .

In This Chapter

▶ Creating standard Outlook items

▶ Extending the user interface with Form Regions

▶ Using Ribbon Designer

▶ Putting all this knowledge to practical use

. . . .

Many people use Outlook every day. We're pretty sure that we're not the only ones who spend hours every day using Outlook to write e-mails, create calendar entries and tasks, and so on. The wide usage of Outlook makes it a perfect candidate for extending its functionality and customizing it.

With add-ins for Outlook, you can extend the existing functionality and customize it to your needs or your customers' needs. In this chapter, we focus on development tasks in Microsoft Outlook, and you build a sample VSTO Outlook add-in project.

This chapter is a little different than the ones that cover Excel or Word solution development. In this chapter, you develop an application-level customization add-in, while in the other chapters about Excel and Word, you develop document-level customizations.

Creating a Quick Example of an Outlook Add-in

In this chapter, you use the Outlook object model to access methods and properties and respond to events Outlook raises. Pause for a moment and think about what you can actually do in Outlook. Sure, you can receive and send e-mails, create tasks, send meeting requests, use calendars and appointments, and manipulate contacts, but those features are only a small subset of the items you can use.

The best part is that practically everything you can do as a regular Outlook user, you can also do through VSTO by accessing Outlook's object model. Not only can you create new items, you can modify the existing items and also change and extend the user interface.

You can start discovering the Outlook model by creating a simple add-in that displays a message when Outlook 2010 starts:

1. **In Visual Studio 2010, choose File⇨New⇨Project.**

   The New Project dialog box appears.

2. **In the Project Types pane, expand Visual Basic node and inside the Office node, select 2010.**

   You see a list of different VSTO projects you can create.

3. **From the projects list, select Outlook 2010 Add-in.**

4. **In Name text box, type the project name.**

   We named our project `HelloOutlook`.

5. **Click OK to create the project.**

   Visual Studio 2010 creates the new project and opens the `ThisAddIn.vb` file. You can imagine this class as the entry point for your add-in. The class comes out-of-the-box with the `ThisAddIn_Startup` method, which handles the `Startup` event of the add-in. This runs your code when Outlook loads the add-in.

In order for your add-in to load when you start Outlook, you have to either run the solution from Visual Studio or install the add-in. If you want to find out more about deployment, see Chapter 17.

Because the method for displaying message boxes is located inside the `System.Windows.Forms` namespace, you have to add this line of code above the `Public Class ThisAddIn`:

```
Imports System.Windows.Forms
```

With the `Imports` statement inside the code file, you're telling your code where to look for specific methods. Instead of using `System.Windows.Forms.MessageBox`, you can add the `Import` statement. After adding the `Import` statement, you can display a message box by simply writing `MessageBox.Show`.

The preceding line tells your add-in where to look for the message box. Now you can type the code to display the message box when the user starts or closes Outlook. Type this line of code inside the `ThisAddIn_Startup` method:

```
MessageBox.Show ("Hello Outlook")
```

If you run your add-in with Ctrl+F5, Outlook starts, and the first message box appears. It's not a lot, but it's a start.

Outlook no longer supports the `Shutdown` methods. Apparently, lots of badly behaving add-ins were trying to do tons of work in the `Shutdown` methods, causing Outlook to close slowly. Therefore, Microsoft told Outlook to not support it any more! You can find out more information at `http://msdn.microsoft.com/en-us/library/ee720183.aspx`.

Creating Outlook Items

E-mail messages are a popular feature that users work with in Outlook. Of course, e-mails aren't the only items you can use inside Outlook. Contacts are just another type of items. You can also manage your Tasks and use the Calendar for appointments. How about Notes and Journal Entries? Because you're a developer, you're probably wondering how can you create all these different items from add-ins. The answer is short: easy!

Every item inside Outlook has a corresponding class that you use to create and manipulate the item. These classes are located inside the Outlook namespace. Every class has a set of properties and methods that are specific to the item, and a couple of them are the same for every item.

How do you think these classes are named if we're referencing them as *items*? If you thought the word *item* is inside the class name, you're right. For example, the class that represents an e-mail message is named `MailItem`, while the class for tasks is `TaskItem`. All other Outlook items are named similarly.

Send me an e-mail

You are beginning a project for creating a new e-mail message. You can create a new add-in project or just use the one you created in "Creating a Quick Example of an Outlook Add-in." Use the previously created project and add this code inside `ThisAddIn_Startup` method:

```
Dim mailItem As Outlook.MailItem
mailItem = CType(Application.CreateItem(Outlook.OlItemType.olMailItem), Outlook.
    MailItem)
```

In the first line of the preceding code, you create a new instance of `MailItem`, which represents an e-mail message. The second line is a bit more complicated than the first. This code casts objects to the appropriate types, just as we did back in "Creating a Quick Example of an Outlook Add-in." Inside the parentheses, add the following line:

```
Application.CreateItem(Outlook.OlItemType.olMailItem)
```

This uses the `Application` object and passes in the type of the item you want to create to a `CreateItem` method. This line of code is inside the `CType` method, and the purpose of this method is to cast from the object type to `Outlook.MailItem` type.

Items in Outlook are always returned as objects and therefore you must use the `CType` method to cast the object type to the appropriate Outlook item.

The next step is to set properties for e-mail and display the created e-mail to the user:

```
mailItem.Subject = "I am learning about VSTO"
mailItem.Body = "VSTO is really cool!"
mailItem.To = "peterj@vstofordummies.net"
mailItem.Display()
```

With the first three lines, you set the subject, body, and recipient of your e-mail. The last line displays the created e-mail message to the user.

If you want to send your e-mail to the recipient, you can put in this line of code:

```
mailItem.Send()
```

Got e-mail?

Sending e-mails is nice, but if you have hundreds of thousands of them, accessing existing e-mails is also very useful. For that reason, the `GetDefaultFolder` method returns the default e-mail folder. You can use the following code to get the number of e-mails in your Inbox folder:

```
Application.Session.GetDefaultFolder (Outlook.OlDefaultFolders.olFolderInbox).
          Items.Count
```

You can access this method from the `Session` object. In order to get to the Inbox folder, you must pass an `enum` called `olFolderInbox` to the method. After you get the folder, you access the e-mails through the `Items` property. And finally, to get the count of e-mails, you use the `Count` property.

You can access other folders in Outlook by passing a different parameter to `GetDefaultFolder` method. For example, you can use `olFolderOutbox` to access the Outbox folder or `olFolderSentMail` to access e-mails in the Sent folder.

Oh, I got so much to do. . . .

From Outlook, you can easily forward a task to somebody else. In VSTO, all you need is a piece of code that goes through all your tasks, reads the task subject, and inserts everything inside an e-mail message.

Look how easy it is to go through items in a specific folder:

```
Dim task As Outlook.TaskItem
Dim taskFolder As Outlook.MAPIFolder
taskFolder = Application.Session.GetDefaultFolder (Outlook.OlDefaultFolders.
          olFolderTasks)


For Each task In taskFolder.Items
          MessageBox.Show (task.Subject)
Next
```

The third line of code is almost the same as the code you used to get to the Inbox folder. The only difference is that in this example, you're passing the `olFolderTasks` parameter to `GetDefaultFolder` method.

Next, you're using the `For Each` loop to go through each task in the folder and display the task subject.

Because you already know how to create new e-mail messages and how to iterate through tasks, you can put everything together and insert task subjects into the e-mail. Here is the code:

```
' Define and create new e-mail
Dim mailItem As Outlook.MailItem
mailItem = CType(Application.CreateItem(Outlook.OlItemType.olMailItem), Outlook.
          MailItem)

Dim task As Outlook.TaskItem
Dim taskFolder As Outlook.MAPIFolder
' Get the task folder
taskFolder = Application.Session.GetDefaultFolder (Outlook.OlDefaultFolders.
          olFolderTasks)
' Go through tasks and insert the subject to e-mail body
For Each task In taskFolder.Items
          mailItem.Body += task.Subject & Environment.NewLine
Next
```

```
mailItem.Subject = "Help me out!"
mailItem.To = "volunteers@example.com"
mailItem.Display()
```

All you have to do now is wait and see whether someone else will do your work.

Using Form Regions

With the help of VSTO and Visual Studio 2010, you can use Form Regions to present your user interface inside Outlook 2010. Form Regions are nothing but a user control that you can use to customize, replace, or enhance any standard form inside Outlook 2010.

 When we say *standard form,* we mean the form or window that appears when you create a new e-mail message, task, calendar entry, and so on. For example, you can use Form Regions to display your custom user interface in the Outlook 2010 Reading Pane.

Adding a new Form Region

For example, say that you want to display additional information while users are composing e-mail messages. Form Region is a perfect candidate for the job.

Using the `HelloOutlook` example, follow these steps to add a new Form Region to the project:

1. **Right-click the project name.**

2. **Choose Add➪New Item.**

   The Add New Item dialog box appears with the list of different items you can add to your project.

3. **Click the Office category and in the Templates pane, select Outlook Form Region.**

4. **In Name text box, enter the name for your Form Region.**

   We named our Form Region simply `MyFormRegion`.

5. **Click Add.**

   As you click the Add button, a wizard for new Outlook Form Region appears, as shown in Figure 10-1.

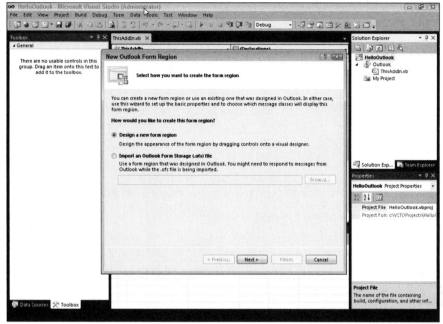

Figure 10-1:
The New
Outlook
Form Region
wizard.

On the first page of the wizard, you can select whether you want to design a new Form Region or import an already created Form Region from the Outlook Form Storage file. (An Outlook Form Storage file [.ofs] contains a Form Region designed in Outlook.)

6. **Because you want to design the form within Visual Studio, make sure that the first option (Design a New Form Region) is selected and then click the Next button.**

As you click the button, a screen similar to Figure 10-2 appears. On this wizard page, you can fine-tune the settings of a Form Region.

Options on this page determine where the Form Region appears when you open a specific item, such as an e-mail or task, in Outlook. You have four options:

- **Separate:** The Form Region appears in a new page inside an Outlook item.

- **Adjoining:** The Form Region is appended to the bottom of an Outlook item.

- **Replacement:** Compared to the Separate type of Form Region, this type of form region replaces the default page of the item.

- **Replace-all:** This option is the same as the previous one except it also removes the tabs from the Ribbon.

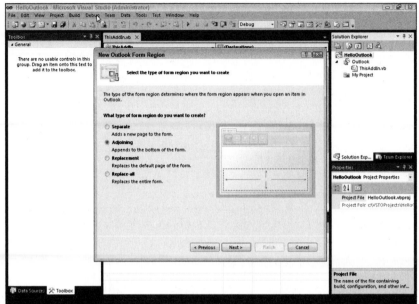

Figure 10-2:
Selecting
the type of
Form Region
you want to
create.

7. **Because you want the user interface to be at the bottom of e-mail messages, select the Adjoining type and click Next.**

   The next wizard page, shown in Figure 10-3, appears.

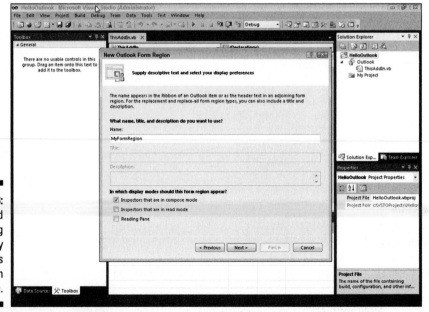

Figure 10-3:
Naming and
selecting
the display
modes
for Form
Region.

On this wizard page, you can specify the name of the Form Region. Notice that the Title and Description text boxes are grayed out because you can set them for only replacement or replace-all Form Region types.

Below the Description text box are three check boxes that you can use to select where the Form Region should appear. By default, all three display mode options are checked, so the Form Region appears when you're creating or reading an Outlook item; with the last option, you can check whether the Form Region also appears in the Reading Pane.

TIP

When you double-click an e-mail message and the form opens up, the Outlook item is in reading mode. The Reading Pane is the form that appears when you click an e-mail message in the list of e-mails.

8. **Because you want your Form Region to appear when users are creating an e-mail message, you should uncheck the second and third option and leave the first option checked; click Next.**

   The last step in the wizard, shown in Figure 10-4, appears.

   Select the message classes that cause the Form Region to appear.

   You can decide to check all eight check boxes, which means that the Form Region appears for every message class, or you can leave Mail Message selected.

9. **Click Finish to close the wizard.**

   Congratulations! You just created your first Form Region. If you followed the steps, you see the Form Designer shown in Figure 10-5.

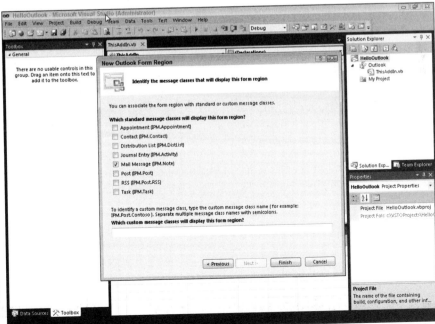

Figure 10-4:
Selecting when the Form Region should appear.

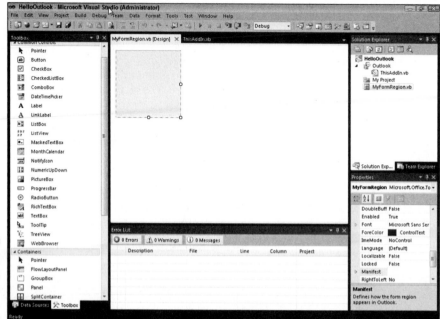

A *message class* is used to distinguish one type of Outlook item from another. The message class for a specific Outlook item determines the form that Outlook uses to display the item. (For example, the message class for an e-mail message is IPM, which stands for interpersonal message.) In addition to the standard message classes, you can also define your own classes that are based on the standard ones. You can create a custom task item for projects called IPM.Task.ProjectTask. Designer for ProjectTask form is based on IPM.Task form.

Adding controls to the Designer

An empty Form Region isn't that appealing. You can add controls to the Designer in order to make it somewhat usable. For this example, you're placing a button on the Form Region. When the user clicks the button, you change the text in subject text box of the e-mail message. Follow these steps:

1. **Choose View⇨Toolbox.**

   The Toolbox window appears.

2. **From the Common Controls category, select the Button control and drag and drop it to the Form Region.**

3. **Select the button on the Form Region and press F4 to open the Properties window.**

You can use the Properties window to change the control's properties, such as Text, Color, Font, and so on.

4. **Change the button's `Text` property to `Click Me!`.**

When you change the text inside the Properties window, the actual button's text updates.

5. **Double-click the button.**

The event for the button click is added to the code, and the current view changes from Designer to Code.

6. **Add the following lines to the newly created event handler:**

```
Dim currentItem As Outlook.MailItem
currentItem = CType (Globals.ThisAddIn.Application.ActiveInspector().
       CurrentItem, Outlook.MailItem)
currentItem.Subject = "This is my email subject!"
```

The first line of code in Step 6 is fairly straightforward; you're creating a new instance of `MailItem`, which represents the e-mail message the user created.

Take a look at the second line, especially the code inside the parenthesis:

```
Globals.ThisAddIn.Application.ActiveInspector().CurrentItem
```

With this line, you're accessing the `ActiveInspector` method, which is inside the `Application` class. (In this case, the `Application` is Outlook.) After you have the `ActiveInspector`, you can get the `CurrentItem`, which represents the item currently opened. Once again, you're using the `CType` method to cast from object type to `Outlook.MailItem`.

Because the Form Region appears only on e-mail messages, you don't need to check which item you cast the object to. If you create a Form Region that appears on different standard item forms, you have to check for the correct type before casting the object.

From here on the code is simple. Because you have the correct item type, you can use the `Subject` property to set the text of the Subject text box in the e-mail message. Set the Subject line text to `This is my e-mail subject!`.

You can use other properties to modify the e-mail message. For example, you can use the `Body` property to set the message body or `To` to set the e-mail recipient. Exploring the properties you can set is the best way to learn the object model.

Press Ctrl+F5 or F5 to run the add-in to see how it works. Outlook 2010 should start. When you create a new e-mail message, your Form Region should be visible at the bottom of the form. You can start typing your message, and if you want to set the Subject line, just click the button. Your e-mail message should look similar to Figure 10-6.

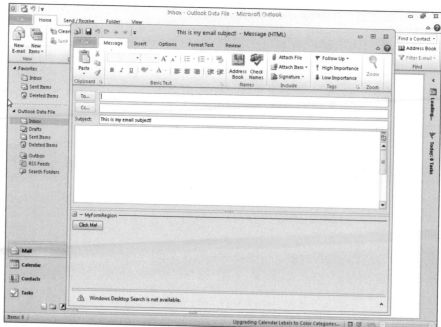

Figure 10-6:
The Form
Region in
action.

Building the Job Jar

With two simple examples in this chapter so far and some code snippets, you have enough information and knowledge to start creating the Outlook Job Jar add-in.

Getting the requirements together

When you think about a Job Jar in the context of Outlook, you probably have Tasks in your mind. The Job Jar you're creating contains a set of uncompleted tasks. With the help of some code and VSTO, you can build an add-in that lets you select a task from a Job Jar and attach it to the e-mail you're writing. You can select tasks based on different criteria, but for the sake of simplicity, we are going to pick out the tasks randomly.

Start by writing small portions of code and at the end, tie everything together with a simple user interface.

Here are the tasks you may find on your burn-down chart:

1. **Create a new Outlook add-in project named JobJarAddIn.**

When the project is created, the file `ThisAddIn.vb` opens. If not, double-click the `ThisAddIn.vb` file in the Solution Explorer.

2. **Get all uncompleted tasks from Outlook.**

   Use the `List` class to store uncompleted tasks.

3. **Randomly select a task from this list when the user clicks a button.**

   Use a built-in class named `Random` to generate a random number (between 0 and number of tasks) to be used as an index in the task list.

4. **Build a user interface.**

   The user interface is pretty simple. It consists of a button on the Ribbon. When the user clicks the button, the code runs and randomly selects a task and attaches it to the e-mail you're creating.

Writing code for your Job Jar

Now it is time to start writing some code. In order to use the `List` class, you need to insert an `Imports` statement before the class definition. Open `ThisAddIn.vb` file and add the following `Imports` statement before the `ThisAddIn` class declaration:

```
Imports System.Collections
```

Rather than declaring the list on the method level, you should declare it at the class level because you want to use the list throughout the add-in. Type the following code immediately after the class declaration:

```
Private listOfTasks As New List (Of Outlook.TaskItem)
```

After you declare the list, continue with creating the first method inside `ThisAddIn.vb` class:

```
Public Sub FillUncompletedTasks ()
listOfTasks.Clear ()
Dim task As Outlook.TaskItem
Dim tasksFolder As Outlook.MAPIFolder

tasksFolder = Application.Session.GetDefaultFolder(Outlook.OlDefaultFolders.
            olFolderTasks)

For Each task In tasksFolder.Items
    If Not task.Complete Then
        listOfTasks.Add (task)
    End If
Next

End Sub
```

The preceding code is almost the same as the one used throughout the book. The first line of code deletes all the items from the list. This way, every time the method executes, you get an updated list of tasks. The rest of the code takes care of getting the default task folder and iterating through all tasks in that folder. If the task isn't completed, you're adding it to the task list.

To get a random task from the list, you can use this method:

```
Public Function PickATask () As Outlook.TaskItem
    Dim randomNum As New Random ()
    Dim taskIndex As Integer = randomNum.Next (0, listOfTasks.Count)

    Return listOfTasks (taskIndex)
End Function
```

You can also create a more sophisticated algorithm to select your task. For example, you can take into account the tasks category or return the tasks that are more than 50 percent complete. Despite all the many available options, we're treating tasks equally and just randomly select one task.

In the preceding method, you initialize the new instance of Random class and pick one random number in the range from 0 and listOfTasks.Count. When you have the random number, you return the task that is in that location. If you have ten tasks in the list, you're choosing a random number between 0 and 9. You can use that number as an index in the list of tasks.

Setting up the user interface

Office 2010 has completely recreated the user interface. Instead of toolbars and button, Office 2010 has a Ribbon, tabs, and chunks. Maybe it's not apparent, but the Ribbon is much easier to use then the old user interface. In the Ribbon, you can find the functionality much faster than if you had to drill through the toolbars, menus, and option dialog boxes. You can use Visual Studio 2010 to create and customize Ribbons. Visual Studio 2010 also contains a built-in visual Ribbon Designer!

To use the Ribbon Designer, right click the project name and choose Add⇨New Item. In the Add New Item dialog box, select the Office node. On the right hand side is a Ribbon (Visual Designer) item. Don't worry about the name of the control; just select it and click Add. The Visual Designer for the Ribbon appears in Visual Studio 2010.

You can set some properties, customize the Ribbon, and write more code:

1. **Click the `Group1` on the Ribbon and open the Properties window.**

   You can open the Properties window by clicking on the control and pressing F4.

2. **Change the property `Label` from `Group1` to `JobJar`.**

3. **Drag and drop the button control to the `JobJar` group control on the Ribbon.**

4. **Select the button, open the Properties window, and change the button `Label` property to `Pick a task`.**

   Your Ribbon with a single group and a button should look like Figure 10-7.

5. **Double-click the button.**

   Visual Studio switches to the Code View, and the cursor appears inside the newly created `Button1_Click` handler.

6. **Add this piece of code inside the click handler method `Button1_Click`:**

```
Private Sub Button1_Click(ByVal sender As System.Object, ByVal e As
        Microsoft.Office.Tools.Ribbon.RibbonControlEventArgs) Handles
        Button1.Click

    Globals.ThisAddIn.FillUncompletedTasks ()

    Dim selectedTask As Outlook.TaskItem
    selectedTask = Globals.ThisAddIn.PickATask

    Dim currentItem As Outlook.MailItem
    currentItem = CType (Globals.ThisAddIn.Application.ActiveInspector().
        CurrentItem, Outlook.MailItem)

    currentItem.Attachments.Add (selectedTask)
End Sub
```

   When the user clicks the button, the code fills the list of uncompleted tasks and then randomly picks one task from the list. Because you're composing an e-mail message, you obtain the reference to the mail item and add the selected task as attachment.

If you run the code now, no custom Ribbon would appear when you try to create a new e-mail. You did not do anything wrong. The Ribbon isn't displayed because you didn't choose when to display it. Ribbons you add to your Outlook add-in projects are by default configured to appear only when you're reading an e-mail item. Double-clicking an e-mail in your Inbox and it opening in a separate window is considered *reading* an e-mail item.

Changing other settings

To show the Ribbon when creating a new e-mail, you have to change a property on the Ribbon Designer. First, open the Ribbon Designer, click it, and press F4 to display the Properties window. Take a closer look at the property named `RibbonType`. This property tells your add-in when to display the Ribbon. If you open that property, you see a bunch of check boxes. By default, the `Microsoft.Outlook.Mail.Read` check box is selected. This means that your custom Ribbon appears when you're reading an e-mail message. Because you want to use the Ribbon when composing an e-mail, you should clear that check box and select the check box named `Microsoft.Outlook.Mail.Compose`.

Another setting that is interesting is `Microsoft.Outlook.Explorer`. Use this setting if you want to modify the main Ribbon in Outlook 2010. This setting is new because in previous versions, Outlook didn't support Ribbons in the main Explorer window.

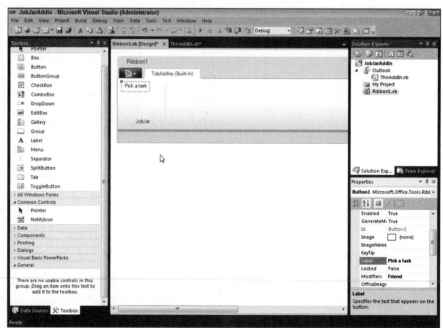

Figure 10-7:
A Ribbon with a group and button.

Running the add-in

Run the add-in and create a new e-mail message. If you click the Add-ins tab, you see your custom Ribbon group and button (see Figure 10-8).

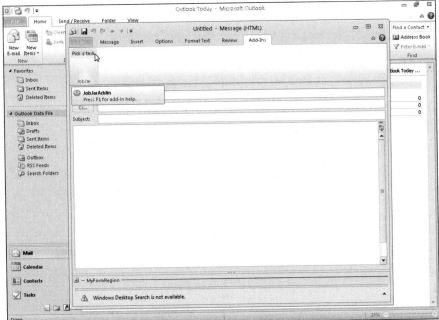

Click Pick a task. Try clicking it once more — nice, isn't it? As you click the button, the code fills the list of uncompleted tasks, randomly selects a task, and then attaches the task to the e-mail.

Chapter 11

Creating a Project Project

* *

In This Chapter

▶ Digging into the Project object model

▶ Visualizing the Project data

▶ Integrating Project with Office software

* *

M icrosoft Project isn't the most used Office software, which is a shame. Fact it, Project is a program that fills a specific need for a specific kind of work, so you typically use it only if you do that type of work. Nonetheless, if everyone used Project more often to accomplish their projects, they'd be more effective at accomplishing tasks.

Whenever you need to do something that has more than one step, Project has a way to organize it. Although you can use Outlook or Excel to track projects, Project does the job so much better. In fact, Project is like a pre-designed database that is specifically tasked with getting things done.

Add-ins for Project were new in VSTO 3.0 with Office 2007. As a result, the database that makes up the project file is available for integration in neat, new ways, and you can integrate information in Outlook, Word, Excel, and PowerPoint even easier than in the past.

The Project add-on template also brings normal features to the table, such as the use of Windows Forms and Form controls. The addition of Project Server, which we cover briefly, brings a whole new piece to the table, too. In this chapter, we delve into the features exposed by VSTO.

Breaking Down the Object Model

Project is designed to organize lists of tasks. The VSTO Object Model for Project is also well organized. Because Project is kind of a what-you-see-is-what-you-get program, it doesn't provide many behind-the-scenes tricky concepts to model in code.

The simple object model pretty much includes projects, calendars, resources and tasks, and then a few stragglers. Figure 11-1 shows the organization.

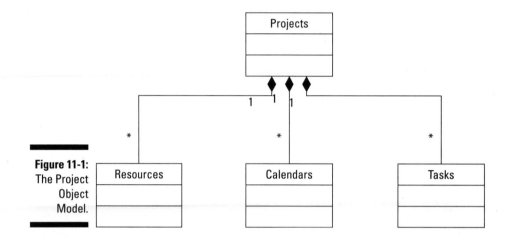

Figure 11-1:
The Project
Object
Model.

The Project object model is complex; it comes from the COM world just like the other Office products. Nonetheless, the managed code that wraps the COM interfaces is well organized, and you can quickly design and implement common operations. Just make sure that you take the time to design and research. Make the tools work for you.

Projects

`Projects` is the top-level object in Project and contains most of the application-level functionality. Just like all the other Office object models, `Projects` — the collection of `Project` objects — is technically a subobject of `Application`. You can reference all the objects under `Application` on a project level, too, because they're logically equivalent.

Application-level objects refer to all the Project files open at the same time. `Project` objects usually represent exactly one file. Because Project isn't the kind of program where you generally have more than one file open, the distinction isn't that much of an issue.

`Filter` is a good example of an object that is present at both the application and project level. Figure 11-2 shows the Filters tool in Project. You can check up on the `TaskFilters` collection, which is a collection of the filters used in the current file.

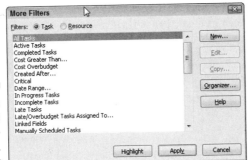

Figure 11-2:
The More
Filters dia-
log box.

For example, if you wanted to reformat the look of the tasks in the Gantt chart, you may want to delete or apply certain filters before you perform the reformatting and then put it back the way it was after the reformat.

```
For Each currentFilter As MSProject.Filter In Application.ActiveProject.
            TaskFilters
    currentFilter.Delete()
Next
'Apply your formatting here!
Application.ActiveProject.TaskFilters("Critical").Apply()
```

The `Project` object is best used out of the `Application` object, with the `ActiveProject` property just as we did in the preceding listing. In 90 percent of all cases, using the `Application` object will covers you.

Calendars

A calendar is like the table structure for a project. It maintains the days, times, work shifts, and spans that various groups are working. The calendar is the base you use to calculate how long tasks will take and how much they'll cost — which is what using Project is all about.

Like `Projects`, `Calendars` are a collection of collections. A calendar has a collection of

✔ `Weekdays`

✔ `WorkWeeks`

✔ `Exceptions`

✔ `Years`

After `Years`, it gets fun. `Years` have a collection of `Months`, which have a collection of `Days`. Lots of interesting math can take place here. For example:

```
Function WorkingDays(ByVal selectedResource As MSProject.Resource, ByVal year As
             Integer) As Integer
    Dim selectedYear As MSProject.Year = selectedResource.Calendar.Years(year)
    Dim result As Integer = 0
    For Each countMonth As MSProject.Month In selectedYear.Months
        For Each countDay As MSProject.Day In countMonth.Days
            If countDay.Working Then
                result = result + 1
            End If
        Next
    Next
    Return result
End Function
```

What happens in the preceding code is pretty straightforward. Given a resource (which has a `Calendar` associated with it in `Project`) and a `Year` (so to narrow down the calendar), you can calculate the total working days. You loop through the months in the year and then the days in the month, and then you check the `Working` attribute of the `Day`.

All this calculation is possible because the `Calendar` — like most of the other objects in `Project` — is stored as a collection of collections. The collections are indexed, so you can loop through them with ease to solve your problems.

Resources

Resources are the entities applied to tasks in order to move them toward completion. Resources have such properties as `Name`, `Rate`, and `Availability`. Usually, resources are people, sometimes even programmers.

Like the other classes in the model, the `Resource` properties are largely collections of objects. One of the most interesting is the `Assignment` class, which relates a `Task` and a `Resource`. Both `Tasks` and `Resources` can have `Assignments` because the assignments are the joining table between the `Tasks` and the `Resources`.

The joining table allows for neat leveling code. Sometimes you just need to cut down on overtime, you know. You can get a resource's overtime using their assignments!

```
Function CalcOvertime(ByVal selectedResource As MSProject.Resource) As Integer
    Dim result As Double = 0.0
    For Each currentAssignment As MSProject.Assignment _
In selectedResource.Assignments
        result = result + CDbl(currentAssignment.OvertimeCost)
    Next
    Return result
End Function
```

This whole system of resources and projects is based on shelves holding books of information, and you can sort through those books for information that pertains to your topic. Pots of soup works, too. Linked lists, friends of friends . . . whatever your simile, what you're dealing with is properties as collections of objects. When the application is well organized, it is a thing of beauty.

Tasks

`Tasks` also are built on the collection of objects model, as shown by the `Assignments` collection in `Resources` (see preceding section). Remember, `Tasks` have `Assignments`, too!.

A new collection for Project 2010 in `Tasks` is the `StartDrivers`. `StartDrivers` are the predecessors to tasks, as shown in Figure 11-3. A task is assigned tasks that must come before it. This assignment is one way that priority is determined.

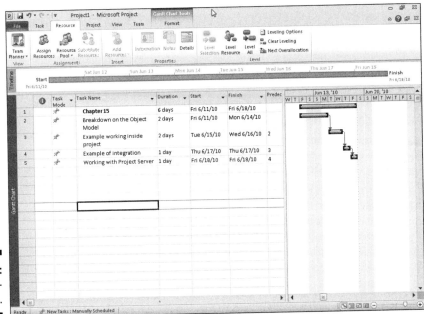

Figure 11-3:
Task prede-
cessors.

`StartDrivers` are made up of two primary kinds of information:

- ✔ `CalendarDrivers` are created when the user specifies that a task must be started or completed by a certain date.
- ✔ `TaskDrivers` are created when the user specifies that a certain task must occur before the specified task.

You can use the `StartDrivers` collection to loop through the `StartDriver` objects, as you do with the `Calendar` and `Assignment` objects in the last two sections.

Working Inside Project: An Example

For this project, the requirement is to contact the owners of a late task. The following steps show you how to send the owners an e-mail:

1. **Create a new Project add-in by selecting Create Project from the Start page.**

   For this example (to keep things simple), you can just put the function code in the `ThisAddIn_Startup` event handler.

2. **Start with your cursor at the `ThisAddIn_Startup` event handler.**

3. **Get a reference to the loaded project:**

   ```
   Dim currentProject As MSProject.Project =
   Application.ActiveProject
   ```

4. **Loop through the tasks.**

   ```
   For Each currentTask As MSProject.Task In
   currentProject.Tasks
   ```

5. **Check to see whether the task is late:**

   ```
   If currentTask.LateStart Then
   ```

6. **Get a reference to the first resource and get its e-mail address:**

   ```
   Dim currentResource As MSProject.Resource =
   currentTask.Resources(0)
   Dim theirEmail As String = currentResource.EMailAddress
   ```

7. **Let the person know via e-mail that the task is late:**

   ```
   Dim outgoingMail As New System.Net.Mail.SmtpClient
   outgoingMail.Send("bill@pointweb.net",
           theirEmail,
           "This task is late",
           "This task is in the collection of late tasks.  Do
       something!")
   ```

The whole code base looks like

```
Dim currentProject As MSProject.Project = Application.ActiveProject
For Each currentTask As MSProject.Task In currentProject.Tasks
    If currentTask.LateStart Then
        'just get the latest one
        Dim currentResource As MSProject.Resource = currentTask.Resources(0)
        Dim theirEmail As String = currentResource.EMailAddress
        Dim outgoingMail As New System.Net.Mail.SmtpClient
        outgoingMail.Send("bill@pointweb.net",
                    theirEmail,
                    "This task is late",
                    "This task is in the collection of late tasks.  Do something!")
    End If
Next
```

Project works just like all the other VSTO object models — collections of collections. All you need to do is organize the information that you're trying to access, and you're done. The collections are almost all indexed, so you can access the information with For Each loops.

Working with Server

Project Server is a slick SharePoint application that supports Project files. In Part III, you can create Document Workspaces for generic documents. These Document Workspaces have events that handle tasks such as changing or moving the document. Project Server has events that are specific to Project files, such as tasks being completed and resources becoming overwhelmed.

Here is a possible list of user stories:

1. **A project manager makes a project.**
2. **He uploads the project to Project Server.**
3. **SharePoint assigns tasks to users based on the document.**
4. **The users have the tasks synced to their Outlook.**
5. **The programmer finishes a function.**
6. **The programmer marks the task off in Outlook.**
7. **SharePoint picks up the change.**
8. **The project file gets updated.**
9. **The Task Complete event is fired.**
10. **A Workflow launches to notify a tester.**
11. **The task gets added to the tester's task list from the project file.**
12. **The process repeats.**

You gotta admit, this scenario is a project manager's dream, and not really that tough. We won't give you all the code here because it would be a whole new book to explain all the ins and outs, but we can talk about the event handler.

Responding to events

We were going to write a list of all the events that the `Microsoft.Office.Project.Server.Events` class has delegates for, but then we discovered that it is 15 printed pages of more than 160 events. In all honesty, you can look up this list in the MSDN Library. Some of our favorites include

- ✔ `ProjectSavedHandler`
- ✔ `ProjectSaveFailedHandler`
- ✔ `ResourceChangingHandler`
- ✔ `TimesheetReviewedHandler`
- ✔ `CustomFieldsUpdatingHandler`

Some events are in past tense (`ProjectSaved`), while others are in present perfect tense (`ProjectSaving`). This difference is because most events have a post-event (the past tense) and pre-event (the present perfect tense) version. It's a pretty complete solution.

Event handling in Project Server works almost like any other event handler — such as handling a button push or a timer going off. Event handlers in VB use the `Handles` statement. In C#, they use the colon (`:`).

To handle events in Project Server, you need to inherit from one of the base classes that have your event handler in them, such as `TimesheetEvents Receiver`. In that class, you can find the `TimesheetSubmitted` event, which you can then override:

```
Imports Microsoft.Office.Project.Server.Events

Public Class TimeSheetFunctions
    Inherits TimesheetEventReceiver
    Public Overrides Sub OnSubmitted(ByVal contextInfo As PsContextInfo,
ByVal e As TimeSheetPostEventArgs)
        'Talk to Accounting
        Dim currentAccountingSystem As MyCompany.Accounting.System
        currentAccountingSystem.HandleThisTimesheet(e.TsUID)
    End Sub
End Class
```

Clearly, this code is just an example; Project Server is a little out of the scope of this book. We, however, have been asked by a number of clients how to do this exact thing and were surprised to find out how complex it really is — at least in terms of the number of products you need to use to do it.

Chapter 12

Developing for Visio

· ·

· ·

*F*ew people know that Visio is a phenomenal development platform, with a vibrant community and a number of coding options. You can do a lot with databases and Visio diagrams without doing a stitch of code, and adding a little VBA to the mix makes Visio a surprisingly powerful tool.

What Visio does so well is, unsurprisingly, visualization. Visio helps the end user get a visual grip on a whole host of things, from software to bridges to networks to department hierarchy.

Like most people, you probably use Visio to design data schemas, UML diagrams, and user interfaces. Maybe you do flowcharts and network diagrams, too. What we didn't know until recently is that Visio can use all kinds of information to generate these kinds of diagrams — and a lot more — for the user, on the fly.

Add the ability to insert Visio into other programs as an ActiveX control, and you have a formidable environment. Add insertion to a complete managed API, and you have a Visualization Toolset.

Visio provides a boatload of diagramming power. VSTO provides a mechanism for harnessing it in managed code. If your users need to see something, and your .NET code can see it, Visio can provide a window into it.

In this chapter, we look into Visio extensibility, focusing (of course) on VSTO. Then we check in with the object model, accessible by managed code, and finally put all these to use.

Exploring Your Visio Development

Although this book is about Visual Studio Tools for Office, you have a lot of other ways to get to Office products. To make sure that you're using the right tool for the job, the following sections describe the options you have when developing for Visio.

Add-ons

Add-ons aren't add-ins.

Well, that was simple.

Seriously, *add-ons* are specific to Visio and are not the same as add-ins. Add-ons are an encapsulation of certain parts of Visio that you can use in a couple of different ways. The cool Web Site Map is an add-on. The Database Reverse Engineering is an add-on.

Visio add-ons were available before COM add-ins were available. In fact, they were available before Visio was a Microsoft product. Because add-ons are such a good way to model certain things inside Visio, they're still around — in two different forms, in fact:

- **Visio Library files:** VSLs are in-process types of add-ons, written in a special format of DLL. (A `.vsl` file is just a `.dll` with a different extension.) VSLs are loaded a lot like COM add-ins, but they don't use the add-in framework; they use the add-on framework.

  Make sense? It didn't to us, either. Just remember that COM is for shared add-ins — it's a *common* architecture. VSLs are just for Visio and are fast and have the benefit of having a design that is well suited to Visio.

- **Standalone programs:** You can also implement add-ons as standalone `.exe` files. The `.exe` are really just programs that happen to work with Visio. If you need to cross over various Visio APIs (like the automation model and managed code), a standalone program may be a valid option.

VBA

Most office programmers are familiar with Visual Basic for Applications. By far the most popular way to customize any Office application, VBA uses scripting to give you the programmer access to most of the Visio model.

VBA has its problems, though. The code is embedded with the file, so no global functionality applies to all drawings. VBA is also slow and insecure (relatively speaking).

VBA does offer some benefits and is great for really specific jobs in small environments. Don't let the anti-script people convince you — VBA has its uses.

COM add-ins

COM is the common denominator. Office is still programmed in COM, not .NET, so COM add-ins are native language. .NET is still running through a translator. Without fail, COM is still the king of Visio automation.

COM add-ins have a lot of problems that need to be fixed, though. Bad programming can really be a problem because a bad COM add-in can render the whole application useless even if it isn't directly being used. COM can be a security hassle or a security hole.

COM is still the only way to implement a shared add-in in Visio. (You can write an add-in in managed code, but it still comes out COM.) Also, if you plan to use any unmanaged code, COM is the best way to go.

Largely, from a functionality standpoint, everything that you can do in COM you can do in VSTO and vice versa. Only the ease of use and implementation are different.

Shared add-ins

Effectively, *shared add-ins* are managed code written, COM accessible versions of add-ins. They're .NET coded, but use the COM model, not VSTO. The reason they exist is to build functionality that will work on all Office products.

You won't find much use for these add-ins anymore, unless you need one to work in several Office applications.

The Drawing Control

The Visio Drawing Control (VDC) is a cool tweak to Visio that allows you to effectively host most of its functionality in another container. VDC is just an ActiveX control — COM again — that allows you to code it like a Windows Control. Although very cool, this tool is outside the scope of this book. For more information, search "Visio Drawing Control" in the MSDN library.

Visual Studio Tools for Office (VSTO)

As with the other Office components, VSTO is a purpose-built set of managed objects that directly interfaces with the COM API of Visio. Because of the common model for creation of add-ins, and the power that the VSTO controls add (as far as the visual designers and what-not), VSTO is the best way to do 80 percent of what you need to do with Visio.

VSTO just makes add-ins for Visio; it has no document option like there is for Word and Excel. To make an add-in, simply access the New➪Office 2010 Application folder. Generally speaking, VSTO for Visio works the same way.

Other than the add-in model, you have Windows Forms if you need them, along with the Task pane, menus, and everything else. The only significant difference is the Visio API, which we cover in depth in the next section.

Without a doubt, VSTO is *the* way to extend Visio unless you expressly need something that one of the other six extensibility options provides.

Harnessing the Power of the Visio Model

Aside from the usual managed code controls that the VSTO engine brings to add-ins, you have access to Visio, too. Much in the vein of the other Office applications, a managed wrapper to the same Visio API that VBA uses is available.

With this managed wrapper, you can get to both the current document that you're working on, and the types that make up the shapes and words. The ability to connect to databases and export the project fit into use of the wrapper, too. Anything that is specific to Visio (pretty much everything anyway) can be accessed through the Visio Object Model.

To get started with the Visio object model, make a new Visio add-in project:

1. **In Visual Studio 2010, click Create➪Project in the Recent Projects section.**

2. **Select Visio 2010 Add-In, as shown in Figure 12-1.**

3. **Type a name in the Name text box.**

4. **Click OK.**

   Visual Studio creates a new VSTO project for you, and you see the familiar two starting event handlers: `ThisAddIn_Startup` and `ThisAddIn_Shutdown`.

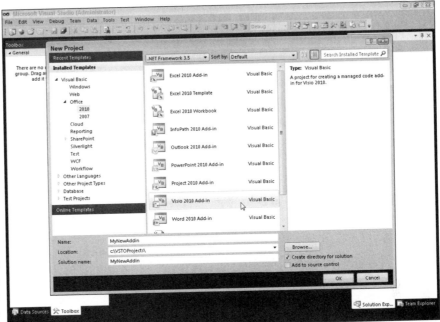

Figure 12-1:
A new Visio
2001 add-in.

Managing the document and pages

The `Visio.Document` object is where the shapes, text, and data connections of the actively loaded project are stored. This object represents the file that you want to work on. To get to the `Visio.Document` that is loaded at the moment, from your add-in, use the `Application` object. This code goes in the `ThisAddIn_Startup` subroutine:

```
Dim currentDocument as Visio.Document
currentDocument = Application.ActiveDocument
```

You probably recognize this code — it's the common way to do just about everything with relation to documents in VSTO. After you have access to the document, you can change global parts of the document, such as margins and data connections.

To do anything interesting, though, you need to specify the page. Because Visio uses a paged format (with the tabs on the bottom), the `Document` itself lets you specify only global information. To get access to the `Page`, use this code:

```
Dim currentPage as Visio.Page
currentPage = Application.ActivePage
```

After you have access to the current page, you can actually draw on the page. The ability to draw on the page is for drawing-level features, such as adding shapes.

A `Window` object also allows you to do tasks such as selecting and copying items. For example, to select all the items on the page, enter

```
Application.ActiveWindow.SelectAll()
Dim everything As Visio.Shapes
everything = Application.ActiveWindow.Selection
everything.Copy()
```

Adding basic shapes to a diagram

Most of the shapes in Visio have `Draw` methods associated with them. After you have a handle to the current page of the document, you can just draw the shape, and it returns a `Shape` object that you can use to change the color and what-not.

For example, say that you want to draw a circle in the upper left-hand corner of the page. You can use `DrawOval` and give it the upper left and lower right coordinates of the square that would go over the circle. (See Figure 12-2 to see what we mean.)

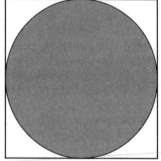

Figure 12-2:
How the circle size is calculated.

To draw this circle (because you have a handle to the `currentPage`), you just define a new `Shape` and then draw:

```
Dim circleShape As Visio.Shape
circleShape = Application.ActivePage.DrawOval( 100, 100, 200, 200)
```

Now you have `currentShape`. That `Shape` object gives you a handle to the specific circle, which gives you all kinds of properties:

✔ `Connections`

✔ `Fill`

✔ `LineStyle`

✔ `Picture`

✔ `Style`

✔ `Text`

Part of the problem in coding for Visio is that you have so many options. What we're hoping to do is narrow them down for you a little.

Adding neat shapes to a diagram

Using the built-in draw functions to draw is easy, but what if you want to add a neat shape, such as something from the Computers and Monitors collection?

The first thing you need to understand is the `Master`. `Masters` define *items,* which are the static parts of Visio. An example of an item is a shape in various categories. You can get to an item three ways:

✔ Iterate through a collection

✔ Specify with an index

✔ Access it via its name

The second thing you need to know is where you want to drop the shape. The XY coordinates are from the top left corner and are in inches, unlike most graphics objects, which are via pixels.

The following code drops a PC shape on the page. Note that this code assumes that the Computers and Monitors shape category is part of the document in question. Otherwise, you'd have to build a little extra code to look up the shape.

```
'Get an object to hold the shape
Dim neatShape As Visio.Shape
'Instead of using a Draw method that will give us a shape
'we go get a copy of it.
neatShape = currentDocument.Masters.ItemU("PC")
'Use the Drop method to place the shape.
currentPage.Drop(neatShape, 4, 4)
```

Putting type on the page

You can put type on the page in a few different ways, but we want to focus on two in particular:

- ✔ Putting title text (a textbox) right on the page
- ✔ Adding text to a shape

Either way, the Characters collection of a shape is where you're headed. To make a title, just use an invisible rectangle. Other shapes react just as you're used to — some inside and some at the bottom.

To add a title text:

1. **Draw a new rectangle.**

   ```
   Dim squareShape As Visio.Shape
   squareShape = Application.ActivePage.DrawRectangle( 600, 100, 620, 300)
   ```

2. **Set up the rectangle as a text box:**

   ```
   With squareShape
     .TextStyle = "Basic"
     .LineStyle = "TextOnly"
     .FillStyle = "TextOnly"
   End With
   ```

3. **Declare a new Characters collection:**

   ```
   Dim titleChars As Visio.Characters
   ```

4. **Set it to the Characters collection of the rectangle:**

   ```
   titleChars = squareShape.Characters
   ```

5. **Change the properties of the Characters collection to show what you want:**

   ```
   With titleChars
     'set the text
     .Text = "This is the title"
     'Set the font to 18
     .CharProps(CShort( _
         Visio.VisCellIndices.visCharacterSize)) = _
         CShort(18)
   End With
   ```

Adding label style text to something works very much the same way. Because they're shapes, they all have a Characters collection. The shape's setup in the template is how the text knows where to sit. All you have to do is get the Characters collection and write to it.

For example, if you want to add a label to the PC shape you added in "Adding neat shapes to a diagram," we would just declare a new `Characters` collection and set the properties:

```
Dim labelChars As Visio.Characters
labelChars = neatShape.Characters
'Just for fun, we will use this computers name.
labelChars.Text = My.Computer.Name
```

Making data connections

Because Visio is in COM, it uses ADO, not ADO.NET. If you haven't had the pleasure of coding in Visual Basic 6 (or another ADO language), a *recordset* is a binary object that is usually stored in one table of data, with no visibility through XML. Recordsets had their problems.

Data in Visio is handled with recordsets, and you make them happen using the `DataRecordsets` collection of the `Document` object. This collection holds the recordsets (think of them as the results from a SQL Statement) that you can use with the shapes in your diagram.

You can use data in other ways with Visio, some of which require no programming. Take a look at the Visio pages in `http://Microsoft.com` for more information.

`DataRecordsets` are used on a document-by-document basis. They're part of the file itself — they don't stick around from file to file. Your add-in allows the `DataRecordsets` to be created in several different files, though.

To create a new `DataRecordset` that populates shapes and other page entities, just `Add` it to the collection. The `Add` method takes a connection string, a command string (such as a stored procedure), an option code, and an optional name. The option code defines a few characteristics that assist with security.

Saving and exporting the project

After you're done changing things on the drawing, you need to let the document author save the document. Of course, the author can save using the Save button, but what fun is that?

Seriously, sometimes you need to let the user do a process that ends with a saved document, backup copy, or export. The `Application` object has some really wild ways to do so, while the `Document` object has more typical methods.

First, save with the `Save` command:

```
currentDocument.Save()
```

You can also save with a new name:

```
currentDocument.SaveAs("A new name.vsd")
```

Pretty boring, but useful nonetheless. Exporting is a new trip, though. To save as a Web page, for example, do the following:

1. **Add the Visio Save as Web Type Library to the solution, as shown in Figure 12-3.**

2. **Get the `SaveAsWeb` object from the `Application`.**

3. **Get the `SaveAsWeb` settings from the `SaveAsWeb` object.**

4. **Name the Web page you're saving.**

5. **Make sure the browser opens up.**

The code looks like

```
Dim gonnaSaveAsWeb as Visio.SaveAsWeb.VisSaveAsWeb
gonnaSaveAsWeb = Application.SaveAsWebObject
Dim currentSettings as Visio.SaveAsWeb.VisWebPageSettings
currentSettings = gonnaSaveAsWeb.WebPageSettings
currentSettings.TargetPath = "c:\Websites\visio.htm"
currentSettings.OpenBrowser = 1
```

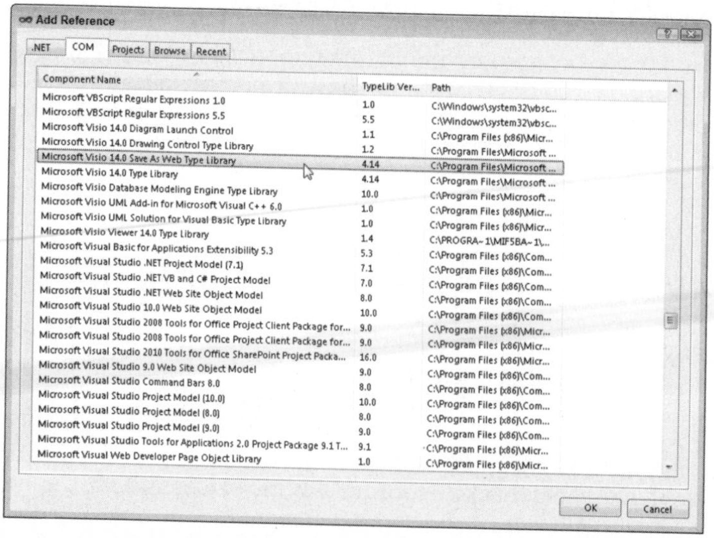

Figure 12-3:
Adding the Visio Save As Web library.

Getting Visualization into the Business Process

From the design perspective, visualizing the business process is a two-part process. You first have to get data, and then you have to make shapes to represent it. On the surface, that task seems pretty simple, and it is!

You could get shapes on the page with just ADO.NET, but Visio has a feature here that is important. Because you're effectively binding the shapes to data items, when the data changes, the shapes change. In order to do the visualization this way, the drawing itself needs to be data aware, which means you use `DataRecordsets`. If you want to grab a little data and then draw a shape, you can use ADO.NET and then set the shape's properties, but you need to be familiar with `DataRecordsets` in case you need them later.

For this example, you're trying to meet this requirement: Adventure Works wants to get a little visualization into its customer store sales. The company wants to see a chart where the square footage of the store is represented by the size of the shape, and the salesare printed next to the shape.

You can meet this requirement using Visio and data-adapted shapes, with the core AdventureWorks database. You use the `LinkToData` method. (You can use `DropLinked`, if you want — look them both up in MSDN to see the difference.)

Getting data into that drawing

First, make a recordset in the add-in that the document can use:

1. **Set up a connection string.**

   Your connection string (unless you're using SQLExpress) is probably

   ```
   Dim connectionString As String
   connectionString = "Data Source=(local);Initial Catalog=" &
   "AdventureWorks;Integrated Security=True"
   ```

2. **Set up a command string:**

   ```
   Dim commandString As String
   commandString = " SELECT DISTINCT Name, SquareFeet, " &
   "AnnualRevenue FROM vStoreWithDemographics " &
   "WHERE EmailPromotion = 1"
   ```

3. **Get a handle on the active document:**

   ```
   Dim currentDocument As Visio.Document
   currentDocument = Application.ActiveDocument
   ```

4. Build yourself a recordset:

```
Dim storeData As Visio.DataRecordset
storeData = currentDocument.DataRecordsets.Add(
connectionString, commandString, 0, "Store Data")
```

Now you have data! The data that comes back looks like Table 12-1.

Table 12-1	Data from vStoreWithDemographics	
Name	*SquareFeet*	*AnnualRevenue*
A Bicycle Association	19000	80000.0000
Acclaimed Bicycle Company	73000	300000.0000
Advanced Bike Components	38000	150000.0000
All Cycle Shop	25000	100000.0000

Making a subroutine to draw the store

The next major step in the process is to build a function that you can call every time that you want to:

1. Place a global position placeholder right under the class declaration:

```
Dim xcoord As Double = 2
Dim ycoord As Double = 2
```

2. Set up a new Subroutine signature.

```
Private Sub DrawStore(ByVal sqFoot As Double, ByVal sales As Double, ByVal
          rowId As Integer)
End Sub
```

3. Declare a new variable for the Page, the Document, and the Shape.

```
Dim currentPage As Visio.Page = Application.ActivePage
Dim currentDocument As Visio.Document = _
          Application.ActiveDocument
Dim storeShape As Visio.Shape
```

4. Compute the lower right-hand corner of the shape.

This calculation uses the sales figure to make sure that each shape is proportionate based on its annual sales:

```
Dim newx As Integer = xcoord + (10 * (sales / 1000000))
Dim newy As Integer = ycoord + (10 * (sales / 1000000))
```

5. Draw the rectangle to the page.

```
storeShape = currentPage.DrawRectangle( _
            xcoord, ycoord, newx, newy)
```

6. Link the shape to its row in the DataRecordset.

This function takes the index of the DataRecordset (this example has only one, so it is 1), the Row ID number you pass into the function, and a Boolean that describes if you're to paint the data text every time the data changes:

```
storeShape.LinkToData(1, rowId, True)
```

The preceding code generates one shape in your chart.

Visualizing the product

The last step is to actually run through the recordset and draw a shape for every row. Handing a recordset is in the VisualizeSales method.

1. Get an array to hold the row IDs.

This step is the only way to iterate through the rows. Remember, you're in COM, not ADO.NET.

```
Dim currentRows As Array
currentRows = storeData.GetDataRowIDs("")
```

2. Make an array to hold the data after it comes out.

This array will be one row:

```
Dim currentDataRow as Object
```

3. Loop through the rows.

```
For counter As Integer = 1 To 10 'Just the first ten
```

4. Get the data row:

```
currentDataRow = salespersonData.GetRowData(counter)
```

5. Call the DrawStore method:

```
DrawStore(CDbl(currentDataRow(1)), CDbl(currentDataRow(2)), counter)
```

6. Move the xcoord up by 2 inches.

You want a new shape every two inches:

```
xcoord = xcoord + 2
```

And that is the end of the loop.

7. **Turn on the visibility on the external data.**

   This step is important because it makes the graphic text on the side of the images stand out.

   ```
   Application.ActiveWindow.Windows.ItemFromID( _
   Visio.VisWinTypes.visWinIDExternalData).Visible = True
   ```

Making a button in a toolbar

Actually, that wasn't the last step. You need a way to run the VisualizeSales button! This little bit of code goes in the ThisAddIn_Startup subroutine, and it is the same as the other VSTO / Office projects. Peter and I discuss various parts of the ribbon throughout the book, so this is just a quick and dirty example so that you can run the program.

To get started adding a Ribbon to your solution:

1. **Right-click the project in Solution Explorer and click Add New item.**

2. **Select Ribbon (Visual Designer) from the list in the center of the Add New Item dialog box and click the Add button.**

   Visual Studio adds the Ribbon files Ribbon1.vb and Ribbon1.Designer.vb to your project.

3. **Drag a Button control from the Office Ribbon Controls section of the Toolbox into the design surface, above where the Group 1 label is.**

   We aren't going to rename things for this simple example — all the text fields are as expected, and you can change them in the Properties panel, if you wish.

4. **Double-click the Button control to generate the Button1_Click event in the Ribbon1 class.**

5. **Add the VisualizeSales() method to the event handler, like this:**

   ```
   Private Sub Button1_Click(ByVal sender As System.
       Object, ByVal e As Microsoft.Office.Tools.
       Ribbon.RibbonControlEventArgs) Handles
       Button1.Click
       VisualizeSales()
   End Sub
   ```

And that is all there is to it. If you're working in Office 2007, it's a lot more complex: You have to deal with the CommandBars collection. That is not a pretty sight. In case you ever have to do it, here is the equivalent code for Office 2007:

```
Dim commandBars As Office.CommandBars
Dim commandBar As Office.CommandBar
Dim runStoreReport As Office.CommandBarButton
commandBars = CType(Application.CommandBars, _
              Microsoft.Office.Core.CommandBars)
commandBar = commandBars.Add("VSTOAddinToolbar", _
              Office.MsoBarPosition.msoBarTop, , True)
commandBar.Context = Visio.VisUIObjSets.visUIObjSetDrawing & "*"
runStoreReport = CType(commandBar.Controls.Add( _
              Office.MsoControlType.msoControlButton), _
              Microsoft.Office.Core.CommandBarButton)
runStoreReport.Tag = "Store Report"
AddHandler runStoreReport.Click, AddressOf VisualizeSales
```

Running the example

Click the F5 or choose Debug⇨Start Debugging, and Visio runs. Make a new blank Basic Diagram and press the blank button in the single button toolbar.

If everything goes right, you see Figure 12-4. If not, check your data connection — that's what got me for a while.

This is an advanced example for a *For Dummies* book, but Visio is an advanced program. You can try a lot of other neat data visualization examples.

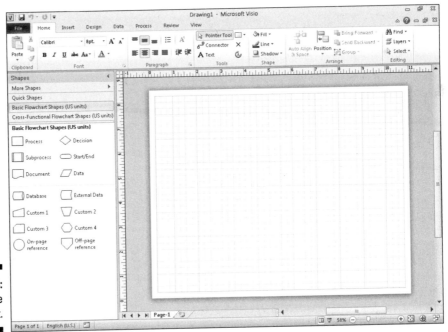

Figure 12-4:
The Store
Report.

Part III
Developing for SharePoint

The 5th Wave   By Rich Tennant

"I'm not saying I believe in anything. All I know is since it's been there our server is running 50% faster."

In this part . . .

This part started as one chapter. After we really understood how powerful the VSTO tools for SharePoint are, we decided to turn it into a whole part. That tells you how much information there is! There are a completely new set of project templates — which we cover — alongside the original workflow templates.

VSTO and SharePoint are made for each other. There is enough for a whole book in here, but until that book gets written, Part III gets you started!

Chapter 13

Working with SharePoint

In This Chapter

▶ Setting up for development

▶ Building SharePoint projects

▶ Reviewing the templates for SharePoint

*V*isual Studio 2010 ships with project templates and project item templates that enable developing for SharePoint 2010. Although support for SharePoint existed in the previous version of Visual Studio, it was limited only to developing SharePoint 2007 workflows. In this chapter, we describe the different development concepts for SharePoint development and use examples to explain how to use SharePoint project templates that are available in Visual Studio 2010.

SharePoint itself (without even discussing SharePoint development) is a very big subject, and it's impossible to explain it in only one chapter, so we made it a whole part. In these chapters, we assume that you have some knowledge about the SharePoint basics (sites, lists, and so on) and that you know how to create lists, libraries, and items in SharePoint. If you want to find out more about SharePoint 2010, we suggest Vanessa William's excellent book *SharePoint 2010 For Dummies* (Wiley).

Getting Started with Microsoft SharePoint Foundation 2010

SharePoint 2010 comes in two flavors: Microsoft SharePoint Foundation 2010 and Microsoft SharePoint Server 2010. For the purpose of this chapter, we use Microsoft SharePoint Foundation 2010. Throughout the chapter, we use SharePoint 2010 to refer to the Microsoft SharePoint Foundation 2010.

You need to install a couple of things on your development machine in order to start using SharePoint project templates.

Just as VSTO does, SharePoint requires Microsoft Office on the machine. To take advantage of new SharePoint project templates, you need to install SharePoint Server on your development machine. Previous versions of Visual Studio required SharePoint (as well as Visual Studio) to be installed on the server operating system (for example, Windows Server 2003 or Windows Server 2008). Luckily, you can install a new version of SharePoint on a client operating system, such as Windows Vista or Windows 7. Another difference between SharePoint 2007 and SharePoint 2010 is that your machine has to support a 64-bit environment — you have to install a 64-bit operating system (either client or server) in order to install SharePoint 2010.

Note that you should install SharePoint 2010 on a client operating system to use it only for your development environment. SharePoint 2010 installed on a client operating system for production environment isn't supported.

We assume that you're using Windows 7, Windows Vista, or even a server operating system, such as Windows Server 2008, and you already have Visual Studio 2010 installed. The steps for installing SharePoint on a client or server operating system are different.

Preparing to install SharePoint 2010

In this section, we explain how to install SharePoint 2010 and its prerequisites on the client operating system.

You can download Microsoft SharePoint Foundation 2010 for free from

```
http://www.microsoft.com/downloads/details.aspx?displaylang=en&FamilyID=49c79
            a8a-4612-4e7d-a0b4-3bb429b46595
```

The package file is about 170MB. The recommended hardware requirements for installing SharePoint 2010 are the following:

- 64-bit processor
- 4GB of RAM for development
- 80GB for system drive

Create a new folder on your hard drive and call it `SharePointFiles` (for example `C:\SharePointFiles`). Next, download the `SharePoint Foundation.exe` file from the Microsoft Web site and save it to that folder. Now you need to extract this file to be able to install the prerequisites for Microsoft SharePoint Foundation 2010. To do so, follow these steps:

1. **Open Command Prompt by choosing Start⇨All Programs⇨ Accessories⇨Command Prompt.**

2. **Navigate to the `C:\SharePointFiles` folder you created by typing the following command in the Command Prompt window:**

   ```
   cd C:\SharePointFiles
   ```

3. **Type the following command to extract the files and then press Enter:**

   ```
   SharePointFoundation.exe /Extract:C:\SharePointFiles
   ```

   This command extracts the files from the `SharePointFoundation. exe` package to the `C:\SharePointFiles` folder.

4. **Open the `C:\SharePointFiles` folder in Windows Explorer and navigate to the `Files\Setup` subfolder.**

5. **Open the `config.xml` file with Notepad (or any other text editor you prefer) and add the following line of XML right above the `</Configuration>` tag:**

   ```
   <Setting Id="AllowWindowsClientInstall" Value="True"/>
   ```

Listing 13-1 shows the contents of the `config.xml` file. The line added in Step 5 appears in bold.

Listing 13-1

```
<Configuration>
<Package Id="sts">
  <Setting Id="SETUPTYPE" Value="CLEAN_INSTALL"/>
</Package>
<DATADIR Value="%CommonProgramFiles%\Microsoft Shared\Web Server Extensions\14\
              Data"/>
  <Logging Type="verbose" Path="%temp%" Template="Microsoft SharePoint
              Foundation 2010 Setup *.log"/>
  <Setting Id="UsingUIInstallMode" Value="1"/>
  <Setting Id="SETUP_REBOOT" Value="Never" />
  <Setting Id="AllowWindowsClientInstall" Value="True"/>
</Configuration>
```

This line of XML tells the SharePoint installer to allow you to install the SharePoint 2010 on the client operating system. You can save the `config. xml` file and then install the prerequisites.

Installing SharePoint prerequisites on Windows 7

Installing SharePoint prerequisites on a server operating system is much easier and more straightforward than installing on a desktop system because a dedicated prerequisites installer takes care of everything. If you're installing SharePoint on a server operating system, double-click the `PrerequisitesInstaller` file and follow the wizard to install all the prerequisites.

If you're installing on a client operating system, you can't use the prerequisites installer; you have to install all the prerequisites manually. Follow these steps to install SharePoint 2010 prerequisites on a Windows 7 operating system:

1. **Run the Microsoft Filter Pack 2.0 installer by double-clicking the MSI file in the `C:\SharePointFiles\PrerequisiteInstallerFiles\FilterPack` folder.**

   You'll have to reboot after this step.

2. **Install the Microsoft Sync Framework Runtime (if needed) from this location:**

   ```
   http://go.microsoft.com/fwlink/?LinkID=141237
   ```

3. **Install Microsoft SQL Server 2008 Native Client support (unless you already have the latest version) from the following location:**

   ```
   http://go.microsoft.com/fwlink/?LinkId=123718
   ```

4. **Install Windows Identity Foundation from the following location:**

   ```
   http://www.microsoft.com/downloads/details.aspx?FamilyID=eb9c345f-e830-
           40b8-a5fe-ae7a864c4d76
   ```

5. **Install Microsoft ADO.NET Data Services Update (KB976127):**

   ```
   http://www.microsoft.com/downloads/details.aspx?familyid=79D7F6F8-D6E9-
           4B8C-8640-17F89452148E&displaylang=en
   ```

   This update is required for the REST support that is part of SharePoint.

6. **Turn on the required Windows features.**

   a. **Choose Start➪Control Panel➪Programs.**

   b. **From the Programs window, select Turn Windows Features On or Off.**

   c. **Select all the features under Internet Information Services (see Figure 13-1) and then click OK.**

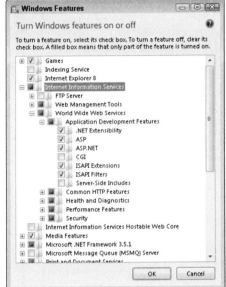

Figure 13-1:
Turning on
Internet
Information
Services
feature.

7. **If you're installing SharePoint on the Windows 7 operating system, install the KB976462 from**

```
http://code.msdn.microsoft.com/KB976462/Release/ProjectReleases.
        aspx?ReleaseId=4317
```

Installing SharePoint

After you install the prerequisites, you can continue installing SharePoint:

1. **Navigate to the folder where you extracted the SharePoint files (C:\ SharePointFiles) and double-click the setup.exe file to start the installation.**

   An Installation Wizard window, shown in Figure 13-2, appears.

2. **After you accept the license agreement, click Continue.**

   A dialog box, shown in Figure 13-3, appears.

3. **Choose the Standalone option to begin installing SharePoint 2010.**

   The SharePoint 2010 installation is usually quite fast.

4. **After the setup is completed, leave the selected option to configure SharePoint checked, as shown in Figure 13-3, and click the Close button.**

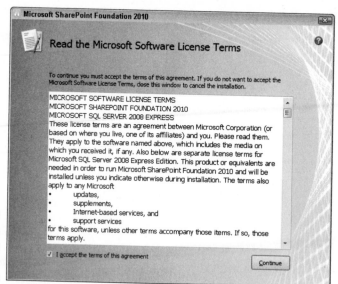

Figure 13-2:
SharePoint
installation.

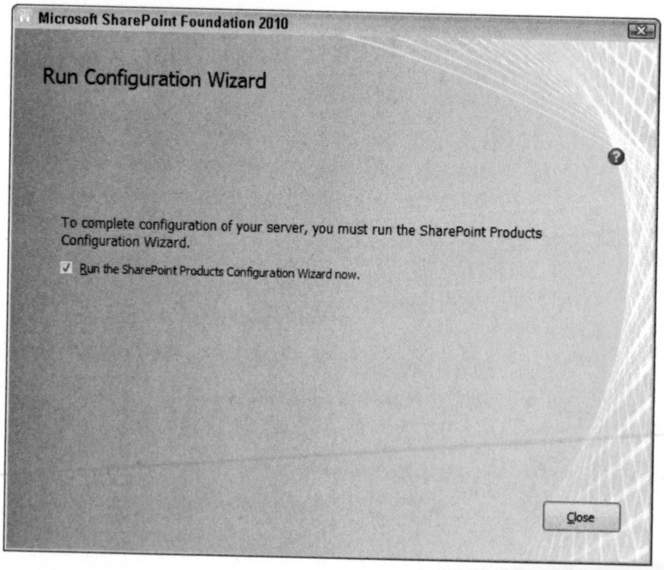

Figure 13-3:
The
SharePoint
installation
completed.

The SharePoint Configuration Wizard dialog box, shown in Figure 13-4, opens. The Configuration Wizard sets up everything required for SharePoint to work: It creates the configuration database, registers SharePoint services, and sets up the server.

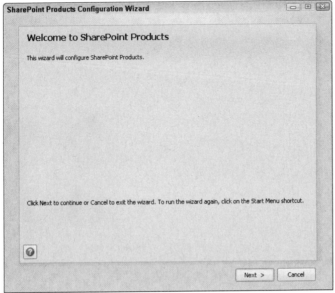

Figure 13-4:
The
SharePoint
Configuration
Wizard.

5. **Click the Next button.**

   You're warned that installation on Windows 7 or Windows Vista is intended for use only on developer workstations (see Figure 13-5).

6. **Click OK to close the dialog box and continue with the SharePoint configuration.**

   Another dialog box informs you that you may have to start or reset the listed services.

7. **Click Yes to continue the configuration.**

8. **When the configuration finishes, click the Finish button.**

   The Internet browser opens, and you're redirected to the SharePoint home site (see Figure 13-6).

Figure 13-5:
Installing
on client
operating
systems is
fordeveloper
worksta-
tions only.

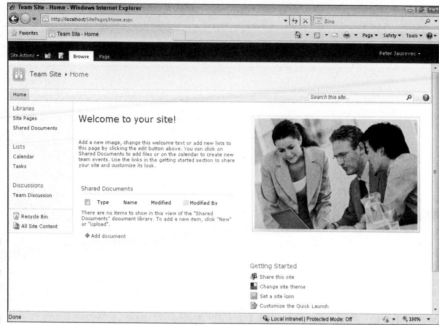

Figure 13-6:
The
SharePoint
team site.

Assuming that you already installed Visual Studio 2010, you're all set and ready to develop for SharePoint 2010.

Working with SharePoint 2010 Projects in Visual Studio 2010

Apart from developing SharePoint 2010 workflows in Visual Studio 2010, you can also develop the following SharePoint projects:

- Empty SharePoint Project
- Content Type
- List Definition
- Module
- SharePoint Sequential Workflow
- SharePoint State Machine Workflow
- Site Definition

✔ Import a SharePoint Solution Package

✔ Visual Web Part

✔ Event Receiver

✔ Business Data Connectivity Model

All these project templates are available in the New Project dialog box under the SharePoint 2010 node, as shown in Figure 13-7.

The following sections explain the SharePoint project templates and how you can use them.

Exploring the SharePoint project structure

If you've used the SharePoint workflow template in previous versions of Visual Studio, the new project structure may surprise you. Moving away from the flat project structure in Visual Studio 2008, the new SharePoint 2010 project templates in Visual Studio 2010 have a completely different, more organized, and easier to understand project structure. Figure 13-8 shows the layout of the new SharePoint project structure.

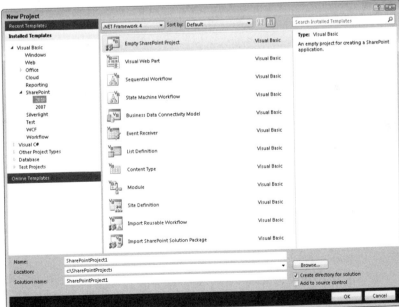

Figure 13-7: SharePoint project templates in Visual Studio.

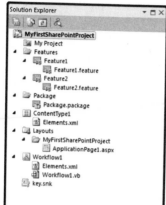

Figure 13-8:
The
SharePoint
project
structure.

Each SharePoint project has at least two special folders: Features and Package. These two folders are automatically created when you use new SharePoint project templates. These folders let you organize different SharePoint building blocks and decide how to package and deploy them.

A Features folder can hold one or more features. (A *feature* in SharePoint can be anything from a workflow to list instances and content types.) You can have multiple different features in your SharePoint project, and you can group them into a package. Each SharePoint project can have only one package. Don't think that this limitation blocks you in any way; just imagine that you have multiple SharePoint projects in a solution, and each of those projects has multiple features. What you can do is mix and match features from different SharePoint projects into the same package.

When a SharePoint project is built, it gets packaged into a WSP file. The WSP file holds all the information necessary to deploy the solution to the SharePoint server.

A *WSP file* is technically a cabinet file (`.CAB`). The use of the Cabinet format gives you the ability to rename the WSP file to a CAB file and extract its contents.

Don't worry — you don't have to master XML in order to work with the Features and Packages folders in Visual Studio 2010. The team at Microsoft who developed the tools for SharePoint development did a great job and provided both Feature and Package designers!

Taking a closer look at the Feature Designer

You can use the SharePoint Feature Designer, shown in Figure 13-9, to edit features inside a SharePoint project.

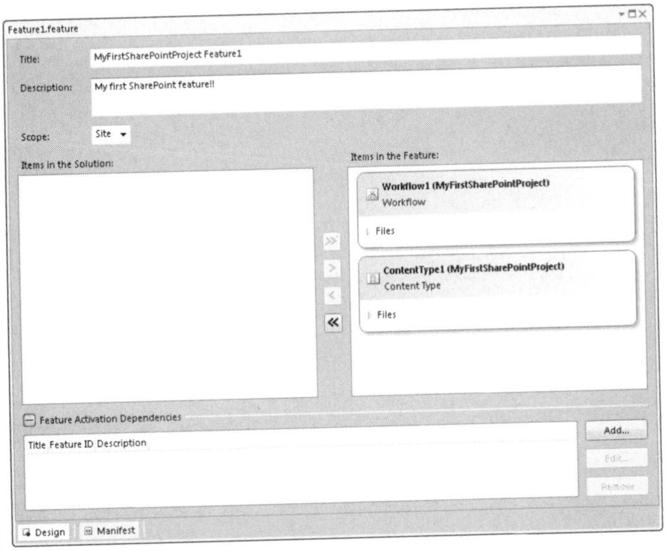

Figure 13-9:
The
SharePoint
Feature
Designer.

In Figure 13-9, two SharePoint project items are inside the feature. A simple double-click on any feature removes or adds the project item to the feature. From the Designer, you can also easily change the feature's title and description.

At the bottom part of the Designer, you can define the so-called *feature activation dependencies*. When a SharePoint solution is deployed to the SharePoint server, you need to activate it before you can use it. With feature activation dependencies, you can make one or more features depend on another feature.

For example, say that you have a feature with a list instance and another feature with workflow. You're also using a feature event receiver to associate the workflow with the list instance at activation time. What happens if workflow is deployed before the list instance? You get errors because you can't associate a workflow to something that doesn't exist.

This is the time to use a feature activation dependency. You should make your list instance feature dependent on the workflow feature. The dependency means that you can activate the workflow feature only if the list instance is activated first. Figure 13-10 shows how to add a feature activation dependency — more precisely, a dependency on `MyFirstSharePoint ProjectFeature2`.

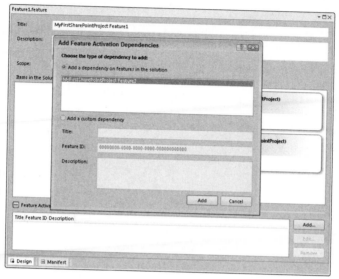

Figure 13-10:
Adding a
feature
activation
dependency.

Looking at project items

Every SharePoint project can contain zero, one, or more SharePoint project items. You can think of a SharePoint *project item* just like you did for feature — a SharePoint project item can be a workflow, Web part, content type, and so on.

Each SharePoint project item can be in its own feature, or you can group multiple SharePoint project items into the same feature. A SharePoint project item usually consists of an `Elements.xml` file and other supporting files — for example, code files in workflows.

An `Elements.xml` file is an XML file that describes the SharePoint project item and holds information that SharePoint reads when SharePoint solution is installed on the SharePoint server. In a way, you can think of an `Elements.xml` file almost like a code file when you're developing for SharePoint because, in most cases, the brains of your SharePoint project are in the `Elements.xml`.

In other SharePoint projects — workflows, event receivers, feature event receivers, and web parts — the brains are still in code files. Nonetheless, the `Elements.xml` file is still there because SharePoint needs it to correctly install and use the SharePoint features you develop.

More control for advanced users

If you're an advanced user who needs even more control, you can click the Manifest tab at the bottom of the Feature Designer. You see another view of the Feature Designer, as shown in the figure.

A feature's Advanced or Manifest view displays the exact same features as you see in

Figure 13-9. From the Manifest view, you can manually edit the feature manifest file, which represents a feature. We recommend making changes in this view only if you really know what you're doing. The Feature view in Figure 13-9 is more than enough for basic SharePoint development.

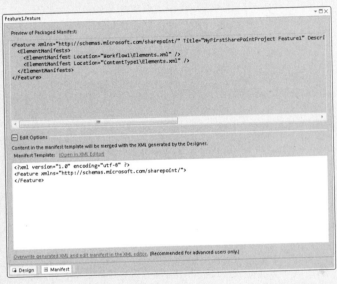

Meeting the Package Designer

SharePoint packages have a designer, too. To open the Package Designer, double-click the Package folder (or a Feature folder, if you want to open a designer for that feature). Figure 13-11 shows a Package Designer inside Visual Studio 2010.

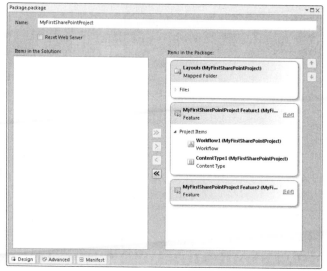

In Package Designer, you can add or remove features from a package just like you can add and remove project items in the Feature Designer. The Package Designer has two more views you can use:

- **Advanced view:** In the Advanced view (see Figure 13-12), you can add assemblies to the package. An assembly added to the package gets installed in either the Global Assembly Cache (GAC) or the Web application.

  Using the Add button, you can either add an assembly from the project in your solution or add any other assembly that is not part of the project. The dialog box for adding assemblies looks like the one shown in Figure 13-13.

- **Manifest view:** The Manifest view of a package, shown in Figure 13-14, is similar to the Manifest view in the Feature Designer. The only difference is that in the package Manifest view, you can edit package manifests.

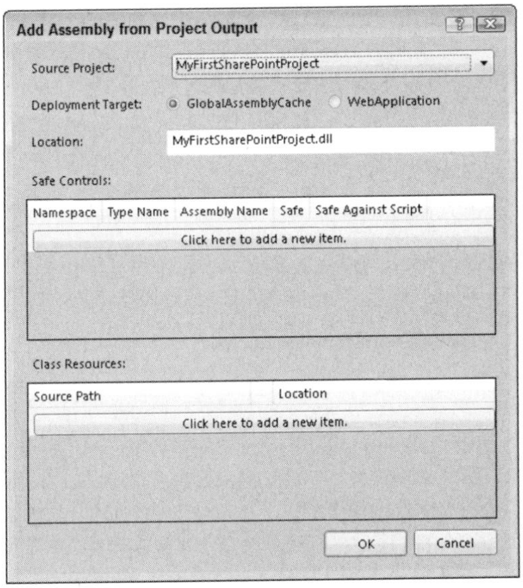

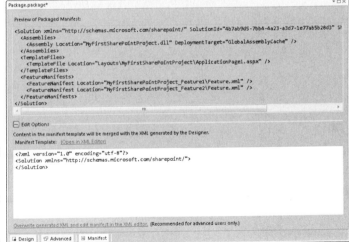

Figure 13-13: Adding assemblies to the package.

Figure 13-14: The Manifest view of a package.

Deploying SharePoint Projects

Deploying a SharePoint project is totally different than deploying a VSTO project or any other project in Visual Studio. If you've ever developed any SharePoint solutions (with or without Visual Studio), you probably know how tough and complicated the SharePoint project development process can be. But you're lucky if you're using Visual Studio 2010.

Deploying a SharePoint project from Visual Studio 2010 is fast and simple. You only have to press F5, and you're done! Visual Studio does everything else for you. And when we say everything else, we mean these steps, which are required for the SharePoint project to get deployed:

- ✔ Packaging the SharePoint project
- ✔ Recycling the IIS application pool
- ✔ Retracting the solution from the SharePoint server (if the solution doesn't exist on the server, this deployment step doesn't need to happen)
- ✔ Adding the solution to the SharePoint server
- ✔ Activating the feature from the SharePoint solution

Because deployment involves so many steps, you may be thinking how nice it would be if a reverse deployment action existed — something that would remove and clean the deployment solution from the SharePoint solution. Well, a reverse deployment action does exist, and it's called Retraction. If you want to clean and remove your solution from the SharePoint server, you can execute the Retract command that is available either from the Build menu or the Context menu when you right-click the project name in the Solution Explorer.

The deployment mechanism for SharePoint projects in Visual Studio 2010 is called *configurable deployment*. And it's rightfully called configurable, as you can see in Figure 13-15.

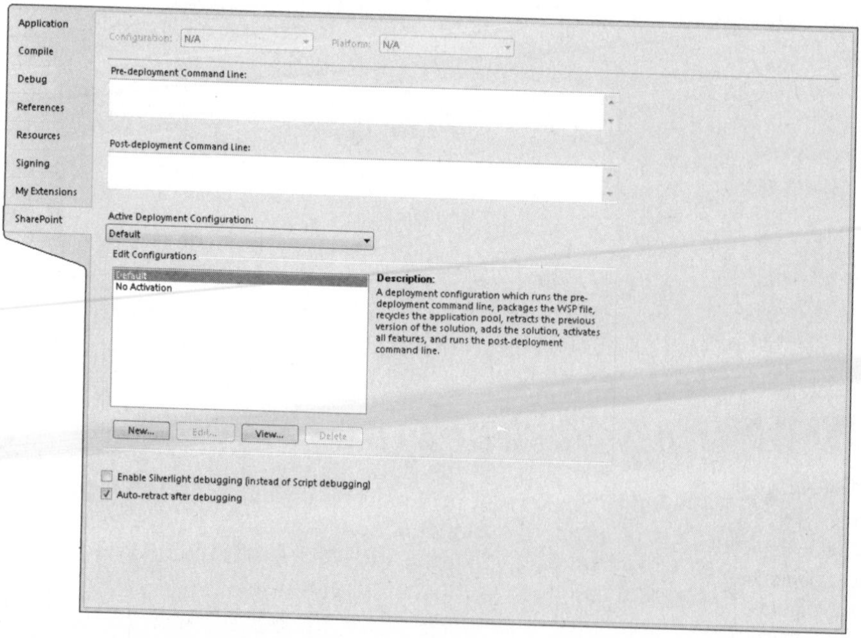

Figure 13-15:
The
SharePoint
tab in
Project
properties.

SharePoint projects have their own tab in Project properties that you can access by right-clicking the project name and choosing Properties from the context menu. The SharePoint tab shows you the deployment configurations that are available for your SharePoint project.

Each deployment configuration consists of a number of ordered steps that are executed either when you deploy the SharePoint project or you retract it. The list of automatic deployment steps we mention previously in this section represents the so-called default deployment configuration. However, Visual Studio has another deployment configuration: the No Activation deployment. This deployment configuration is similar to the default; the only difference is the absence of the last step, which activates the features.

If the stepped deployment isn't enough, you can also create your own deployment configurations. On the SharePoint tab, you can click the new button to open the Add New Deployment Configuration dialog box, shown in Figure 13-16.

From the dialog box in Figure 13-16, you can select which steps you want to execute when the SharePoint project is deployed and what steps to execute when the retract command is called.

In addition, the entire SharePoint feature in Visual Studio has its own object model and API. You can use that API to extend the functionality of not just projects and project items but also the deployment. Developing your own deployment steps and even deployment configurations isn't so difficult.

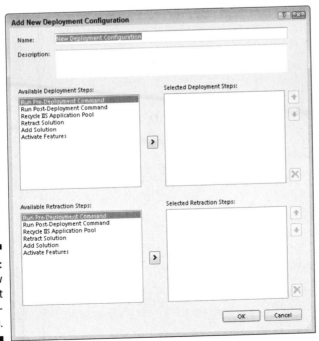

Figure 13-16:
Adding new deployment configurations.

Chapter 14

Building SharePoint Workflows

In This Chapter

▶ Scanning the workflow options

▶ Coding workflows in VSTO

▶ Putting workflows to work

*U*sers can build simple workflows in SharePoint Designer, but to create workflows that integrate with other services or program code, you have to use Visual Studio. You can build a workflow in Visual Studio using the New Project template for SharePoint workflows.

Workflow templates come in two types:

✔ The **Sequential workflow** is like a flowchart. It's triggered by one event and goes from the top to the bottom, making decisions and transformations as it goes. It's just a line of `If` statements.

✔ The **State Machine workflow** is like a pinball machine. It starts in one place and then is bounced around from state to state by events. This workflow works like a Windows application with buttons.

Starting a Fresh Workflow

For this example, you start with a simple sequential workflow. Workflows are complicated enough that you aren't going to find out everything that they can do in this chapter, but we give you enough to get you started. MSDN can help you from there on out.

To start a workflow:

1. **Click Create Project in the Visual Studio Start Page.**

2. **Select SharePoint and then 2010 from the tree view on the left side of the New Project dialog box.**

3. **Select the Sequential Workflow and name the project Example Workflow.**

The name isn't very original, we know.

4. **Accept the defaults for the name and the trust level and click Next.**

5. **Accept the defaults in the Workflow Type Selection dialog box and click Next.**

   You're creating a List workflow.

6. **Accept the defaults in the Workflow List Selection dialog box and click Next.**

   This steps sets the initial lists that you want to associate your workflow with. (If you add a new list, you have the option to select your workflow.)

7. **In the You Can Specify The Conditions For How Your Workflow Is Started dialog box, check the When the Item Is Changed check box.**

   This step adds the event handlers to your workflow, which you can ignore, if you want.

8. **Click Finish.**

   You see the Workflow Designer.

The Workflow Designer, shown in Figure 14-1, works a lot like the Windows or Web Forms Designer screens. A toolbox contains all the controls that you need for SharePoint or workflows in general, and the Properties box appears on the right. In the center is a design surface.

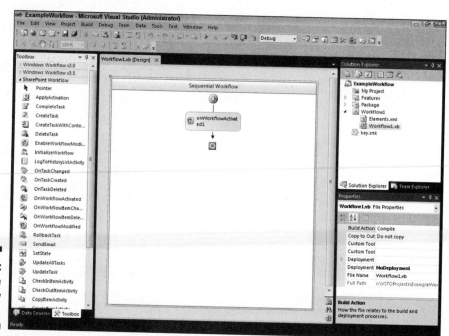

Figure 14-1: The Workflow Designer.

Knowing What You Have to Work With

Starting a new Workflow project is a bit confusing. Even the `ToolBox` is different. We knew what a `TextBox` was, but a `SharePointSequential WorkflowActivity`? It's a whole new world, unless you already know SharePoint controls.

To start with, everything that starts with `On` — `OnTaskChanged`, `OnWorkflowItemChanged` — is an event handler. These event handlers change the state of the workflow. In a sequential workflow, these event handlers move the workflow from step to step.

The first workflow step is always `OnWorkflowActivated`. You can use the first step to initialize values and the like. `OnWorkflowActivated` is like `Form.Load` for workflows.

When an event occurs, you can put code in the event handler (by double-clicking the event icon) or use one of the activity controls. These controls do necessary functions, such as making log messages, handling exceptions, or sending e-mails.

When you're done coding the workflow, you assign this workflow to a document list. When a document is added to the list, the workflow starts. The document is the subject of the workflow. (For more information, see the upcoming section "Using a Workflow.")

Building a Simple Workflow

This example keeps things simple. When the workflow is activated, a task is added. This example gives you a chance to use the designer a little, use the code a little, and deploy and test.

Follow these steps to build a `Hello World` type workflow:

1. **Create a new sequential workflow.**

   If you're not sure how, see the steps in the "Starting a Fresh Workflow" section, earlier in this chapter.

2. **Drag a `CreateTask` activity to the designer surface and float it over the arrow under the `onWorkflowActivated1` activity, as shown in Figure 14-2.**

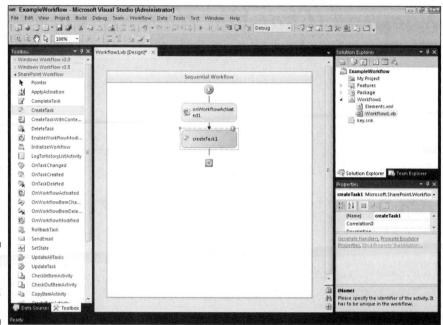

Figure 14-2:
Adding a
Create Task
activity.

3. **In the Properties pane, type `taskToken` into the correlation token.**

   The *correlation token* is a unique keyword that enables mapping between the objects in a workflow and SharePoint (in this case). Workflow items and SharePoint activities should have different tokens, which is why you don't use the default `workflowToken`.

4. **Click the plus sign next to the correlation token in the Properties pane and fill out the Owner Activity.**

5. **Click the drop-down list box and accept the default name, `Workflow1`.**

6. **Click the continuation button (. . .) next to Task Properties.**

   The Task Properties dialog box lets you tell SharePoint where to get the properties for the task — not set the properties directly.

7. **Click the Bind to a New Member tab.**

8. **Accept the default name (`createTask1_TaskProperties1`) and click OK.**

   If you go back and look at the properties, you can see that the new member is selected, as shown in Figure 14-3.

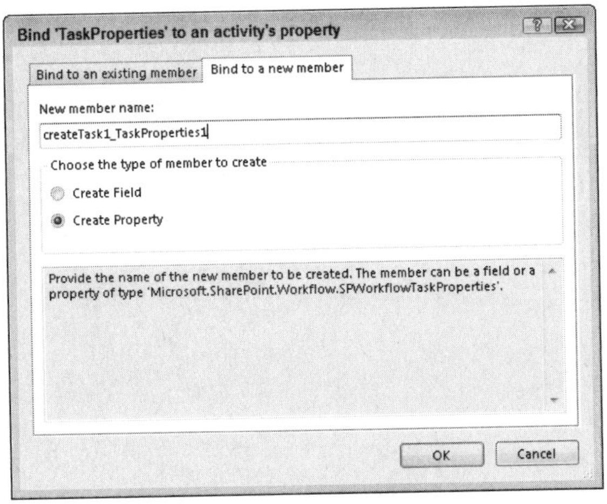

Bind 'TaskProperties' to an activity's property

Bind to an existing member | **Bind to a new member**

New member name:

createTask1_TaskProperties1

Choose the type of member to create

○ Create Field

● Create Property

Provide the name of the new member to be created. The member can be a field or a property of type 'Microsoft.SharePoint.Workflow.SPWorkflowTaskProperties'.

OK | Cancel

Figure 14-3:
Binding
to a new
member.

9. **Repeat Steps 6 through 8 but instead of clicking the button next to Task Properties in Step 6, click the button next to the `TaskId` property.**

Now you have a workflow that compiles.

Setting the Workflow's Task Properties

The problem with the workflow created in the preceding section is that it doesn't do anything because you haven't set the `Task` properties. The previous steps tell the workflow what property to get the task information from, but you still have to set up that property.

To do so, you need to go into Code View and set up the `Task` properties. Setting `Task` properties isn't all you can do in Code View, but it is all you're doing here because that's all the requirements say to do.

1. **In Solution Explorer, right-click the `Workflow1.vb` file and choose View Code.**

2. **Confirm that the code contains a new Public property called `create Task1_TaskProperties1` in the code.**

The method header should look like this:

```
<DesignerSerializationVisibilityAttribute(_
DesignerSerializationVisibility.Visible)> _
<.BrowsableAttribute(True)> _
<CategoryAttribute("Misc")> _
Public Property createTask1_TaskProperties1() As _
SPWorkflowTaskProperties
```

```
      Get
            Return CType(MyBase.GetValue(_
Example_Workflow.Workflow1.createTask1_TaskProperties1Property), _
 Microsoft.SharePoint.Workflow.SPWorkflowTaskProperties)
      End Get

    Set(ByVal value As _
SPWorkflowTaskProperties)
        MyBase.SetValue( _
Example_Workflow.Workflow1.createTask1_TaskProperties1Property, value)
      End Set

End Property
```

3. **In Workflow Designer, double-click the `createTask1` activity to add an event handler and fill out the `Task` properties:**

```
Private Sub createTask1_MethodInvoking ( _
ByVal sender As System.Object, ByVal e As System.EventArgs)
    createTask1_TaskId1 = Guid.NewGuid()
    createTask1_TaskProperties1 = new SPWorkflowTaskProperties()
    With createTask1_TaskProperties1
        .Title = "Workflow created task "
        .StartDate = Now()
        .Description = "This task was created by a workflow "
    End With
End Sub
```

4. **Choose Build➪Build Example Workflow.**

   The workflow is ready for use on SharePoint!

Using a Workflow

Generally, in order to use the workflow, you need to associate it to a list on the SharePoint Server site. But by default, workflow is already associated to the list selected in the Workflow Project Wizard — the Shared Documents list.

To get started using the project created in this chapter, you have to deploy. Because you're actually on the server where you'll be deploying, Visual Studio helps you out. Choose Build➪Deploy Workflow Example to run a build and then register the workflow as a component accessible to SharePoint.

If you want to debug the project before you deploy, you can press F5 to start debugging the project, and Internet Explorer opens and navigates to the SharePoint site.

Verifying Your Workflow

After you deploy the workflow, you can verify whether your workflow is really associated to the Shared Documents list:

1. **In Internet Explorer, type http://localhost or the name of your machine into the address bar to bring up the SharePoint default site.**

2. **Select Shared Documents list in the navigation bar on the right side.**

3. **Select Library.**

4. **Select Workflow Settings.**

   Your screen should look similar to Figure 14-4.

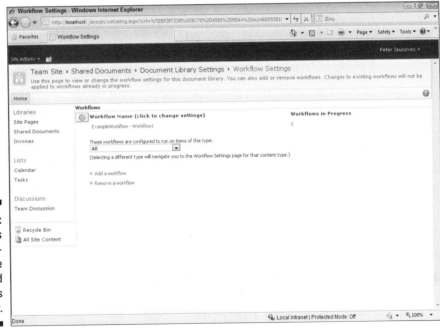

Figure 14-4:
Workflows associated to the Shared Documents list.

Starting the Workflow

To start the workflow, go to the Shared Documents list and upload a sample document. Click the Shared Documents link again and then click the Add document link to add a document to the list.

If you refresh the Web page, you see the ExampleWorkflow — the Workflow1 column has been added to the list and contains the value Completed, as shown in Figure 14-5.

The workflow you created was completed successfully, and a task was created in the Task list. You can quickly verify the task creation by clicking the Tasks link under the Lists header in the navigation bar on the right side of the page. You see something similar to Figure 14-6.

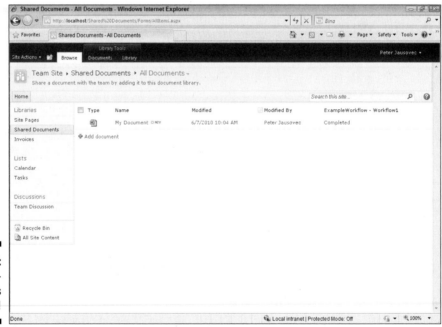

Figure 14-5: The workflow is completed!

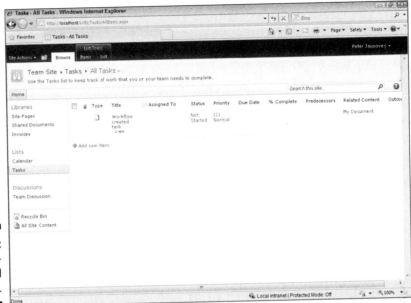

Figure 14-6:
The work-
flow created
a task.

Managing SharePoint Content Types

Content types in the SharePoint world represent a way to manage the content on SharePoint sites. Say, for example, that you have a document library where all your company invoices are stored. Just by looking at the list of documents, you can't easily figure out the company the invoice was sent to or the name of the person who prepared the invoice. With the help of content types, you can add information to each invoice stored in the document library, and that information shows up in the columns of the document library.

By default, each document library on SharePoint supports a default content type called Document. The Document content type can hold information such as a document title, date the document was created, and the name of the person who uploaded the document. If you want to show the company name for each invoice in the document library, for example, you'd need to create a new content type.

You can define what data you'd like to have in the Invoice document library:

✔ Name of the invoice

✔ Date created

✔ Person who created the invoice

✔ Name of the company where invoice was sent

✔ Total amount on the invoice

The first three items in the preceding list are already included in the default Document content type. Because of the hierarchical organization of content types in SharePoint, each content type has to inherit from an existing content type. So, instead of creating new columns for the name, date, and person, you can inherit the new Invoice content type from an existing Document content type, and you get those columns for free.

How about the remaining two columns — company name and total amount? Well, you can create new columns and add them to your new Invoice content type.

Adding a Content Type project

After you have all the requirements and an idea how they work, start by creating a new SharePoint Content Type project in Visual Studio 2010 and add a new SharePoint project item to the project that will create new columns on the SharePoint. Here's how:

1. **In Visual Studio 2010, create a new project named InvoiceContentType and click OK.**

    The SharePoint Customization Wizard appears, as shown in Figure 14-7.

2. **Leave the option Deploy As a Sandboxed Solution checked and click Next.**

    Visual Studio verifies the connection to the SharePoint. The second page of the Customization Wizard appears, as shown in Figure 14-8.

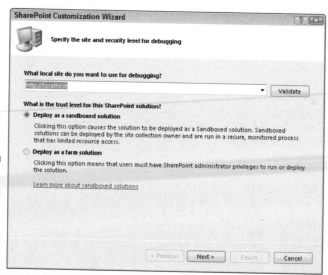

Figure 14-7: The first page of the SharePoint Customization Wizard.

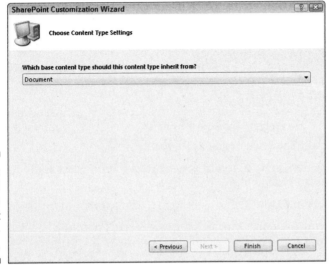

Sandboxed and *farm solutions* — what? With Visual Studio 2010, you can create almost all SharePoint projects as either a sandboxed solution or a farm solution. The main difference between sandboxed and farm solutions is that the sandboxed solutions run in a secure process and have limited access to the resource on the SharePoint. In order to run and deploy a farm solution, you must have SharePoint administrator privileges.

3. From the drop-down box, select `Document` content type.

You want your `Invoice` content type to be based on the existing `Document` content type.

4. Click Finish to close the wizard.

When you click Finish, the SharePoint content type project is created, and the `Elements.xml` file opens automatically.

Adding columns

Notice some of the values in the `Elements.xml`, such as the content type name, description, group, and other values. The one XML element you're interested in is the `FieldRefs`. The value inside the `FieldRefs` element tells SharePoint which columns our content type is referencing.

In order for the content type to reference any of the columns, those columns need to be on the SharePoint site already. Out of the original five columns in the document library, three are already on the SharePoint site, so you need to add only two new columns.

To add new columns to the SharePoint, you use the empty element project item. Follow these steps to add a new empty element project item to your existing content type project:

1. **Right-click the `InvoiceContentType` project name in the Solution Explorer.**

   A context menu appears.

2. **Choose Add⇨New Item.**

   The Add New Item dialog box appears.

3. **Select the Empty Element project item template from the list of templates and name it `InvoiceColumns`.**

4. **Click Add to add the project item to the project.**

   The empty element project item is exactly what the name implies — it's an empty `Elements.xml` file.

To add new columns to the SharePoint, you use the `Field` XML element. The `Field` element with its attributes and values tells SharePoint how to create the field. To create the new field, you have to specify the following values to the `Field` XML element:

✔ ID

✔ Name

✔ Type

✔ DisplayName

If you put the preceding list into the XML, it looks like

```
<Field ID="[ID]" Name="[NAME]" Type="[TYPE]" DisplayName="[DISPLAY NAME]"/>
```

Of course, you need to substitute the values in `[]` with the actual values. Here's what the XML looks like when you do for your two fields:

```
<?xml version="1.0" encoding="utf-8"?>
<Elements xmlns="http://schemas.microsoft.com/sharepoint/">
  <Field ID="{98D7454B-A3E3-4F2D-BD79-1DA518D884FF}"
         Name="InvoiceCompanyName"
         Type="Text"
         Group="Invoice Columns"
         DisplayName="Company Name"/>
  <Field ID="{3E0F4CF2-A391-480E-B6D4-01F3042359DF}"
         Name="InvoiceTotalAmount"
         Type="Currency"
         Group="Invoice Columns"
         DisplayName="Total Amount"/>
</Elements>
```

Notice the `Group` attribute, which tells SharePoint how to group the new columns. When you deploy the empty element, SharePoint creates a new group called `Invoice Columns`, and the group contains both columns you created.

How do you get the ID value? No, we didn't come up with the value for the `ID` attribute. A nice tool inside Visual Studio creates the ID values for you. Choose Tools⇨Create GUID to open the dialog box for creating GUIDs.

Referencing columns

After you create the columns, you can reference them in the content types' `Elements.xml` file. Open the `Elements.xml` file inside the `ContentType1` folder. Add the following XML inside the `FieldRefs` XML element:

```
<FieldRef ID="{98D7454B-A3E3-4F2D-BD79-1DA518D884FF}"
          Name="InvoiceCompanyName"/>
<FieldRef ID="{3E0F4CF2-A391-480E-B6D4-01F3042359DF}"
          Name="InvoiceTotalAmount"/>
```

It's that easy! To reference an existing field on SharePoint, you provide only the ID and the name of the field.

Deploying the solution

You're ready to deploy the SharePoint solution and try it out. Press F5 to start debugging and to deploy the solution to the SharePoint. The Internet browser opens on the Site Content Types page, as shown in Figure 14-9.

Click the content type — `InvoiceContentType` — `ContentType1` — appears under the Custom Content Types heading. You see the Site Content Type Information page. From the Content Type Information page, you can change the settings of the content type as well as add, remove, or change the order of columns in the content type. In Figure 14-10, the Company Name and Total Amount site columns are part of your content type.

Content type by itself isn't useful. To bring the content type to life, you need to associate it with a SharePoint library or list.

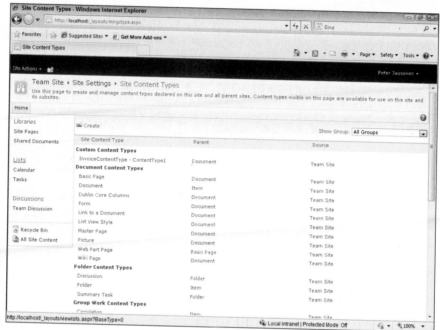

Figure 14-9:
The Site
Content
Types page.

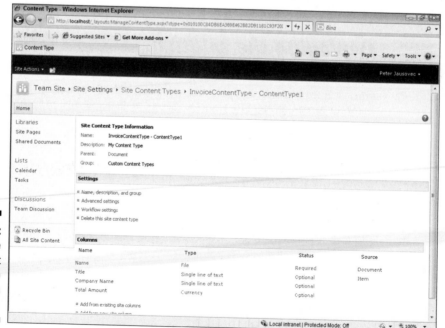

Figure 14-10:
The Invoice
Content
Type with
custom
columns.

Chapter 15

Building SharePoint Lists and Libraries

. . . .

. . . .

You've probably figured out that SharePoint is all about lists and items in those lists. Visual Studio 2010 contains two project templates specifically targeted toward creating lists in SharePoint:

✓ **SharePoint List Definition template:** As the name suggests, you can use the SharePoint List Definition template to define SharePoint lists. This template is similar to a Word template. You can create a template for a SharePoint list and use it when creating new list instances.

✓ **SharePoint List Instance template:** This supports a predefined list inside SharePoint.

Adding a List Definition to a Project

When you can make the Invoice document library in Chapter 14, you create an instance of the Invoice library and a content type and then associate that type with the list. If you want, you can create a list definition that already has the required content type in it. That way, you can create as many Invoice list instances on the SharePoint as you want with a single mouse click.

You can also use the List Definition from a Content Type template to solve the list creation dilemma. A Visual Studio template automatically creates a list definition from your content type.

In the following steps, you use the `Invoice` content type project from the previous section and add a `List` definition from a content type project item:

1. **Open the `InvoiceContentType` project.**

2. **Right-click the `InvoiceContentType` project name in the Solution Explorer and choose Add⇨New Item.**

   The Add New Item dialog box appears.

3. **Click the `List Definition From Content Type` project item template.**

4. **Name the project item `InvoiceListDefinition`.**

5. **Click Add.**

   The SharePoint Customization Wizard appears, as shown in Figure 15-1.

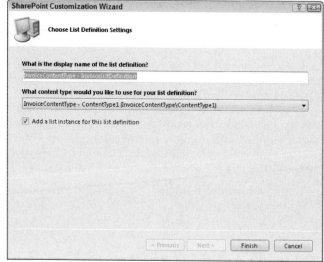

Figure 15-1:
The List
Definition
From
Content
Type Wizard
page.

6. **Type the display name for the list definition: `InvoiceList Definition`.**

   The `Invoice` content type is already selected in the drop-down box, so you don't have to do anything else. Any content type project items in your project show up in this drop-down box.

7. **Make sure that the Add A List instance for this list definition is selected.**

   When the Add a List Instance for This List Definition option is selected, a new list instance based on the list definition is created when we deploy the project.

8. Click Finish.

A new SharePoint project item, named `InvoiceListDefinition`, is added to your project. The newly added item also contains a subfolder called `ListInstance1`. Yes, that list instance is going to be created based on the list definition.

Believe it or not, you only need to press F5 to start debugging and to deploy the project, and you can see your list definition and list instance in action.

Changing the Startup Item

You can change the startup project item to the list instance. When you press F5, the Site content type page opens. Well, if you change the startup item to the list instance, that list instance opens when the Internet browser loads the page.

To set the startup item, right-click the `ListInstance1` project item folder and select Set as Startup Item from the context menu, as shown in Figure 15-2.

Now when you press F5, the Internet browser takes you directly to the `InvoiceContentType — ListInstance1` page, as shown in Figure 15-3.

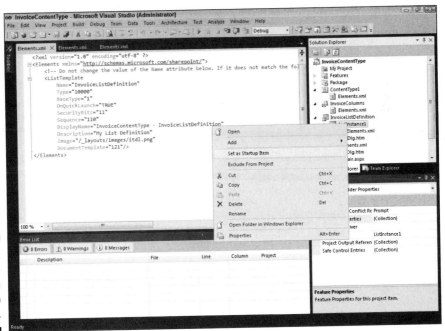

Figure 15-2:
Setting the list instance as a startup item.

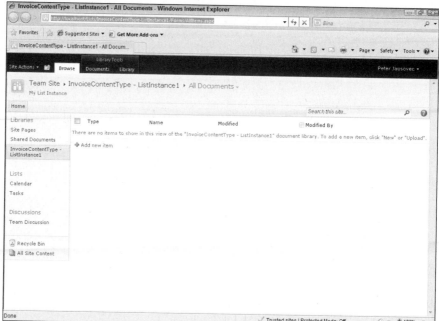

Figure 15-3:
The
`Invoice`
list instance.

Uploading an Invoice to a Library

You can upload an invoice to a library to verify how the `Invoice` content type works. Follow these steps to upload a new document (invoice) to the invoice list instance:

1. **Click the Documents tab on the Ribbon.**

   The Ribbon changes, and the Documents tab becomes active.

2. **Click the Upload Document button.**

   The Upload Document window appears, as shown in Figure 15-4.

3. **Click Browse and browse to the invoice or a document you want to upload.**

4. **Click OK to upload the document.**

   As soon as you click OK to the upload the document, the content type magic happens. The document is uploaded to the list, and another dialog box opens, prompting you to enter the Company Name and the Total Amount, as shown in Figure 15-5.

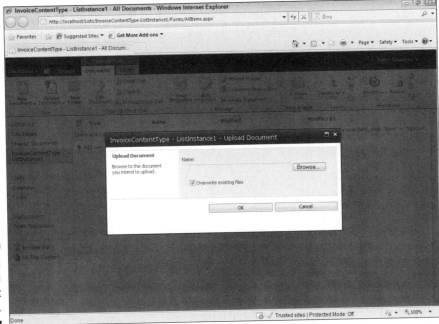

Figure 15-4:
The Upload
Document
window.

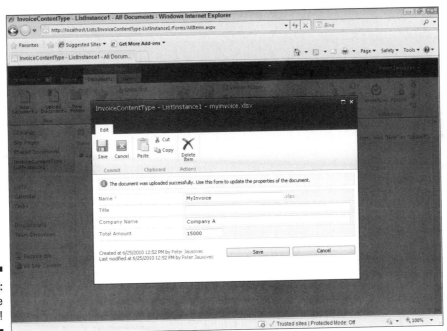

Figure 15-5:
Content type
magic!

Adding Libraries to the Default View

When you click the OK button, the company name and total amount values are stored in the library. The new columns added to the SharePoint don't appear in the libraries default view. Follow these steps to fix this issue:

1. **In the Internet browser, navigate to the library list instance.**

   In this example, its `InvoiceContentType — ListInstance1`.

2. **Click the Library tab on the Ribbon.**

   The Ribbon in the Internet browser changes, as shown in Figure 15-6.

3. **Click the Modify View button.**

   The Edit View site opens, as shown in Figure 15-7. From this site, you can decide which columns to show in the default view.

4. **Under the Columns heading, find the Company Name and Total Amount columns and put a checkmark in the Display column.**

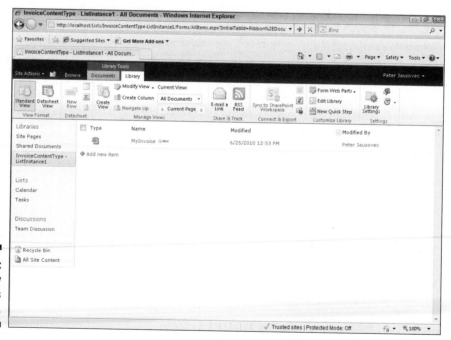

Figure 15-6: Library settings Ribbon.

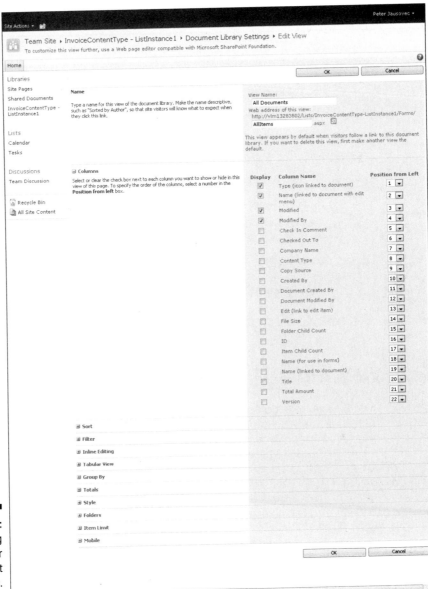

5. Click OK to save the changes.

You return to the library, and the Company Name and Total Amount columns are displayed in the default view, as shown in Figure 15-8.

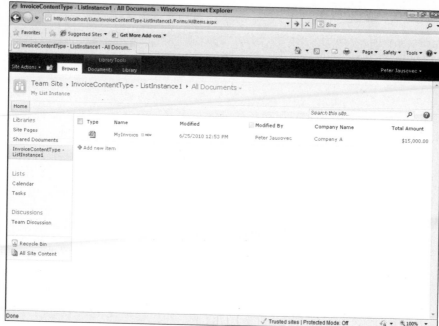

Figure 15-8:
New
columns
in the
default
view.

Working with Visual Web Parts

Say, for example, that everyone likes the SharePoint invoice solution you developed in this chapter. The solution starts to spread throughout the company, and suddenly almost every department of the company has its own Invoice library where they store their invoices.

As a manager, you'd like to get the following information: the total number of all invoices across the company, the total value for all invoices, and the invoice with the highest total amount. You could browse through all invoice libraries, sort the library, get the highest amount, compare it to the amounts in other libraries, and so on, but that process sounds like too much work, doesn't it?

Ideally, you could capture all this information in one place. That's where the power of Web parts comes in. Technically, *Web parts* are ASP.NET server side controls that are part of a Web part page. A *Web part page* is an ASP.NET page that is capable of hosting the Web part controls. Each Web part page in SharePoint consists of different zones that act as placeholders for Web parts, as shown in Figure 15-9.

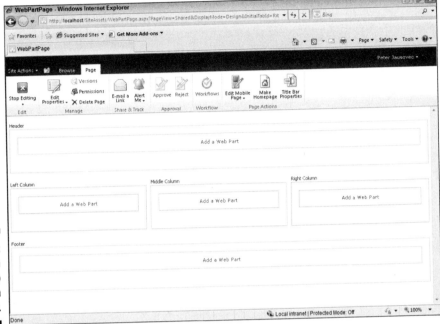

Figure 15-9:
Zones on
the Web
part page in
SharePoint.

Creating a visual Web part

You can create a visual Web part for your invoice solution using the project you develop earlier in this chapter.

You're probably wondering about the word *visual* in the name of the visual Web part. The Web part is called visual because you can use the Web designer in Visual Studio to design the Web part. Other types of Web parts, called simply *Web parts,* don't have a designer, and are developed with code.

To add a visual Web part to the project:

1. **Open the invoice project in Visual Studio 2010.**

   You can also create a new project, but make sure that the SharePoint items from the previous project (site columns, content types, list definition, and list instance) are deployed to SharePoint.

2. **Right-click the project name in the Solution Explorer.**

   The context menu appears.

3. **Choose Add⇨New Item.**

   The Add New Item dialog box appears, as shown in Figure 15-10.

Figure 15-10:
Adding a
new visual
Web part
project item.

4. **Select the visual Web part item.**

5. **Name the Web part InvoiceWebPart.**

6. **Click Add to add the visual Web part to the project.**

   The `InvoiceWebPart` project item is added to the Solution Explorer, and the ASP.NET User Control Designer opens in Markup View.

To switch to Design View, click the Design button at the bottom of the Markup View. The Design View for the visual Web part appears, as shown in Figure 15-11.

Working with the visual Web part designer isn't that much different than working with Windows Forms Designer, for example. The principle is the same: You can drag and drop controls from the toolbox onto the Designer and change controls' properties from the Properties window.

Designing controls that work

The goal of this Web part is to show the following information to the users:

- ✔ Number of all invoices
- ✔ Total value of all invoices
- ✔ Invoice with the highest amount

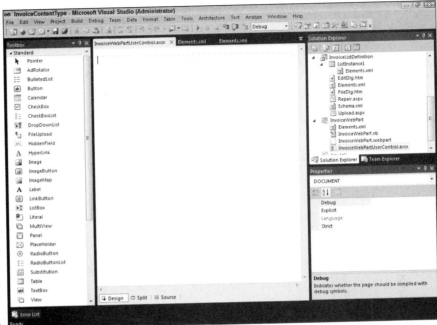

Figure 15-11:
The visual
Web part
Design
View.

To achieve this goal, you need to add a couple of controls to the Web Designer and write code that retrieves that information and then displays it in the Web part: Start by building the visual Web part control:

1. **Type text into the Designer to make it clear to the user what data you're showing.**

   You can change the font sizes, types, and colors; we went with a very simple design, as shown in Figure 15-12.

2. **Drag and drop `Label` controls that will hold the data you want to show to the users.**

   After you drag and drop the `Label` controls, change the (ID) property of each `Label` control from the Properties window. Here's what each `Label` control should be named:

   • Number of all invoices: `lblAllInvoices`

   • For total value: `lblTotalValue`

   • For an invoice with the highest amount: `lblHighestAmount`

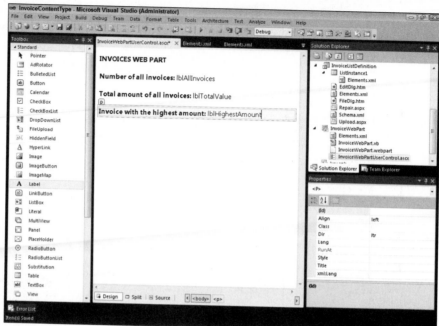

Figure 15-12:
Controls on
the visual
Web part
Designer.

Now it's time to start coding! Double-click the visual Web part Designer to open the Code View. You have to get to the invoice list instance you created in the Workflow example, get the total number of items in the list, calculate the total value of all invoices, and finally get the invoice name with the highest amount.

Start with the first snippet of code for getting all SharePoint libraries that store invoices. To make it simple, assume that each list that contains the word Invoice has invoices stored in it. Here's the first snippet of code:

```
Dim site As New SPSite("http://localhost")
Dim web = site.AllWebs.First()

Dim invoiceLists = From list As SPList In web.Lists _
        Where list.Title.Contains("Invoice") _
                Select list
```

The first two lines get you to the SharePoint site and then the default site. You use the LINQ query to get all lists from the Web that contain the word Invoice in the title. The LINQ query is straightforward — you get all lists in the Lists collection that contain the word Invoice, and you add them to the collection of lists called invoiceLists.

LINQ is short for Language Integrated Query, a cool new technology that adds dynamic queries to all kinds of objects. If you've done any SQL programming, the queries probably look familiar to you.

Now you have to define some variables to hold the data you want to show on the Label controls.

```
Dim allInvoices As Integer = 0
Dim totalValue As Double = 0.0
Dim maxValue As Double = 0.0
Dim companyNameWithMaxAmount As String = String.Empty
```

The first three variables are self-explanatory. The allInvoices variable holds the number of all invoices across all lists that contain invoices. The totalValue variable holds the total value of all invoices, and the maxValue variable holds the highest amount of the invoice. The last variable, company NameWithMaxAmount, is used to store the company name to which the invoice with the highest amount was issued.

Finally, here's the last part of the code where you actually count and calculate the values.

```
For Each invoiceList In invoiceLists
  allInvoices += invoiceList.ItemCount
  For Each listItem In invoiceList.Items
    Dim amount As Double = CType(listItem("Total Amount"), Double)
    If (amount > maxValue) Then
      maxValue = amount
      companyNameWithMaxAmount = CType(listItem("Company Name"), String)
    End If
    totalValue += amount
  Next
Next
```

You use two For Each loops to iterate through all lists and then through all items. The If statement inside the second For Each loop checks whether the amount of the current item is greater than the current max amount value. If it is, you set the current item amount as the max value and store the company name in the companyNameWithMaxAmount variable.

Getting to the values is simple as well: You're passing in the column display name and then casting the value (which is object) to either a Double or String. In the last line, you add the current amount to the total value.

Finally, you need to show the variable values on the Labels on your Designer. Here's the code that sets the variable values on the label controls:

```
lblAllInvoices.Text = allInvoices.ToString()
lblHighestAmount.Text = maxValue & ", company: " & companyNameWithMaxAmount
lblTotalValue.Text = totalValue.ToString()
```

The preceding three lines are simple. You're setting the variable values to the Text property on Label controls. You're all done, but before you press F5 to see your visual Web part in action, you need to do one more thing.

Changing your solution type

You can deploy a visual Web part only as a farm solution. Because your project is configured as a sandboxed solution, you have to change the solution type in order to deploy the visual Web part. Changing the solution to a farm solution goes like this:

1. **Click the project name in Solution Explorer.**

2. **Open the Properties window.**

3. **Change the Sandboxed Solution property value from True to False.**

   A dialog box, shown in Figure 15-13, appears and prompts you to confirm the change.

4. **Click Yes to close the dialog box.**

Figure 15-13:
Changing
the
Sandboxed
Solution
property.

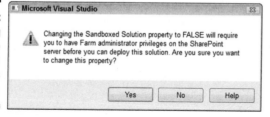

Deploying your project

Now you're all set to press F5 and deploy the project. You have a couple of options on how and where to display the visual Web part. The most effective place to show your Web part is on the main SharePoint page. Here's how:

1. **Navigate to the SharePoint home page at `http://localhost`.**

2. **Click the Page tab on the Ribbon.**

   The controls shown in Figure 15-14 appear on the Ribbon.

3. **Click the Edit button to edit the page.**

   The Editing Tools tab appears on the Ribbon, as shown in Figure 15-15.

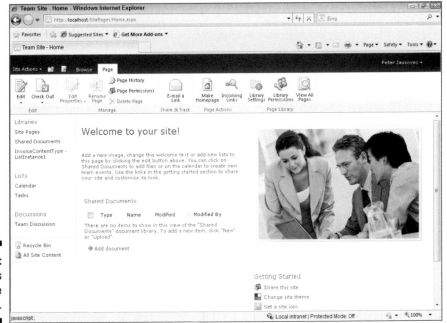

Figure 15-14:
The controls
on the
Page tab.

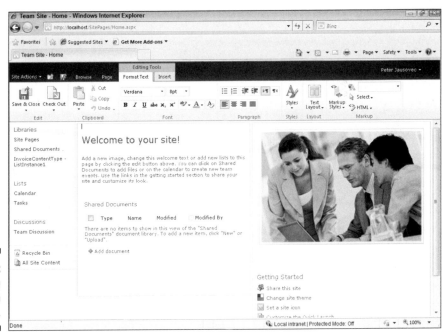

Figure 15-15:
The Editing
Tools tab on
the Ribbon.

4. **Click the Insert tab.**

From the Insert tab, you can insert various items to the SharePoint page. Of course, the Web Part button allows you to insert a Web part to the page.

5. **Click the Web Part button.**

The list of Web parts and categories appears at the top of the page, as shown in Figure 15-16.

6. **From the Categories control, click the Custom item.**

By default, all Web parts created in Visual Studio 2010 have the category assigned to Custom.

7. **Select the `InvoiceWebPart` item in the Web Parts list.**

8. **Click the Add button to insert the Web part to the page.**

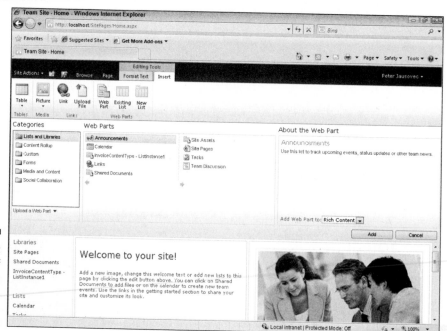

Figure 15-16:
The list of
Web parts
and its
categories.

At this point, the Web part appears on the SharePoint page and looks similar to the one in Figure 15-17.

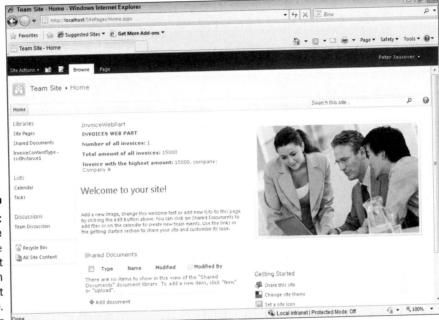

Figure 15-17:
The
`Invoice`
Web part
on the main
SharePoint
page.

Deploying Files to SharePoint

If you want to deploy additional files with your SharePoint project, you can take advantage of a SharePoint project item template called `Module`, which is specifically designed for deploying various files to the SharePoint server.

Say, for example, that you want to deploy a couple of images to the SharePoint server. With the Module project item, you can easily accomplish this task:

1. **In Visual Studio 2010, choose File⇨New Project.**

   The New Project dialog box appears.

2. **Select SharePoint and then 2010 from the tree view.**

3. **Select the Module project template.**

4. **Name the project `MyImages`.**

5. **Click OK to create the project.**

   The SharePoint Wizard appears.

6. **Leave all the default settings in the wizard selected and click Finish to create the project.**

Visual Studio creates a new Module project that contains an `Elements.xml` file and `Sample.txt` file inside the `Module1` project item folder.

The `Elements.xml` file opens by default, and the contents of the file look like this:

```xml
<?xml version="1.0" encoding="utf-8"?>
<Elements xmlns="http://schemas.microsoft.com/sharepoint/">
  <Module Name="Module1">
    <File Path="Module1\Sample.txt" Url="Module1/Sample.txt" />
  </Module>
</Elements>
```

Inside the Elements XML element, the `Module` element is defined. The Module element in the XML file contains all the files you want to deploy to the SharePoint server. After the module is deployed, you can access the deployed files with the following URL:

```
http://localhost/Module1/Sample.txt.
```

Delete the `Sample.txt` file from the Solution Explorer because you don't need it. Click the `Sample.txt` file and press the Delete key to delete it. As soon as you delete the file, you'll notice that the contents of the `Elements.xml` file change accordingly.

The File XML tag is removed from the `Elements.xml` file. You can imagine that something similar happens when you add files to the Module1 SharePoint project item. Follow these steps to add an image to the Module1 SharePoint project item:

1. **Right-click the Module1 folder in the Solution Explorer.**

   The context menu appears.

2. **Choose Add⇨Existing Item.**

   The Add Existing Item dialog box appears.

3. **Browse to an existing image on your computer and click the Add button to add the image to the project item folder.**

We added an image named `Maks.jpg` to the project, and our workspace looks like the one in Figure 15-18.

Notice how the new entry for the `Maks.jpg` file is added to the `Elements.xml`. It looks exactly the same as the entry for the `Sample.txt` you removed previously.

Press F5 now to deploy the project. The SharePoint home page opens in the Internet browser. If everything works as expected, the `Maks.jpg` file you deployed should appear in the Internet browser when you open the URL `http://localhost/Module1/Maks.jpg`, as shown in Figure 15-19.

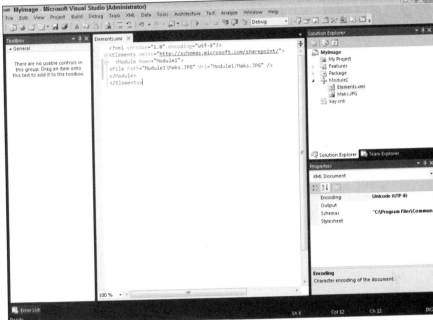

Figure 15-18:
The Module
project
item with
`Maks.`
`jpg` file.

Figure 15-19:
The
deployed
image on
SharePoint.

Handling Events in SharePoint

Events in SharePoint, as name suggests, have something to do with events that are happening on the SharePoint. There are many places and items in SharePoint, such as SharePoint site collections, lists, items in those lists, and so on, where events can be triggered. For example, you can respond to an event that happens when a SharePoint workflow is started, or when an item is uploaded to the list.

The following list contains five categories of events you can respond to using the Event Receiver project template in Visual Studio:

- List Events
- List Item Events
- List Email Events
- Web Events
- List Workflow Events

Each category from this list contains one or more events you can respond to using the Event Receiver project template. You can separate most events in those categories into synchronous and asynchronous events.

An example of a *synchronous* event is the `ItemDeleting` event from the List Item Events group. This event is called a before event because it occurs before the actual item is deleted from the list.

The *asynchronous events* are called after events because they occur after the action happens. The after event is the `ItemDeleted` event. At the time the `ItemDeleted` event occurs, the item is deleted from the list.

Here are some of the interesting scenarios where you can use events from the event categories:

- An item is being added to the list.
- An item is being deleted from the list.
- An item is being checked in or checked out.
- A field is being added to the list.
- A field is being removed from the list.
- A list was added to the SharePoint.
- A list was removed from the SharePoint.
- A site was deleted.
- A workflow was started.
- A workflow was completed.

Creating an event receiver

To understand these events a bit more, we expand on the SharePoint invoice scenario we use throughout this chapter. Say that you only want invoiced uploaded with names that start with `Invoice`. If a user uploads a file with a name that doesn't start with Invoice, a custom error message appears, and the uploaded item is deleted.

The first part of the scenario checks the file name and uses the `ItemUpdating` event. To display an error message if the file isn't uploaded, you use an Application Page, another SharePoint project item that's available in the Visual Studio 2010:

1. **Create a new Event Receiver project in Visual Studio.**

2. **Select the Event Receiver project template.**

3. **Name the project `InvoiceEventReceiver`.**

4. **Click OK to create the project.**

   The SharePoint Customization Wizard appears.

5. **In the SharePoint Customization Wizard, select the Deploy As A Farm Solution.**

   You select the farm solution because you later add an application page to the project, and application pages can be deployed only as part of farm solutions.

6. **Click Next to continue to the next page of the SharePoint Customization Wizard.**

   The second page of the SharePoint Customization Wizard appears (see Figure 15-20). From the wizard page in Figure 15-20, you can select one of the event categories, the item that is going to act as an event source, and the events you want to handle.

7. **Select the List Item Events from the first drop-down box in the wizard.**

8. **Select the `InvoiceContentType` — `InvoiceListDefinition` as the source for our events from the second drop-down box in the wizard.**

9. **From the list of events, select the An Item Is Being Updated event.**

   Your selection in the wizard should look similar to Figure 15-21.

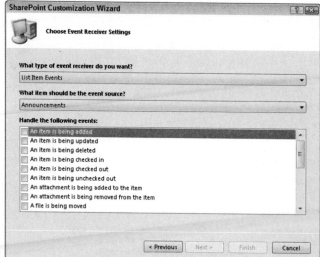

Figure 15-20:
SharePoint
Event
Receiver
Wizard.

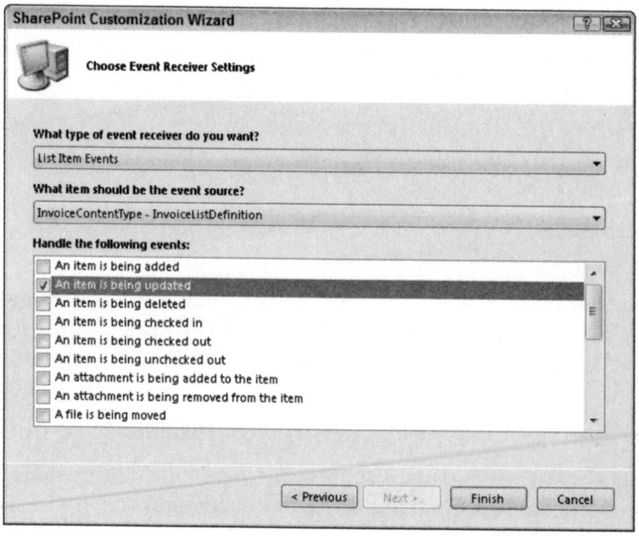

Figure 15-21:
The Event
Receiver
wizard set-
tings for
Invoices.

10. Click Finish to create the Event receiver project.

When the project is created, the EventReceiver1.vb code file opens automatically.

Adding an application page

The `EventReceiver1.vb` file is the place where you write the code to check whether the name of the file being uploaded to the invoice list starts with Invoice and either cancel the upload and delete the item or allow the user to upload the document. Before writing any code, add an application page to the project:

1. **Right-click the `InvoiceEventReceiver` project name in Solution Explorer.**

2. **Choose Add⇨New Item.**

3. **Select the Application Page project item from the dialog box that appears.**

4. **Name the application page `InvalidItem.aspx`.**

5. **Click Add to add the application page to the project.**

You next show this application page to the users in case the name of the file they are trying to upload to the invoice list doesn't start with Invoice. Locate the `asp:Content ID="Main"` element in the `InvalidItem.aspx` file and add the following HTML:

```
<h1>Error occurred!</h1>
<b>Document name has to begin with the word "Invoice" in order to be uploaded.
        </b>
```

The error message is very simple and very minimal — you're informing users that the file they were trying to upload doesn't begin with the word Invoice.

Changing the event status

To get back to the `EventReceiver1.vb`, add the following code to the `ItemUpdating` method:

```
MyBase.ItemUpdating(properties)

Dim itemName As String = properties.ListItem.DisplayName

If (itemName.StartsWith("Invoice") = False) Then
    properties.ListItem.Delete()
  properties.Cancel = True
  properties.Status = SPEventReceiverStatus.CancelWithRedirectUrl
  properties.RedirectUrl = "/_layouts/InvoiceEventReceiver/InvalidItem.aspx"
End If
```

The first line of code already appeared in the method when the project was created. It's just calling the same method in the base class. The next line gets the display name of the list item. The `properties` variable is being passed to the `ItemUpdating` method and contains all the necessary information about the list and item. After you have the name of the item, if it doesn't starts with the word `Invoice`, you execute the code inside the `If` statement.

A couple of properties on the `properties` parameter cancel the event. Because `ItemUpdating` is a synchronous event, you can cancel it and not allow the item to get updated, which means it isn't added to the list. Therefore, you set the `Cancel` property to `True`. Because you want to redirect users to the custom-made application page called `InvalidItem.aspx`, you set the `Status` property value to `CancelWithRedirectUrl`. And finally, you set the `RedirectUrl`. By default, all application pages are deployed inside the `_layouts` folder.

You're probably wondering why we're using the `ItemUpdating` method and not the `ItemAdding` method. The event receiver works a bit differently if you're uploading a file or just creating an item in the list (for example, creating a new announcement in the announcements list). You can't use the `ItemAdding` event to check the filename because the `ListItem` property is empty. Remember, the `ItemAdding` event is called before the actual item is created and file uploaded; therefore, there's no list item yet. Because `ItemUpdating` is the event that gets called right after `ItemAdding`, it's safe to use it. However, if you're not uploading a document and you're just creating a normal item in the SharePoint list, use the `ItemAdding` event by all means.

Deploying the event receiver

Press F5 now to deploy the event receiver and verify whether you get the error page when trying to upload a document that doesn't start with the word `Invoice`. As you press F5, the Internet browser opens at the SharePoint home page. Click the `InvoiceContentType — ListInstance1` page you created in the Workflow example. Next, click the Add New Item link to upload a document. Browse to an existing document with a name that doesn't start with the word `Invoice`. As the file is uploaded, the application page appears, as shown in Figure 15-22.

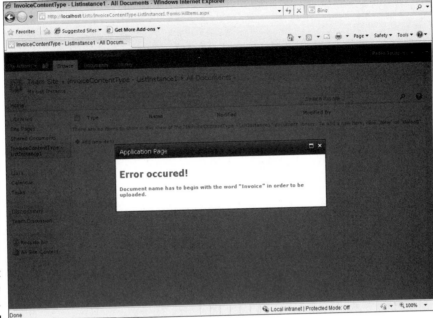

Part IV
Finishing Up

The 5th Wave   By Rich Tennant

"I hate when you bring 'Office' with you on camping trips."

In this part . . .

Security and deployment are neat topics? We think so! Security is so easy in this edition of VSTO that there isn't much to write about, but you'll find some good tips. And deployment is covered in some depth, too.

Chapter 16

Security

Secure coding should be forefront in every programmer's mind. Bad people out there are paid well to find weaknesses in software security and create exploits that can be monetized for reasons ranging from simple theft to creation of massive spam networks.

The VSTO team certainly had this on their mind when creating VSTO. The first three versions of VSTO were so secure, they were almost unusable. VSTO 4 doesn't have this problem at all. The common scenarios for VSTO deployment are now much more straightforward.

This straightforwardness isn't to say that there aren't more complex scenarios. There are, and an excellent section in the MSDN library describes them well. This chapter shows how the common scenarios are handled with VSTO and Visual Studio 2010.

Checking Security with CAS

Code Access Security (CAS) is a role-based security system that uses code groups to deal with permissions. In the past, VSTO security relied on CAS policy to determine whether customization was permitted to run. When VSTO shipped with Visual Studio 2005, it required all the assemblies in the customization to be granted full trust in order to run. The tool named caspol provided the evidence that served as a basis for granting full trust.

As evidence, you could use either the location of the assembly, its strong name, or a combination of both. (A strong name is a digitally signed value that uniquely described the installable component.) The existence of the evidence means that you could have a specific folder on your computer, and every VSTO customization in that folder had permissions to run. In cases when you deployed a VSTO customization to a network share, the evidence used was in the form of a URL.

CAS isn't used anymore in Visual Studio 2010. Instead, the ClickOnce security model stores the evidence. ClickOnce security model certificates determine whether the VSTO customization is trusted to run.

You may be wondering what kind of magic happens when you press F5 and run your solution from within Visual Studio 2010. When running a VSTO add-in or a document customization, a test certificate is automatically created. When you publish your customization, you use the test certificate to sign the VSTO deployment manifest.

This automatically generated test certificate sounds like a good solution if you're deploying your project to your own computer or within your company, but we don't suggest using a test certificate for solutions that are being distributed outside of your intranet. If you want to distribute your VSTO solution wider, you should consider and obtain a publisher certificate from VeriSign, for example.

Creating Test Certificate Settings

From Visual Studio 2010, you can create a new test certificate or select a certificate from the certificate store or from a file.

To open Signing settings inside Visual Studio 2010, follow these steps:

1. **In Visual Studio 2010, right-click the VSTO project name and choose Properties.**

   The property pages for your project appear.

2. **Click the Signing tab.**

   Figure 16-1 shows the Signing tab and the available options.

If you want to generate a new test certificate, you can click the Create Test Certificate button. When you close the dialog box, a new `.pfx` file is created in Solution Explorer. Similarly, you can click the Select from Store or Select from File button to select a certificate that is either in your computer's certificate store or a certificate stored in a `.pfx` file.

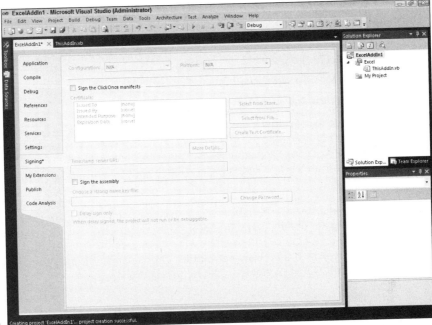

Figure 16-1:
Signing
settings.

Generating Manifests and the Trust Prompt

Both deployment and application manifest files are generated when you publish your customization. As the name suggests, a *deployment manifest* describes the deployment and contains the customization version number as well as a pointer to the application manifest. Just as the deployment manifest describes deployment, an *application manifest* describes the application being deployed.

When you try to install the customization, the deployment and application manifests are downloaded. After the files are on your computer, you can evaluate the security and verify that the customizations have enough privileges to be installed. At this time, a so-called trust prompt appears. This dialog box contains the name of the customization and publisher of the solution.

Trust prompting works based on five zones that you can customize:

- Internet
- Untrusted Sites
- My Computer
- Local Intranet
- Trusted Sites

You can change the zone setting and disable the Trust Prompt dialog box or prompt only when a specific certificate signs a solution.

If, for any reason, the certificate can't access customization, an inclusion list is used. The *inclusion list* is a registry key that contains all trust decisions the users made when installing VSTO customizations.

To see how the inclusion list looks, choose Start⇨Run⇨ regedit to open RegEdit () and navigate to the following registry key:

```
HKEY_CURRENT_USER\Software\Microsoft\VSTO\Security\Inclusion
```

Instead of manually poking through the registry, you can also modify the inclusion list programmatically. You can use the `AddInEntrySecurity` class to add or remove items from the inclusion list.

Office Trust Center

Due to an Office requirement, you have to open a customized document from either a local computer or a trusted location. Although you can still open a customized document that isn't on a local computer or in trusted location, an error message appears.

Because Office requires a document to be in a trusted location, an Office dialog box lets you edit that trusted location. You can access the Trusted Location dialog box in Excel (or Word) using the following steps:

1. **In Excel 2010, choose File.**

   The Excel menu appears.

2. **Click Options.**

   The Excel Options dialog box opens.

3. **Select Trust Center.**

4. **Click the Trust Center Settings button.**

   The Trust Center dialog box opens.

5. **From the list on the left side, select Trusted Locations, as shown in Figure 16-2.**

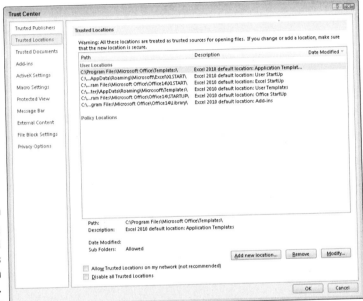

Figure 16-2:
Trusted
Locations
dialog box in
Excel.

Security in Visual Studio 2010 has become much more sophisticated compared to earlier versions. In order to install and run VSTO customization, deployment manifests need to be signed with a certificate. From Office, you need to save your document-level customizations in a trusted location. So multiple checks occur before the customization is allowed to run and install.

On the other hand, the security model is subtle — for example, similar security checks occur when you F5 your VSTO solution, yet you don't see any security prompts. These security checks enable developers to be more productive when developing and implementing their solutions because they don't have to think about certificates, signing, and the inclusion list. An automatically generated test certificate is created and used for debugging. After the developers are ready to publish the solution to a wider audience, then they should consider using a publisher certificate.

Chapter 17

Deploying VSTO Solutions

. . . .

In This Chapter

▶ Taking a look at ClickOnce

▶ Deploying your add-in

▶ Changing your settings

▶ Solving problems

. . . .

*A*fter you create your Visual Studio for Office project, deployment sounds like the last thing you need to do to complete the whole cycle and make your project available to users.

In this chapter, we discuss how to deploy an add-in with ClickOnce. The example we provide shows the deployment on a local computer, but you can see the real value and magic of ClickOnce if you deploy the project on a network share or a Web site.

The process for deploying to different sources is much like the process described in this example. So if you like to deploy your add-in or document solution to your Web site, replace all the references in the example from local disk to Web site, and that's it!

Getting the Scoop on ClickOnce

Because deployment is similar for both VSTO add-ins and VSTO documents, we use the term *customization* for both types. In previous versions of Visual Studio and VSTO, deployment was quite difficult. In order to install your VSTO solution, you had to take care of several prerequisites like .NET 3.5 framework, Visual Studio Tools for Office Runtime, and more. In addition, you had to manually set the CAS policy. (For more on CAS, see Chapter 16.)

To install all those prerequisites, you had to create custom install actions and new bootstrapper packages that Visual Studio uses.

Thanks to ClickOnce, you don't have to worry about any of these details in Visual Studio 2010. ClickOnce is a technology for deployment. Instead of running an executable file such as `setup.exe` or `setup.msi`, users can click a link on a Web page, and an application or VSTO customization gets installed.

In large enterprises, where administrative IT staff like to have complete control over every desktop for stability, ClickOnce may not be an option. In these cases, you end up building installers and adding them to an application pool. In this case, an installer will have to be built using the Setup Project template in Visual Studio.

One of the biggest benefits of ClickOnce is application updates. For example, say that you created a VSTO solution, and you uploaded the setup file (executable file) to your Web server, or you burned it on a CD that you gave to your users. In the first scenario, users download the executable setup and install the application. In the second case, the same thing happens: The user puts the CD in the drive and runs the setup. So far so good. But what if you have 100 or even more users, and you discover a bug in your customization after all 100 users already installed the application? This situation is a rather big problem. You can spend a couple of days burning CDs with the updated application and sending them out again.

With ClickOnce, users of your VSTO solution get the updates automatically. Because your customization is published on the Web server, you can easily modify it and republish it back to the same server. The next time the user runs your customization, the customization itself checks the Web server for a new version and installs it, if necessary.

Deploying an Add-In with ClickOnce

The idea of ClickOnce is to have one central location for distributing your applications. To create a simple add-in and deploy it:

1. **In Visual Studio 2010, choose File⇨New Project.**

   The New Project dialog box appears.

2. **From the list of templates on the right side, select Word 2010 Add-in.**

3. **Name the add-in as DeploymentTest and click OK.**

   Visual Studio creates a new Word 2010 Add-in project.

This add-in isn't complex at all. When the add-in starts, you see a message box with the add-in version, and that's pretty much all the functionality your add-in will have.

Adding a reference to the add-in project

In order to use the add-in, you have to add a reference to the add-in project:

1. **Right-click the project name and choose Add Reference.**

   The Add Reference dialog box, shown in Figure 17-1, appears.

2. **From the list in the .NET tab, find the component System. Deployment and click OK.**

   You can also double-click the component to add it to the project.

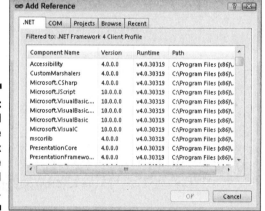

Figure 17-1: The Add Reference dialog box with the selected component.

In order to use the functionality of the System.Deployment namespace, you need to tell the class file to import it. To do so, you have to add the Imports statement at the top of ThisAddIn class in the ThisAddIn.vb file. While you're at it, add another namespace so that you can use the MessageBox class to show a message box:

```
Imports System.Deployment.Application
Imports System.Windows.Forms
```

Deploying the add-in

You can use the `ApplicationDeployment` class to check whether the add-in was deployed from the network and to get the add-in version, check for updates, and more.

Open the `ThisAddIn.vb` file and find the `ThisAddIn_Startup` method. (It should be the first method in the class.) Then, add the following code to the `ThisAddIn_Startup` method:

```
If (ApplicationDeployment.IsNetworkDeployed) Then
    Dim version As String
    version = ApplicationDeployment.CurrentDeployment.CurrentVersion.ToString()

    MessageBox.Show("Add-In version = " + version)
End If
```

Before you show the add-in version to the user, check whether the add-in was even deployed to the network. To do so, use the `IsNetworkDeployed` property that returns `True` if the add-in was deployed to the network or `False` if the add-in wasn't deployed to the network. After you're sure the add-in was deployed to the network, you can display a message box with the current add-in version.

If you press F5 to run the add-in on your machine, the message box doesn't appear. If you want the message box to appear, you have to deploy the add-in first. Here's how you can deploy the add-in:

1. **Right-click the project name and choose Publish.**

   The Publish Wizard, shown in Figure 17-2, appears.

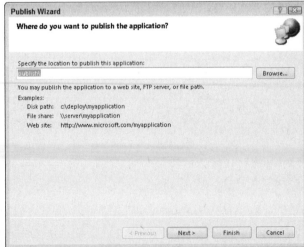

Figure 17-2:
The first page of the Publish Wizard.

On the first page of the wizard, you can select the location where the add-in should be published. You have three options for the publish location: local path, network share, or Web site.

2. **For this example, use the default path, which is the \publish directory, and click Next.**

The wizard looks like the one in Figure 17-3.

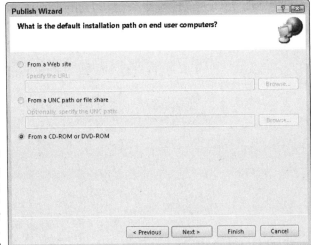

Figure 17-3:
Selecting the installation path for your add-in.

3. **Choose the location where users will install the add-in from and click Next.**

You have three choices on the second page of the Publish Wizard. Leave the default selection, From a CD-ROM or DVD-ROM. The last page of the wizard is the summary page, and it shows the publish location.

4. **Click the Finish button.**

Visual Studio rebuilds the solution and publishes it to the selected location.

Finding additional deployment settings

Of course, you can get to even more deployment settings. The additional deployment and publishing settings are located in the Publish tab in the project properties. Here's how to get there:

1. **Right-click the project name and choose Properties.**

2. **On the Properties window, click the Publish tab.**

   The Publish tab looks similar to Figure 17-4. (For now, you don't have to worry about all those buttons and settings in the Publish tab — we explain them in "Publishing your add-in," later in this chapter.)

3. **Click the Updates button on the Publish tab to configure when the add-in should check for updates.**

   The Customization Updates dialog box, shown in Figure 17-5, appears.

   By default, the interval for checking for updates is set to 7 days, which is too long for this example.

4. **Select the Check Every Time the Customization Runs option and click OK to close the dialog box.**

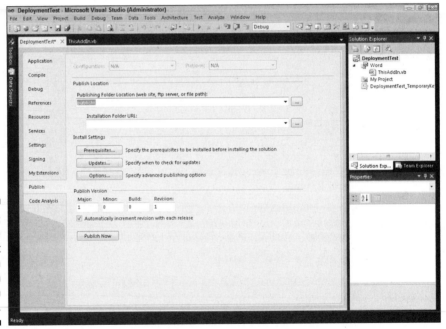

Figure 17-4:
More deployment and publish settings on the Publish tab.

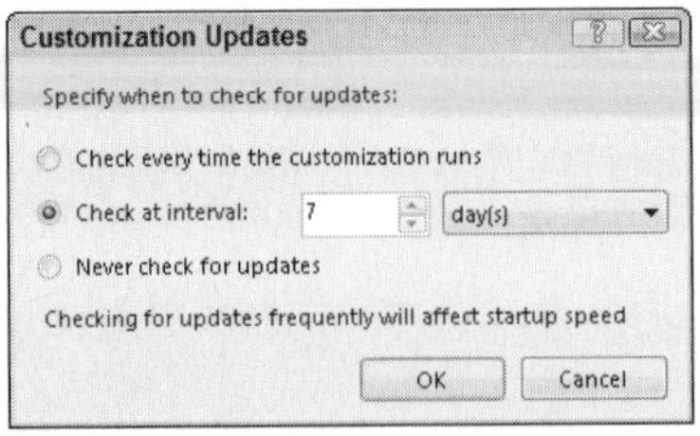

Figure 17-5:
The Customization Updates dialog box.

Publishing your add-in

You can publish the add-in by clicking the Publish Now button on the Publish tab. The Publish Now button does exactly the same as the Publish Wizard: It uses the default settings for the Publish location, rebuilds the project, and publishes it to the selected location.

To publish the add-in:

1. **Browse to the folder where the Visual Studio solution is saved and find the Publish folder.**

   To quickly go to the folder where the Visual Studio solution is located, you can right-click the project name in Solution Explorer and choose Open Folder in Windows Explorer.

2. **Double-click the Publish folder to open it.**

   The Publish folder contains the Application Files folder and a couple more files.

3. **To install the add-in, double click the `DeploymentTest` file.**

   This file is the VSTO Deployment Manifest that you can use to deploy the VSTO customizations.

   The Microsoft Office Customization Installer dialog box, shown in Figure 17-6, appears. The dialog box tells you that the publisher of the Office customization can't be verified. Because you didn't sign your project, the publisher is unknown. This dialog box can protect you from installing any unwanted Office customizations, but because you developed this customization, you know that it's safe.

4. **Click the Install button to continue and install the customization.**

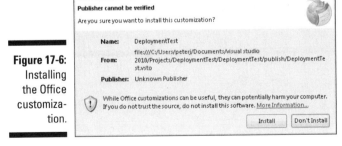

Figure 17-6: Installing the Office customization.

As soon as you click Install, the add-in is installed. After installation completes, a message box appears to confirm the successful installation of the customization.

5. Click Close to close the dialog box.

The add-in customization is installed now.

You can verify this installation by opening Word 2010.

If the message box in Step 4 doesn't appear, don't worry; it just means that Office is concerned about safety, so it doesn't trust any customizations so easily. Because you've already opened Word, click the File button and choose Word Options. From the Options dialog box, select the Trust Center item on the left side. In the Trust Center dialog box, click the Trust Center Settings to button to open the Trusted Locations page. The dialog box shown in Figure 17-7 appears. Close and re-open Word 2010, and the message box should appear. If not, check to see whether any Word 2010 instances are running. If so, close all Word 2010 instances, re-install the add-in, and try again.

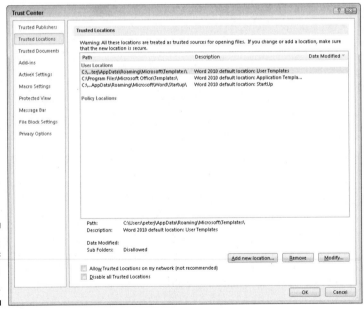

Figure 17-7:
A list of trusted locations.

Adding a folder to the Trusted Location list

You may have noticed that the location of the Publish folder isn't in the Trusted Locations list. To add a folder to the Trusted Location list:

Click the Add New Location button. In the Microsoft Office Trusted Location dialog box that appears, type the location to the `\publish` folder or click the Browse button to browse to the Publish location.

An additional setting, when set, trusts all the subfolders in the selected path. You can also add descriptions, if you like.

Updating and testing an add-in

To make an update to the add-in, all you have to do is rebuild and republish the add-in from Visual Studio. In order to verify that the updates work, you have to login with a different user name on your development computer. Because the location of each installed add-in is stored in the registry, you get an error message when you open Word 2010, and the add-in gets loaded. Each time you run the Build command in Visual Studio, the add-in is registered, and the value, such as the add-in location, is stored in the registry. When you install the add-in, you're already doing the second installation, and you can't install the same add-in twice.

 The simplest way to test the updates is to publish the add-in on the network share or your Web site and then run the VSTO customization installer from another computer.

Modifying Additional Settings

Setting the interval of an add-in isn't the only thing you can modify. If you go to the Publish tab page in Visual Studio 2010, you see a few more buttons and text boxes. The interesting one is the Prerequisites box. Each time you publish an application Visual Studio 2010 creates the setup project. This setup project is published to the same folder as your application. With the help of the setup project you can install prerequisites your application needs to be executed.

 Make sure that VSTO is selected as a prerequisite for your setup project. It isn't by default, and the setup will fail without it!

If you open the Prerequisites box, you see the list of all available prerequisites for you to use in your customizations. A couple of the prerequisites are already selected by default.

You can change one more setting in that dialog box: You can specify where the setup project should look for the prerequisites. By default, prerequisites are downloaded from the vendor's Web site. If you're deploying from CD and the deployment computer doesn't have an Internet connection to download the prerequisites, you can select the Download Prerequisites From The Same Location As My Application checkbox. This setting copies all the selected prerequisites to the Publish folder, and it also installs them from the same location.

If you don't want to use the prerequisites and the setup project, you can simply uncheck the Create Setup Program to install prerequisite components.

If the list of prerequisites doesn't suit your needs, you can create your own prerequisite package and then use it in your projects. The prerequisite files are located in separate folders within the folder `Program Files\Microsoft SDKs\Windows\v6.0A\Bootstrapper\Packages`. Every prerequisite folder contains an XML file named `product.xml`, which contains the information about the dependent components (for example, SQL server depends on .NET Framework installation) and so-called install checks.

The x64 path is `C:\Program Files (x86)\Microsoft SDKs\Windows\v7.0A\Bootstrapper\Packages`.

Install Check can point to a file that checks whether the prerequisite is already installed on the deployment machine. Based on the output of that file, the bootstrapper decides whether a prerequisite should be installed.

Troubleshooting

If you used previous versions of VSTO and Visual Studio, you probably know how deployment evolved from that time. For those who didn't use previous versions, we'll just say that many, many articles were written on deploying VSTO solutions, and you had to follow numerous steps to make the deployment work. The whole process consisted of modifying and extending the setup project, which was automatically added to your project when you created a VSTO project. In order to deploy the solution, you had to create a custom install action, which took care of the deployment of prerequisites and setting the CAS policy. A lot of people had (and still have) problems with deploying VSTO solutions.

Luckily, you can use some great tools to check what's wrong with your deployment and why your add-in doesn't show up or document customization isn't loaded.

One particular set of tools helps you with your VSTO development and deployment. The package consists of nine tools, two of which are specific to deployment.

VSTO Developer Cleaner

VSTO Developer Cleaner can help you discover the build artifacts that are on your development computer, enabling you to remove them with a single mouse click. You should remove those artifacts once in a while, especially if you use your computer to both develop and test your projects. With this tool, you can remove add-in registry entries, temporary certificates, and inclusion lists that are created when you're debugging your VSTO projects.

The tool is pretty straightforward to use. The user interface consists of three tabs that correspond to the artifacts you can remove. To remove an artifact, you click the desired tab, select one or more artifacts from the list, and click the button to remove them.

VSTO Troubleshooter

VSTO Troubleshooter is a diagnostic tool that examines the deployment computer. The tool helps you diagnose issues that may occur when you're deploying VSTO solutions. The tool scans the deployment computer and searches for installed prerequisites. After the search is complete, it generates the report with the state of the prerequisites.

To put it simply, if your VSTO customization isn't working on the deployment computer, run this tool. In a second, you'll know whether any of the prerequisites are missing.

You can download the PowerTools package from this Web site:

```
http://www.microsoft.com/downloads/details.aspx?FamilyId=46B6BF86-E35D-4870-
        B214-4D7B72B02BF9&displaylang=en
```

Creating a separate setup project can take time, especially to get all the prerequisites together. But after your deployment is working as you like it, you can re-use the created setup project as a template for your next project.

Part V
The Part of Tens

The 5th Wave   By Rich Tennant

"I assume everyone on your team is on board with the proposed changes to the office layout."

In this part . . .

What's a *For Dummies* book without a Part of Tens? A lot less fun, that's what! In this part of tens, we give you ten reasons to ditch Web programming and build Office solutions with VSTO instead.

Feeling like you don't have enough to do? Not a problem, we have ten neat project ideas. Finally, to sew up our SharePoint work, we have ten places you can integrate with SharePoint.

Chapter 18

Ten Reasons to Ditch Web Programming

In This Chapter

▶ Opting for Office and VSTO over hand-built ASPX programs

▶ Changing your perspective of Web programming

*W*hen faced with a set of requirements, many developers reach for the nearest tool at hand, ASP.NET. The new Office toolkit is overlooked too often. This chapter is all about looking for ways to use functionality that is already built to solve some problems.

Do we think you should really ditch Web programming? Of course not. The next time a customer comes to you with a fierce set of requirements that includes a tight budget and impossible timeline, though, think VSTO. It may solve those problems a lot better than a Web application!

Smart Clients Are Smarter!

The best reason to ditch Web programming is simply that smart clients are smarter. By using Office as your platform, you combine the low maintenance of the thin client with the solid performance of a fat client.

In a Web environment, even using ASP.NET and the AJAX tools, you're constrained by the Web browser and network environment. In a VSTO environment, you have no such constraints. If you want to pull up a Windows form, you can. If you want to launch a Web browser or use a Web service, you can. And if you want the Office UI to handle things, it can.

Cross-Platform Needs Are (Often) Overstated

The No. 1 argument we hear for Web development is "I don't want to force my users into a browser choice" or "What about Macintosh?" Our answer more often than not is "Who cares?"

You have to be totally honest with yourself and your users about cross-platform support. It's a big-time buzzword that CEOs are learning at management camp, but it doesn't mean a lot, and supporting cross-platform development can add a ton of time to your development effort.

Sure, VSTO will push your users into Office 2010 on Windows 7 or better. But so many situations do this anyway. Would it be cheaper to upgrade the 15 percent of users on old versions than to write your software in a cross-platform style? It probably would.

You Can Save Time and Money

Speaking of cheaper software, we have spent the majority of this book telling you about the great bits in the Office object model that VSTO provides. We didn't get even close to telling you about all the existing Office features that you get to use when you write your program using VSTO:

- If you're building something with a grid requirement for data entry, why not just use Excel? It's a just a big data grid!

- How about a requirement for the user to put items in a certain order? Use Visio!

- Any drawing requirement? How about PowerPoint? It has a strong, codeable drawing engine.

- Did you know that Word is a great HTML generator? If you have a requirement to output HTML, consider Word!

- Don't code your math requirements! Use Excel instead.

You get the idea. If you let VSTO do some of the work for you, you don't have to buy a third-party component, and you don't have to write it yourself. Significant savings are there for the taking.

People Already Know Office

Though it is a continuing debate, Microsoft Office is still the most used office suite by a large margin. Forrester did a study when Office 2007 was still in pre-release, and Microsoft held something like 82 percent of the market for enterprise and mid-market office software. Office is on most machines and is in most companies. While not ubiquitous yet, Microsoft Office is undeniably the most popular software out there for document creation.

This popularity bodes well for the VSTO programmer because the programs you create will have a platform on which to run. The developer faces more than that, however. Office has set the standard for office suite functionality. When a geek suggests Star Office, the first question from a business user is "Does it support Microsoft Office documents?" and with good reason. People know how to use Office.

Because people know how to use Office, they know how to use your software. And the more software that is written with Office in mind, the better it will be. Right now the largest hurdle is getting people to think of Office as a platform.

Web applications, on the other hand, have myriad problems with usability just because of the freedom of design. There is no standard at all as to how things should work, so users are lost upon loading the site. Office solves that problem with a firm grasp on the user interface.

You Can Offer Free Pops and Bangs

Nearly every Web application that we've written had a common request — a spell-checker. Because Web applications are often written to spread the functionality to remote users, you don't get the "eyes over the shoulder" that you get when you're using a client/server application with fewer people able to access it. Missing this functionality leads to spelling mistakes.

Sometimes, we download one of the fine spell-check components available online. Sometimes, we have the users work in Firefox. Sometimes, we point out that the mistakes are in a specialized language subset and a spell-checker wouldn't help anyway. On one occasion, we actually wrote a spell-checker.

Office comes with a spell-checker. And a commenting tool. And drawing tools. And formulas. And HTML export. And on and on. Many features are free in Office, and VSTO can make use of them.

Composite Applications Are the Future

Microsoft may have its problems, but the leaders of the company have been right on in leading the direction of business and personal computing. If you look at the kinds of applications that Microsoft is focusing on right now, composite applications are the thing. *Composite applications* are just large frameworks that tie together several existing applications. SharePoint (see Part III) is just a large composite application. SharePoint has a Web component, but largely it's designed to make existing applications work together better. Windows Live is another example of a composite application for the personal crowd. Heck, even Windows 7 has built-in support for widgets.

The idea is that you should be able to write something in one place and use it in whatever platform that you need it. VSTO is a bridge development environment that supports that style of programming — you can consume SharePoint Services or other Windows Services, make Office applications work together, and still implement a Windows Form if you need to.

You Have No Cross-Browser Issues

Forrester did a study back in 2003 about time spent developing Web applications under various platforms. This data is old now, but one thing is still true: If you want your application to work on various Web browsers, add 30 percent to your development time.

Cross-browser problems may be a thing of the past for basic Web pages, but for AJAX Web applications, they're just getting started. Even if you're concerned only about Windows PCs, Firefox has a significant percent of the market. If you're working for an education organization, you probably have Macs, and they probably run Safari.

Office doesn't have that problem. Even if your users use Firefox, they'll still use Office. Versions are most likely standardized, too, so you'll encounter little problem there. Browser compatibility is another great reason to consider VSTO over Web. Macintosh users are another issue.

New Deployment Features Reduce the Hosted Problem

Chapter 17 covers deployment in depth, and we hope you agree that using ClickOnce is a much better solution to your deployment problems than most other hosted solutions.

Deployment is a big argument for the thin client world. After all, if you can affect 100,000 users by changing the code on one server, why wouldn't you? Now you can deploy like a thin client with VSTO, too.

You Can Combine Windows Forms Features with Your Programs

One thing that Web applications can't easily do is be Windows applications.

As slick as Ajax is, it won't ever be as phat as a fat client. Some things are just best done as a Windows application. Because you can include a Windows Form right in your VSTO application, you can have the best of both worlds. Yes, you get all the freedom of using Office for your platform, but when you need a calendar control, then you can just toss one right on in the Task pane.

You also have other benefits. You can easily integrate SQL Reporting, for example, because it's a Windows Forms application at the root of all of this, right? Using something like SQL Reporting is some reuse for you — how about an Excel add-in that uses existing SQL Reports somehow? Perhaps that add-in is already out there, but you get the idea.

Don't forget about the Windows Presentation Foundation, too! And third-party components — even going back to the COM world — will run in a VSTO environment because they are made for Windows environments. Don't rebuild that old VB6 control into an Ajax control if you don't have to. Just include it in your VSTO environment.

You Can Better Meet Your Customers Requirements

When we get a list of requirements, a timeline, and a budget from a client, we sit down and talk with them. The first sentence usually is "There are three components to software construction — fast, good, and cheap. You can pick two."

Our whole goal as software engineers is to get software construction as close to integrating all three of those components as possible. With the features available as part of VSTO, combined with SharePoint and the rest of the Office Server System, we can offer the client a whole lot of good software, much of it right away, and for a very reasonable cost as compared to building the whole thing from scratch.

Chapter 19

Ten Cool Ideas and Resources for Your Next VSTO Project

In This Chapter
▶ Thinking out of the box for VSTO projects
▶ Exploring tips and resources for Office development

*I*n this chapter, we share ten interesting ideas and resources you can use for your next VSTO project. Some of the ideas may sound weird, but the whole point of this chapter is to show you that you can accomplish even the craziest feats of technology with VSTO by combining other technologies and APIs. We also include more general tips and resources that make developing with VSTO easier.

The possibilities are practically endless.

Create a Macro to Master the Object Model

Throughout the book, we mention several times that if you want to learn the Office object model, the easiest way is to start poking around and trying different things. But this method of learning the object model may take a while. We have another tip for you how you can learn the object model, and this tip involves macros and recording macros.

We could describe a *macro* as set of instructions. Office applications contain a so-called Macro recorder, which enables you to record the instructions. Say that you've applied special formatting to some text in the document. You can start recording a macro, perform the formatting steps, and then save the macros and assign it a button or shortcut key. After you save the macro, you can reuse it as much as you like. Instead of executing several steps to achieve a task, you can perform those steps once, save them as macro, and then reuse them.

Creating a macro

You're probably wondering how creating macros can help you learn the Office object model. When you're recording a macro, the Office application is creating VBA code on the fly, which means that the steps you perform are translated to lines of VBA code. And because the code is in VBA, you can easily modify it to VB.NET — sometimes you don't even have to modify the code. Simply copy the code to your VSTO project, and you're all set!

Recording a macro in Excel is almost exactly the same process as creating a macro in Word:

1. **In Excel 2010, make the Developer tab visible and then start recording your first macro.**

2. **Choose File⇨Options.**

   The Excel Options dialog box, shown in Figure 19-1, appears.

2. **Click the Customize Ribbon option.**

3. **Put a checkmark next to the Developer tab in the list box on the right side of the Excel Options dialog box, as shown in Figure 19-2, and click OK.**

   The Developer tab is unchecked by default. After you check it and close the dialog box, the Developer tab is visible in Excel.

   Before you start recording a macro, you have to decide what you want to record, such as setting the text font size to 15 and the color to red.

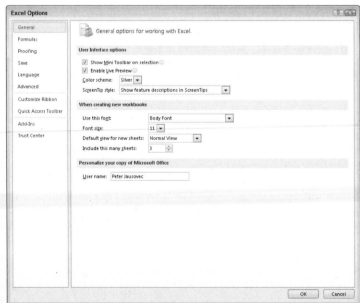

Figure 19-1:
The Excel Options dialog box where you enable the Developer tab.

Figure 19-2:
Enabling the Developer tab.

4. **Click the Record Macro button on the Developer tab.**

   The Record Macro dialog box, shown in Figure 19-3, appears.

Figure 19-3:
The Record Macro dialog box.

5. **Name the macro, describe it, and assign a shortcut to the macro.**

6. **Use the combo box to choose where the macro should reside.**

   You can decide between three places to put the macro:

   • This Workbook

   • New Workbook

   • Personal Macro Workbook

We selected This Workbook, which means that the macro is saved in the current workbook. We can also save the macro in a new workbook or even in a so-called personal macro workbook where we store all our macros.

7. **Click OK.**

The recording of the macro begins. The Macro recorder records everything you do from this point on.

8. **Change the font size to 15 and change the text color to red.**

9. **Switch back to the Developer tab and click the Stop Recording button.**

Congratulations! You've recorded your first macro.

After you record the macro, you can replay the recorded steps anytime.

Working with your macro's code

If you want to see the code that was generated, you can click the Macros button in the Developer tab. The Macro dialog box, shown in Figure 19-4, appears. This dialog box contains all the macros that are in the current workbook. From this dialog box, you can do the following:

✔ Run the macro

✔ Step into it (run the macro step by step)

✔ Edit the macro and see the code

✔ Delete the macro

✔ Set options

Figure 19-4:
Several
options in
the Macro
dialog box.

Because your reason for recording a macro was to get the code, select the recorded macro and click the Edit button. The Microsoft Visual Basic IDE opens (see Figure 19-5).

Instead of opening the Macro dialog box, you can open the Visual Basic IDE by clicking the button Visual Basic in the Developer tab.

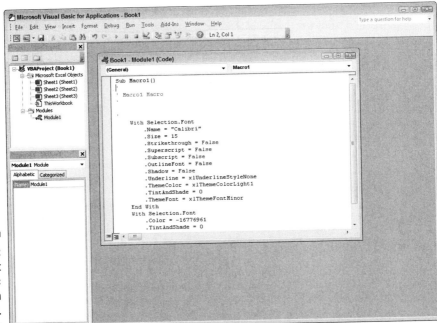

Figure 19-5:
Microsoft
Visual Basic
IDE with
macro code.

The code in the Visual Basic IDE should look similar to this listing:

```
Sub Macro2()
    With Selection.Font
        .Name = "Calibri"
        .Size = 15
        .Strikethrough = False
        .Superscript = False
        .Subscript = False
        .OutlineFont = False
        .Shadow = False
        .Underline = xlUnderlineStyleNone
        .ThemeColor = xlThemeColorLight1
        .TintAndShade = 0
        .ThemeFont = xlThemeFontMinor
    End With
    With Selection.Font
        .Color = -16776961
        .TintAndShade = 0
    End With
End Sub
```

You may have expected only two lines of code — one for setting the font size and the second one for setting the color. The way the macro recorder works is that it doesn't change only the one property (in this case, the text size) but all the properties. That's not necessarily a bad thing because you can see all the properties you can set to the `Font` object. But if you'd like to set the size only, then the line `.Size = 15` is the one to go with.

You may wonder what the `With` statement is for. Because all the properties that start with the dot are located in same object, instead of writing `Selection.Font.Name` or `Selection.Font.Size`, you can use the `With` statement and omit the `Selection.Font` part.

And that's not all — you can probably copy and paste a part of this code to a VSTO project to see whether it works. In most cases, only a couple of tweaks are necessary to make the code compile and run. Isn't that great? If you don't know how to do something, start the Office application, run the Macro recorder, and start recording!

Create Statistics in Outlook

Ever wonder how many e-mails you receive or send? What percentage of your tasks is completed, active, or not even started yet? These examples are only the simple statistics. How about calculating how much time you spent in meetings in one month or a year? You can build an Outlook add-in that creates this statistical information for you.

Here's a code snippet to get you started:

```
Dim inboxFolder As Outlook.MAPIFolder
inboxFolder = Me.Application.Session.GetDefaultFolder(Outlook.OlDefaultFolders.
        olFolderInbox)

Dim emailsInInbox As Integer
emailsInInbox = inboxFolder.Items.Count()
```

The preceding code gets the default Inbox folder and reads the number of all items in the folder. You can do the same with other default folders — for example, for tasks or sent e-mails.

Did you ever wonder how many people in your contact list work at the same company? The following code snippet iterates through the contact list and checks whether the contacts' company name equals My Company. If it does, the code increments the counter. You can do the same for all other fields from contact details.

```
Dim contacts As Outlook.MAPIFolder
contacts = Me.Application.Session.GetDefaultFolder(Outlook.OlDefaultFolders.
            olFolderContacts)

Dim iPeopleFromMyCompany As Integer
iPeopleFromMyCompany = 0

For Each contact As Outlook.ContactItem In contacts.Items
    If contact.CompanyName.Equals("My Company") Then
        iPeopleFromMyCompany = iPeopleFromMyCompany + 1
    End If
Next
```

Protect Your Privacy

Imagine you're in a meeting and are about to give a presentation. As you connect your computer to the projector, you forgot to close Outlook. What happens? Yes, everyone in the meeting can get a glimpse of your e-mails. This mistake can be embarrassing — both for you and the people at the meeting. Even though they don't want to peek at your e-mails, nothing else is on the screen.

To avoid this potential mishap, you can create an Outlook add-in that activates in the event of connecting the external display. As soon as you connect the external display, the event handler code runs and hides Outlook, for example.

Create a Four-in-a-Row Game

Isn't four-in-a-row a game?. Indeed, it is. You can use Excel to create a four-in-a-row game. And best of all, you don't have to use VBA because you can use VB.NET or even C#.

You can use the following code snippet to color the cell in red when the user clicks it:

```
Target.Interior.Color = RGB(255, 0, 0)
```

The type for `Target` is `Range`. A good way to start with the game is to add a named range control to the Excel sheet. This named range represents the playing field for the game. To be honest, the named range control is your good friend here because that control has an event called `BeforeDoubleClick`. If you create an event handler for this event, the parameter `Target` is passed to the event handler.

The only thing missing is some artificial intelligence for playing the game, which you can probably find in almost every book on algorithms, and a simple UI with buttons to start the new game or to display statistics. For the user interface, you can use a Task pane or even a Ribbon.

When you're done with this implementation, you can also think about all the charts and great statistics you can create based on played games if you implement it in Excel. Another idea for a game in Excel is Tic-Tac-Toe or even Tetris!

Search for Some URLs

You can use this really cool idea in Word and Excel. This add-in goes through the Word document and searches for URLs. After a URL is found, an add-in adds it to the collection and displays it on the user interface or even exports the URLs to an appendix of the document. The more we think about this one, the more ideas we get. How about extracting addresses? Or maybe e-mail addresses? This idea can be really useful.

But how would you search for URLs? Anytime you need to find something in text, the magic phrase is regular expressions. A *regular expression* is a special piece of text that describes a search pattern. In a way, you can think of regular expressions as wildcards on steroids — a lot of them! For example, here is a regular expression to find URLs:

```
(([a-zA-Z][0-9a-zA-Z+\\-\\.]*:)?/{0,2}[0-9a-zA-Z;/?:@&=+$\\.\\-_!~*'()%]+)?(#[0-
9a-zA-Z;/?:@&=+$\\.\\-_!~*'()%]+)?
```

Looks like a mess, doesn't it? Well, you can find a lot of resources, examples, and tutorials for learning regular expressions on the Internet. You can use regular expressions for a lot of other things, such as matching phone numbers, postal codes, HTML tags, and so on. The possibilities are endless.

You can also use regular expressions to verify user input. For example, say that you have a text box for entering phone numbers that looks something like

```
(425) 000 - 0000
```

After the user enters the phone number, you can use a regular expression to verify that the input is correct — in other words, whether it conforms to the regular expression.

Find Pictures for Your Presentations

You're in the middle of preparing a PowerPoint presentation, and you think to yourself, "Well, this presentation looks good, but some pictures would make it better.: Wouldn't be great if you could insert pictures from your Flickr account directly from PowerPoint? A FlickrNet API Library is available for download at

```
http://www.codeplex.com/Wiki/View.aspx?ProjectName=FlickrNet
```

With this .NET library, you can access your Flickr account and get the list of your pictures directly from PowerPoint add-in.

Another spin on this idea is to do the opposite thing. Say that you've already created the presentation, and you want to upload it to Flickr. You can write an add-in that takes a snapshot of each slide and then uploads the slides to Flickr.

Read Word Documents or E-Mails

Do you like audio books? How about creating an add-in that reads Word documents or e-mails for you? This add-in may even present something instead of you! also. You can create an add-in that uses Speech API so that a computerized voice reads e-mails to you.

This add-in can also work the opposite way. Imagine speaking into the microphone connected to your computer, and a VSTO add-in recognizes your speech (with some help of Speech API) and converts it to a document or e-mail. You have to admit that this idea is really cool.

Originally, we thought about this idea to be implemented in PowerPoint, but you can use it in Word or Outlook. The idea is the same as with Word or Outlook. But what if the add-in could somehow know what to say after the presentation starts? Reading from slides would be useless. You can write your speech in the comments for each slide, and the add-in reads that text during the presentation. You can also use tags in comments, which would have some special meaning — for example, you can implement the tag `<Speed=10>`, and based on the value, your computerized voice could speed up or slow down. Another idea is to introduce the tag `<Pause=2>` — for example, this add-in pauses the speech for 2 seconds. You can extend this add-in with even more custom tags.

Remember When Your Favorite Show Is On

This idea combines Excel and Outlook. If you can get the TV listings for your favorite TV channels to Excel, you can select your favorite TV show and, with the click of a button, transfer the information about the TV show to your Outlook calendar. Your Outlook client is probably always running. and with the help of this Excel add-in (or even document-level solution), you'd never miss your favorite TV show.

Try to Make Your Own Treasure Map

What do you think about connecting Outlook to Microsoft Windows Live maps? With some help of APIs for Live maps and `FormRegions` in Outlook, you can display a map in contact form. Instead of opening the browser and searching for an address, you can just open the contact and see the map! Not only can you get the map, you can also calculate the route from your location to the location of your contact.

Gather Up Resources for Office Developers

Office, VSTO, and SharePoint developers and users can find numerous resources on the Internet. In particular, the `OfficeZealot.com` Web site is a collection of blogs that mostly talks about development for Office, VSTO, or SharePoint.

A separate Web site for SharePoint-related blogs is `vspug.com`.

If you have any questions about VSTO development, stop by the MSDN VSTO Forums:

```
http://forums.microsoft.com/MSDN/default.aspx?ForumGroupID=4&SiteID=1
```

Microsoft employees and MVPs are regulars on these forums. So if you have any questions, you can get your answers there.

Chapter 20

Ten Ways to Integrate SharePoint

In This Chapter

▶ Digging into the SharePoint object model

▶ Using workflows to route documents

▶ Discovering Excel services

*P*art III covers a whole lot of SharePoint, but we still have a lot more to cover. In this chapter, you find some great ideas on integrating Office and SharePoint using VSTO.

Deploy Word or Excel Files with VSTO Automation to Document Libraries

Making document customizations is one of the newest and neatest things that you can do with VSTO because you could already do add-ins with COM. Now, because document customizations follow the document, you can add them to documents you import to SharePoint document libraries, even as templates.

Think of the circular reference possibilities. The documents have code in them that call on SharePoint services that refer to the lists of documents that call on SharePoint services. This is deep stuff.

Seriously, you can do a lot with the idea of adding documents that are aware of their surroundings to a document library. For example, the document can look up what other documents are in the list where it was accessed. Another idea is to publish Excel spreadsheets that use Excel Services that have also been published to the SharePoint server — the ultimate in flexibility.

We show you how to customize a document in Chapters 3, 6, and 8. To add a document to a document library:

1. **Browse to the library in question.**

2. **Choose Upload Document from the menu bar.**

3. **Pick the custom document you want to upload.**

4. **Click OK.**

The only question is what to do with the DLL that goes with it — the stuff that holds the .NET code. The code is pretty simple, but you need to touch the manifest that VSTO publishes with the document.

1. **Put the DLLs in a file share that the SharePoint folder can see.**

2. **Edit the application manifest to point to the new location of the DLLs.**

3. **Publish the document to SharePoint.**

Look at the SharePoint 2010 Object Model

Even though you probably think that the existing support in Visual Studio 2010 and the existing SharePoint project templates are enough for your needs for SharePoint development, you will eventually need to use the SharePoint object model.

If you read Part III, you got all the lists that start with the word "Invoice" from the SharePoint server. You then used the SharePoint object model to talk to the SharePoint server and to get the information back to your solution. You also used SharePoint server code in the event receiver project in Part III.

If you think you can access the SharePoint 2010 object model only from SharePoint projects, think again! You can use the object model from your VSTO solutions as well. You need to add a reference to the `Microsoft.SharePoint.dll` assembly, located in the X:`\Program Files\Common Files\Microsoft Shared\Web Server Extensions\14\ISAPI`, where X is the name of the hard drive where SharePoint is installed.

With the SharePoint object model, you can create, update, or delete SharePoint lists and libraries, add or remove items from the lists, start workflows, associate workflows, and much more.

Move Documents Around with a Workflow

One of the great uses of workflows (see Chapter 14) is to move documents around. You can use add-ins to expedite this process, but to be honest, Office 2010 does it pretty well without it.

Using a workflow to manage a document process isn't trivial, but it isn't impossible, either. After you write and deploy a workflow, you can assign it to a document when you add that document to a library. In the workflow, you can write functions to handle certain events within the process of handling the document.

Deploy InfoPath Forms to SharePoint

One way of looking at SharePoint is as a database made up of lists. Each list is a table, and items are like rows. The paradigm isn't perfect because of list templates, but it's close enough for government work.

If you have a database, you need a form. InfoPath is the application of choice for building forms for the SharePoint database. Usually, when you add an item to a list, you do it from the Item List screen, using the Datagrid View. With InfoPath, you can even automatically feed it a Web service, database, or XML schema and get a form out of it. You can then write custom code to handle special occurrences.

You can also write workflows in Visual Studio and then apply them to InfoPath forms you created to manage lists. This tie-in is a great link between the power of VSTO, flexibility of SharePoint, and integration ability of InfoPath.

Integrate Security with a Claims-Based Identity Model

CardSpace is Microsoft's entry into the world of claims-based security. SharePoint is moving to use *CardSpace* and other like identity models to provide security.

CardSpace is Microsoft's entry into the Identity Selector market. When a user using CardSpace approaches a Web site, the user produces a virtual identity card that makes certain claims about the user. The Web site can then check a trusted third party for confirmation as to the validity of the claims. Web sites or other applications that use CardSpace reduce the total number of identities the user has to remember by using a common user interface for logins.

You can find a great article about the topic in MSDN at

```
http://msdn2.microsoft.com/en-us/library/aa480189.aspx
```

Build a PowerPoint Show from SharePoint Site Content

Ed Hild has the coolest demonstration of add-in performance that we've ever seen on his blog. Hild shows you how to make a PowerPoint presentation from SharePoint pages. He uses VSTO to build a PowerPoint add-in. (See Chapter 9 to find out how you can build one.) His add-in, however, calls a SharePoint Services Web service to get page data and then uses the new XML format of PowerPoint pages to construct a slideshow with information from the pages. It's slick.

You can see the demo at

```
http://blogs.msdn.com/b/edhild/archive/2008/01/03/video-building-presentations-
                    from-sharepoint-site-content.aspx
```

Use Excel Services in Your VSTO Applications (and Everywhere Else)

In our years of programming, we've seen more sophisticated programs trapped in Excel spreadsheets than you can imagine. Good organizers and power users who don't have access to Visual Basic or think it's over their head use the tools they have at their disposal. This approach leads to big, monster programs written in VBA in a cell in an Excel spreadsheet, which does not lead to scalability.

Excel 2010 allows users to take those big formulas that they've written and make Web services out of them. Those services are then hosted in a SharePoint site.

Publishing to Excel Services is basically saving a spreadsheet to SharePoint. The only difference is the Excel Service options. To save to Excel Services:

1. **Make a new spreadsheet.**
2. **Name the ranges that you want to be made visible to SharePoint users of the spreadsheet.**
3. **Choose File➪Share➪Publish to Excel Services.**
4. **Click the Excel Services Options button.**
5. **Select the items from the workbook.**
6. **Save it to SharePoint.**

Index Your Documents

Indexing your documents is pretty simple, but you can find a thousand uses for the new Microsoft search tools. Though indexing slows down your machine a little, we recommend using it. The search catalogs are accessible from both SharePoint and VSTO. It doesn't matter how many cool VSTO Documents you have out there if you can't find them.

Remove Managed Code Extensions from Documents

After a user finishes using document customizations, you may want to remove the customizations so that users who don't have permissions to run them can use the document after it's posted to SharePoint. You can remove the customizations with the customization itself or with a separate application and the `Microsoft.VisualStudio.Tools.Applications` classes.

1. **Create a new Visual Studio project of your choice.**
2. **Reference the `Microsoft.VisualStudio.Tools.Applications` namespace.**
3. **Get a path to the document:**

```
Dim Path as String = "C:\Document.docx")
```

4. **Get the Runtime Version for that document:**

```
myDocumentVersion = _
ServerDocument.GetCustomizationVersion(Path)
```

This step sees what version of .NET is being used.

5. **Make sure that the document is using at least Version 3:**

```
If myDocumentVersion = 3 Then
```

6. **Remove the document customizations:**

```
ServerDocument.RemoveCustomization(Path)
```

7. **Don't forget to close the If statement:**

```
End If
```

You can find more information about removing customizations at this MSDN article:

```
http://msdn2.microsoft.com/en-us/library/bb772099.aspx.
```

Reference SharePoint Services in a VSTO Program

Amidst all this cool stuff, don't forget the basics of the integration — that SharePoint exposes almost all its resources as an XML Web service. Making that reference is key to writing documents and add-ins that really make use of your SharePoint installation.

Referencing SharePoint services works just like any other service:

1. **Right-click the project in Solution Explorer.**

2. **Select Add Service Reference.**

3. **Browse to the URL of your SharePoint installation.**

4. **Name the service something memorable.**

That's all there is to it.

When you're designing solutions, remember that integration is key, and Services are the lock . . . or something like that. You can easily achieve integration when programs expose their functionality as a service. Just because you're writing for Office doesn't mean that you can't take advantage of exposed functionality.

Index

Notes